GLOBAL CAPITALISM UNBOUND

GLOBAL CAPITALISM UNBOUND

WINNERS AND LOSERS FROM OFFSHORE OUTSOURCING

EDITED BY

EVA PAUS

First published in 2007 by
PALGRAVE MACMILLAN™
175 Fifth Avenue, New York, N.Y. 10010 and
Houndmills, Basingstoke, Hampshire, England RG21 6XS
Companies and representatives throughout the world.

PALGRAVE MACMILLAN is the global academic imprint of the Palgrave Macmillan division of St. Martin's Press, LLC and of Palgrave Macmillan Ltd. Macmillan® is a registered trademark in the United States, United Kingdom and other countries. Palgrave is a registered trademark in the European Union and other countries.

ISBN-13: 978–1–4039–8429–6
ISBN-10: 1–4039–8429–8

Library of Congress Cataloging-in-Publication Data

Global capitalism unbound : winners and losers from offshore outsourcing / Eva Paus, editor.
    p. cm.
    Includes bibliographical references and index.
    ISBN 1–4039–8429–8 (alk. paper)
    1. Contracting out. 2. Offshore outsourcing. 3. Information technology—Management. 4. Globalization—Economic aspects.
    I. Paus, Eva.

HD2365.G55 2007
331.1—dc22   2007009257

A catalogue record for this book is available from the British Library.

Design by Newgen Imaging Systems (P) Ltd., Chennai, India.

First edition: November 2007

10 9 8 7 6 5 4 3 2 1

Transferred to digital printing in 2008.

CONTENTS

List of Contributors

Luis Abugattas Majluf is a Senior Advisor, UNDP Arab States Regional Initiative on Trade, Economic Governance, and Human Development, Cairo. Previously he was a Senior Expert at UNCTAD in the Trade Negotiations and Commercial Diplomacy Branch. He has been a consultant to major international organizations and to private and public sector organizations in many countries.

James Burke received his Ph.D. in economics from the University of Massachusetts at Amherst and currently works at Mount Holyoke College. In work with the Political Economy Research Institute (PERI) at the University of Amherst, his recent research interests have focused on economic globalization and its effects on labor.

Gerald Epstein is Professor of Economics and Codirector of the Political Economy Research Institute at the University of Massachusetts, Amherst. His most recent edited and coauthored books include *Financialization and the World Economy* (edited, E. Elgar, 2005), and *An Employment Targeted Macroeconomic Policy for South Africa* (E. Elgar, 2007), coauthored with Robert Pollin, James Heintz, and Leonce Ndikumana.

Richard B. Freeman is the Herbert Ascherman Chair in Economics, Harvard University, and Program Director, Labor Studies, National Bureau of Economic Research, both in Cambridge, Massachusetts. He is also Senior Research Fellow, Centre for Economic Performance, London School of Economics, London.

Gary H. Jefferson is the Carl Marks Professor of Trade and Finance at Brandeis University, where he holds joint appointments in the Department of Economics and the International Business School. His research focuses primarily on China's industrial sector. He has published widely on the subjects of industrial productivity, enterprise restructuring, foreign direct investment, and technical innovation.

Bartlomiej Kaminski is Associate Professor of government at the University of Maryland, College Park. He has served as a foreign trade consultant for several international organizations including the World Bank, UNDP, and the European Commission. His most recent book *Globalization and Corruption* (coauthored with Antoni Kaminski) was published in Poland in 2004.

Catherine L. Mann is Professor of International Economics and Finance at Brandeis University and a Senior Fellow at the Peter G. Peterson Institute for International Economics in Washington. Previously, she served at the Federal Reserve Board of Governors, the President's Council of Economic Advisors at the White House, and at the World Bank. Her most recent book is *Accelerating the Globalization of America: The Role for Information Technology* (2006).

Hans-Peter Martin has been a party-free, independent member of the European Parliament since 1999. Before that he worked for fifteen years as a foreign correspondent for the German newsmagazine *Der Spiegel*. His book *The Global Trap* (1996) became an international bestseller and was translated into 27 languages. His forthcoming book is entitled *The European Trap—The End of Democracy and Well-Being* to be published by Piper, Munich.

William Milberg is Associate Professor of Economics, New School for Social Research and Schwartz Center for Economic Policy Analysis. Melissa Mahoney, Markus Schneider, and Rudi von Arnim are Research Assistants at the New School's Schwartz Center for Economic Policy Analysis.

Eva Paus is Professor of Economics and the Carol Hoffmann Collins Director of the Dorothy R. and Norman E. McCulloch Center for Global Initiatives at Mount Holyoke College. Her most recent book is *Foreign Investment, Development, and Globalization. Can Costa Rica Become Ireland?* (Palgrave Macmillan, 2005).

Vivien A. Schmidt is Jean Monnet Professor of European Integration at Boston University. She has written extensively on European political economy and public policy. Her most recent books are *Democracy in Europe* (Oxford, 2006) and *The Futures of European Capitalism* (Oxford, 2002).

Helen Shapiro is an Associate Professor at the University of California, Santa Cruz, where she teaches in the departments of Sociology, Latin American and Latino Studies, and Economics. She has published widely on Latin American economic development and industrial policy, including *Engines of Growth: The State and Transnational Auto Companies in Brazil* (Cambridge: Cambridge University Press, 1994).

Guy Standing is Professor of Economic Security, University of Bath, and Professor of Labour Economics, Monash University. He was previously

Director of the Socio-Economic Security Programme of the International Labor Organization. His recent books include *Beyond the New Paternalism. Basic Security as Equality* (London and New York: Verso, 2002).

Navdeep Suri is a serving member of the Indian Foreign Service and is currently India's Consul General in Johannesburg, South Africa. He has previously served in New Delhi and in India's diplomatic missions in Cairo, Damascus, Washington, Dar es Salaam, and London. His study on outsourcing and development was presented at the Inter-Government Experts Meeting at Geneva organized by UNCTAD in February 2005.

LIST OF FIGURES

LIST OF TABLES

Acknowledgments

In editing this book I have incurred many debts, foremost to the contributors who were most cooperative and willing to revise their manuscripts if needed. Many of the contributions are based on presentations at the conference "New Global Realities. Winners and Losers from Offshore Outsourcing," at Mount Holyoke College in March 2006. The conference was hosted by the Dorothy R. and Norman E. McCulloch Center for Global Initiatives. My sincere thanks go to the *New York Times* Knowledge Network and the Rockefeller Brothers Fund for cosponsoring and supporting the conference. I am particularly indebted to Mary E. Tuttle, '37, whose endowed Mary E. Tuttle Colloquium Fund provided important financial support for the conference.

Jean Costello's superb assistance in copyediting this book was indispensable, and Jennifer Medina provided valuable assistance throughout the whole process.

EVA PAUS
Editor

South Hadley, February 2007

PART I
INTRODUCTION

Chapter One

Winners and Losers from Offshore Outsourcing: What Is to Be Done?

Eva Paus

The rapid expansion of offshore outsourcing is the key characteristic of the current process of economic globalization. As production processes become increasingly fragmented across national borders, companies source abroad parts and services they used to produce in-house, at home. The ramifications of globalized production, especially as it moves into the field of IT-enabled services, are the subject of growing concern. On the one hand, the globalization of production offers new opportunities for economic growth, development, and human well-being. But, on the other hand, it poses fundamental challenges, as some countries and groups of people will benefit more than others, some will benefit at the expense of others, and some may simply lose out.

This book brings together different perspectives on the debate. Leading scholars and practitioners from different backgrounds analyze who are the winners and losers in this great transformation and which policies are needed to harness the benefits of globalized production for more people and countries. The cumulative weight of the arguments leaves little doubt that we are at the beginning of a huge transformation, with dramatic distributional consequences within and across countries. It is imperative that we realize the magnitude of what lies ahead and take action to address the consequences. Otherwise major political upheaval seems inevitable.

Offshoring and Globalization: A Sea Change

Outsourcing is integral to the division of labor and thus as old as economic development itself. When a production process can be separated into discrete parts and a producer finds that it is more economical for a part to be produced off-site, then the production of that part is outsourced. Over the last forty to fifty years this age-old process has taken on a significant added dimension, as producers have increasingly outsourced to other countries. The scope and implications of offshore outsourcing are looming particularly large, as offshoring has started to make inroads into the service sector, with huge potential for future expansion.

Back in the 1970s, the coincidence of two trends ushered in a new international division of labor: technological advancements made it increasingly more possible to fragment production processes and produce standardized components and parts on a grand scale, and the development of containerization led to a drastic reduction in shipping costs (e.g., Fröbel et al. 1977). In addition, in the 1980s, developing countries became increasingly more interested in attracting foreign direct investment (FDI), as they liberalized trade, investment, and other markets. In the context of these developments, transnational corporations(TNCs) have built up ever more sophisticated global production networks, with different parts of the value chain produced by affiliates in other countries or by unaffiliated companies through arms-length contracts.

The growth of international trade in parts and components is an indication of the growing fragmentation of production across national borders. In the United States, the share of imported intermediate inputs in total inputs rose from 5.3 percent in 1972 to 7.3 percent in 1979 to 12.1 percent in 1990 (Feenstra and Hanson 1999). By 2003, it had reached 22.7 percent (Burke and Epstein 2006). Studies for other developed countries confirm the trend (e.g., Hummels, Ishii, and Yi 2001).

For a long time, offshoring in manufacturing was concentrated in labor-intensive parts, since they could be produced more cheaply in low-wage developing countries. In recent years, however, this traditional pattern of North-South production allocation and trade has started to break down, as education and training levels in some developing countries have improved considerably, and new countries with large pools of skilled labor have joined the global market. As a result, offshoring is spanning an increasingly broader spectrum of skill and technology-intensive parts and components in manufacturing, accelerating a process of deindustrialization in today's rich countries, increasing international competition in more industries and products, and fuelling the drive in developed countries toward establishing comparative advantages ever higher up the value chain. The flip side of this deindustrialization process in developed countries has been increased industrial upgrading in some of today's developing countries, especially in Asia.

But offshoring is no longer restricted to the manufacturing sector. Since the late 1990s, we have witnessed rapid growth in the offshoring of services, which will ultimately have much more profound implications than off-shoring in manufacturing proper. The diffusion of information and communication technologies (ICT) has made it possible to offshore IT-enabled services, ranging from back office processes (e.g., data entry, call centers, accounting) to software services to online delivery of professional services. In contrast to manufacturing-based offshoring, which generates more intense competition between specific industrial sectors and subsectors across national borders, service-based offshoring cuts across all sectors. In this new world of global competition, any task that can be digitized and does not require face-to-face contact can potentially be offshored.

There are no official data on services offshoring, as the current collection of trade data in services reflects the traditionally held assumption that services are nontradable. Although the available estimates suggest that international trade in IT-enabled services has been growing rapidly, these services still account for only a small share of total world trade. The OECD (2004) estimates the value of globally offshored services at somewhere between $10 billion and $50 billion in 2003 (cited in Abugattas, this volume). Contrary to widespread assumptions, services outsourcing has been predominantly a North-North and not a North-South phenomenon, in spite of India's prominence as an important recipient of off-shored services.

To date, the growth of service offshoring seems to have led to relatively small job losses in developed countries. The widely cited study by Forrester Research (McCarthy 2004) predicted that service offshoring would lead to a loss of 3.3 million jobs in the United States by 2015. That corresponds to roughly 2 percent of the U.S. labor force in 2005. For the EU-15, Forrester (Parker 2004) predicted a job loss of 1.16 million by 2015, coincidentally also the equivalent of around 2 percent of its labor force in 2005 (cited in Kirkegaard 2005, 6).

The potentially profound transformational impact of service offshoring stems from the range and number of jobs that may be threatened by off-shoring in the future, given the job and task characteristics that are needed for IT-enabled international trade. The estimates range from around 20 percent of the total labor force for several OECD countries (van Welsum and Reif 2006) to 11 to 14 percent for the United States (Bardhan and Kroll 2003, Jensen and Kletzer 2006). Blinder (2006, 122) suggests that "the total number of current U.S. service-sector jobs that will be susceptible to offshoring in the electronic future is two to three times the total number of manufacturing jobs (which is about 14 million)."

There are many reasons why susceptibility to offshoring may not translate into actual offshoring, as discussed by Abugattas in this volume. But it is this potential expansion of service offshoring that suggests seismic shifts in the world as we know it, leading Blinder (2006) to refer to the dawn of the Third Industrial Revolution and Baldwin (2006) to call for a new paradigm.

Nonetheless, as several contributors argue in this book, it is the conjuncture of offshoring and other key factors that together promote the sea change in the globalization process, driving at the establishment of a global labor market. One key factor is the entry of China, India, and Central and Eastern Europe into the international market. It has led to an increase of 1.46 billion workers in the global labor force, roughly double its previous size (Freeman, this volume). The second factor is that these countries also have a large number of highly skilled/educated workers. As a result, the "great doubling" has dramatically increased competitive pressures not only in the production of low-wage, unskilled labor-intensive goods, but also in technologically more sophisticated products and in IT-enabled services (Freeman, this volume).

Guy Standing (this volume) argues that we are at the beginning of another "great transformation," with the expansion of global capitalism breaking down the current social order, a process akin to the rise of market economies and nation states destroying the preexisting social system in the nineteenth and early twentieth century. But where Polanyi's *Great Transformation* (1944) was about the development of a national capitalist labor market, the current transformation is about the development of an international capitalist labor market.

Offshoring in Developed Countries

Winners, Losers, and the Undermining of the Social Contract as We Know It

Based on traditional comparative advantage theory, many economists argue that offshore outsourcing can be good for all parties concerned as it leads to a more efficient allocation of resources, which enlarges the size of the economic pie. The dynamic complement to this static equilibrium theory is that offshore outsourcing leads to a decline in input prices, and an increase in profits that will be invested in new competitive areas, thus creating employment and further income growth.

Catherine Mann (this volume) makes this case most emphatically for IT-based services. She analyzes the impact of ICT hardware on the economy and extrapolates from there to IT services. She argues that IT products and services have three characteristics that make offshoring of IT-enabled services a win-win situation: they are price elastic with respect to investment and demand, they are income elastic, and there are network externalities (spillovers among the participants in the network). Thus as offshoring reduces the price of IT products and services, investment goes up more than commensurately, leading to economic growth, employment expansion, and productivity increases.

Milberg et al. (this volume) question the validity of some of Mann's assumptions for IT services, even if they hold in the case of ICT hardware. They argue that investment demand is not necessarily price elastic. In other words, higher profits do not have to lead to greater investment, as shown by the experience in the United States over the last few years. As a result, the expected employment and growth effects have only been realized partially.

But most of the analysis of the impact of offshoring on developed countries, in this volume and beyond, does not focus on the assumptions behind the growth dynamics that are supposed to generate the win-win outcome. Rather it concentrates on the impact of offshoring on the well-being of labor and examines the ability of current social contracts to generate and support needed changes.

There is general agreement about who the big winners and losers are. The big winner, writ large, is capital. Whether explained theoretically as a halving of the global capital labor ratio (Freeman, this volume), or the gain in bargaining power vis-à-vis labor (Standing, Burke and Epstein, Milberg et al., all in this volume), the globalization of the labor market, with near unlimited global mobility of capital but high restrictions on labor mobility, puts capital in the driver seat.

There are two other groups in the winning camp: first, the highly skilled workers whose jobs cannot be offshored, and second, and more ambiguously, the consumers. If offshoring leads indeed to lower prices, then the consumer gains. Yet a consumer always wears another hat that indicates the source of her/his income. The capitalist/consumer may win really big, with rising income and declining prices. But the worker/consumer may lose if her/his income declines relatively more than prices; it is the real wage that matters after all. And the consumer who is not on either side of the labor market may win or lose depending on the income source (e.g., retirement benefits).

The big loser in the offshoring/globalization process is labor; not all workers, of course, but labor as a group. Everybody agrees that there are now more workers in tradable manufacturing sectors and in service jobs with traits that make them potentially offshorable. The key question is how many workers, industries, and tasks will be affected, how rapidly workers' skills become obsolescent, how long it will take them to find new jobs, and how likely it is that the jobs they find will pay as much as the jobs they lost. It is the scale of potential job losses, the speed at which job losses occur, and the difficulty of finding a job at a similar income level as before that puts labor market adjustment and worker retraining in a completely different ball game from what it was before.

Identifying seven forms of labor related securities (income, representation, labor market, employment, job, skill, work security), Standing (this volume) argues that insecurity has grown in all seven forms, not only as a result of offshoring, but more generally due also to the evolvement of a global labor market. Examples abound of producers in developed countries reducing the benefits of their workers, whether due to genuine competitive pressures or because producers' bargaining power allowed them to extract concessions from workers wielding the stick of potential relocation abroad. The common trend, Standing argues, has been a change in the composition of social income, with a decline in enterprise benefits, a shift in state benefits from universal to selective benefits, and an increase in the importance of money wages and the reliance on informal support systems.

Labor is not the only group that has been losing bargaining power vis-à-vis globally mobile capital. Governments find themselves in a weakened position as well. Governments' ability to tax corporations has declined steadily, as capital can always move or threaten to move somewhere else. At the same time, governments often use lower tax rates to compete—at the local, state, and national levels—for productive investment or to retain it within their jurisdictional space (Standing, Burke and Epstein, this volume). The beggar-thy-neighbor policies in labor benefits and corporate tax rates are accelerating the flexibilization of labor markets and job insecurity around the globe, in developed as well as developing countries. As a result, existing social contracts in today's rich countries are increasingly undermined.

Mann, Milberg, Burke, and Epstein focus their analysis primarily on the United States, arguing from economic and political economy perspectives. Schmidt and Martin, in contrast, concentrate on the EU, particularly on the institutional and political context that shapes the responses to offshoring in "Old Europe." In addition to globalization, EU-15 countries also have to contend with Europeanization. On May 1, 2004, ten new countries with much cheaper labor, skilled and unskilled, joined the EU-15; and on January 1, 2007, Rumania and Bulgaria became the latest members. Lower labor costs are only one side of the Europeanization coin for the EU-15. The other side is the labor mobility from the Eastern to the Western part of the Union, which—Martin (this volume) argues—further undermines the current labor standards and is fuelling a political backlash in the EU-15.

Schmidt suggests that the differences in the reactions to offshoring and globalization in the EU-15 countries can partly be explained by the differences in welfare and work reforms implemented in the three different "families" of welfare states: the liberal welfare state (Britain and Ireland), the social-democratic welfare state (Sweden and Denmark), and the conservative welfare state (France, Germany, Italy, and the Netherlands). Though Schmidt highlights the differences in government discourses that legitimize the reforms and shape the public's response to globalization and Europeanization in the different EU-15 countries, such differences may become less important if globalization intensifies. In that case, she concludes that "national work and welfare systems will find it harder and harder to cushion the effects, and national leaders will be increasingly hard put to come up with sufficiently legitimating discourses across Europe."

In contrast to Schmidt, Martin contends that we are already at the point of growing delegitimization. He argues that offshoring and globalization are undermining the welfare states, reducing the size of the middle class, and challenging the very foundations of democracy. The shift in income patterns and the growing frustrations over lack of good jobs are finding their expression in growing disillusion with democracy at the national level, and they are making it increasingly more difficult to legitimize the project of the EU.

What Is to Be Done?

Remarkably, in spite of their differences in background and analysis, none of the contributors argues in favor of protectionism in developed countries as a way to slow down the pace of change and thus provide some breathing space for the needed adjustments in labor markets and otherwise. Some argue explicitly against protectionism on the grounds of maximizing efficiency and growth (Mann, Freeman, Milberg et al.), while others reject it because it hurts developing countries (Freeman, Standing). In addition, it would be rather difficult, if not impossible, to use protectionism to slow down IT-enabled service offshoring.

Broadly speaking, we can distinguish three major challenges that offshoring poses for developed countries: (1) how to increase the likelihood that the growth dynamic behind a potential win-win scenario is realized; (2) how to support workers who are affected negatively by offshoring; and (3) how to counter the unraveling of the current social contract. The authors in this book propose a range of policies to address these challenges. Major differences among policy recommendations stem primarily from the issues the authors identify as the principal challenges that need to be addressed, and only secondarily from differences in policy proposals to address the same particular problem.

Promoting the Growth Dynamic
Milberg et al. argue that, in recent years, high profits in the United States have not resulted in commensurate increases in investment. To spur profit reinvestment and raise the elasticity of investment, they propose expanded coverage of the investment tax credit, a higher tax credit for R&D investment,

accelerated depreciation, and a reversal of the recent reduction in the tax rate on dividend income and capital.

Burke and Epstein identify insufficient aggregate demand as one of the reasons behind labor's weakened position. And the lack of demand they attribute—in turn—to the "neo-liberal trifecta of fiscal austerity, anti-inflationary monetary policy, export-led trade policy." An increase in aggregate demand may or may not strengthen labor's position, but it will certainly increase economic growth. Burke and Epstein recommend abandoning inflation-targeting approaches to central bank policy, more regulations to reduce short-term speculative global capital flows, for example, a Tobin Tax, and a shift away from export-led policies.

Both Freeman and Mann address the challenge of how to remain competitive in high value-added and knowledge-intensive activities, areas in which today's developed countries need to stay ahead of the curve. Freeman advocates increased investment in knowledge, with more graduate fellowships in science and engineering, more basic research—particularly in energy and the environment—and increased investment in public infrastructure. The European countries are, of course, pursuing the same goals. At the Lisbon summit in March 2000, the EU heads of state committed to making the EU "the most competitive and dynamic knowledge-driven economy by 2010."

Mann raises the important question of how we might need to change the educational content, K-16, to prepare our youth for the new global world, how to enhance their ability to learn on an ongoing basis. She stresses the importance of judgment, problem solving, communications, tacit knowledge, and sector-specific knowledge. These sentiments are echoed by Baldwin (2006, 43), who argues that "the educational system should be preparing them for lifetime employability rather than lifetime employment."

Supporting the Adjustment Process for Workers

There is widespread agreement that support needs to be expanded considerably for workers who have been laid off as a result of trade competition. In 1962, the Kennedy administration included Trade Adjustment Assistance (TAA) in the Trade Expansion Act to win congressional support for the tariff cuts in the Kennedy Round. Since then, the TAA has been adjusted periodically, usually with the goal of winning political support for further tariff reductions (Baicker and Rehavi 2004). The most recent expansion occurred in 2002 with the Trade Adjustment Assistance Reform Act. Given the challenges ahead, the TAA is woefully inadequate in its current form, in scope and in resources.

The level of benefits has to be higher, the period of benefit eligibility longer, and the scope broader to include the service sector (e.g., Jensen and

Kletzer 2006, Milberg et al., Burke and Epstein, this volume). Given the difficulty of distinguishing between job losses due to trade competition and due to other reasons, many argue that TAA eligibility should be extended to anybody who is laid off for reasons outside of her/his control.

In recognition of the fact that workers often do not find jobs at the same income level as before, a number of analysts advocate some form of wage insurance, where workers would be paid a portion of the difference between their former and new salary for a limited period of time. While such a wage subsidy currently exists under the TAA for trade-displaced workers over 50 years of age, it is limited in amount (up to a total of $10,000 over two years) and in scope. Germany and France have similar wage support schemes. But as helpful and necessary as such arrangements are for easing the adjustment pain, they do not obliterate the fact that eligible workers will indeed end up with lower wages. Advocates of wage insurance do not address the potentially profound political implications of this reality.

To support retraining on a larger scale, the EU established the European Globalization Adjustment Fund (EGF)—available to all twenty-seven members—which went into effect in January 2007. With a budget of up to €500 million a year, the fund supports only active labor market measures, including training, microcredit, job search, and mobility allowances. To be eligible for EGF support, a member country must show that job losses were due to changes in world trade patterns and that at least 1,000 people are affected in a given sector or company (European Commission 2006a).

One of the countries that seems to have been particularly successful with labor market adjustment policies is Denmark, with its "flexicurity" model of highly flexible labor markets combined with high income support and a very strong focus on active labor market policies (Schmidt, this volume). Where the United States spends .16 percent of GDP on active labor market policies, Denmark spends almost 2 percent (Galax 2007, 33).

Portability of health and pension benefits is a critical element in making job relocations less painful and more possible, and in making corporations more competitive (Milberg et al., this volume). That is particularly important in the United States, where health and pension coverage is much more likely to be tied to specific companies than in Western European countries, where coverage tends to be much broader.

Countering the Unraveling Social Contract
Offshore outsourcing and the evolvement of a global labor market pose a profound challenge to the existing social consensus in developed countries. To counter the unraveling of the social contract, a number of contributors advocate changing the rules of the game so as to reign in capital and empower labor and governments. Martin (this volume) paints the specter of

dramatic political consequences, if we fail to regulate the globalization process as it is unfolding now.

Burke and Epstein brilliantly capture the conflict between unrestrained global capital expansion and a viable political contract to support it: "Globalization precludes the very solutions required to compensate for its negative impacts." The manifold needs for social investments discussed above (from tax credits of various kinds—investment, R&D, human capital—to income support policies to active labor market policies to investment in public infrastructure) require considerable government outlays. But the tax race to the bottom does not allow governments to capture more taxes from those who are benefiting the most from the globalization process. Burke and Epstein advocate a change in U.S. tax laws, eliminating the deferral of taxation on unrepatriated income earned in low-tax countries, tax coordination at the national and international level, and enforcement of tax rules and greater information exchange among tax authorities in different countries.

To counter the huge increase in job and income insecurity, Freeman, Milberg et al. and Standing advocate a minimum set of benefits for everybody, though they have different ideas about what such a set should look like. Freeman urges to increase the basket of nonmarket goods and services for all citizens (including health insurance); and Milberg et al. call for a minimum level of health insurance, pension, and child care irrespective of job and employment status. Standing proposes two possible routes toward a more viable social order. The first route is to extend the benefits of today's full-time employees to employees who are temporary or part-time workers. Some European countries with "flexicurity" models might hold out valuable lessons in this regard (Schmidt, this volume). The second proposal is much more radical: moving beyond the employer-employee relationship, Standing advocates a core of basic rights for everybody—regardless of the work they do, whether they are in the formal labor market or in the broad area of volunteer caregiving.

Offshoring for Development?

While there is a lot of discussion about the potentially dramatic impact of offshoring on the well-being of the average worker and the social fabric in developed countries, there is virtually no debate in the existing literature about offshoring's impact on developing countries. Analysts generally assume, implicitly or explicitly, that developing countries will benefit from offshoring, as a matter of course. Offshoring is thought to bring more investment leading to greater employment and economic growth, a line of reasoning not too dissimilar from what we saw in the context of developed countries. But beyond that, the argument for developing countries differs: it focuses on the potential positive spillovers from offshoring for the advancement of the host country's technological capabilities rather than on the implications for the distribution of income, workers' well-being and social contracts.

Concentrating on spillover effects does not mean that offshoring does not have distributional implications in developing countries, or that these do not matter. But in the context of underdevelopment, the development of a country's technological capabilities is considered the critical element (as it can be the engine for structural change and industrial advancement) that will allow—at least in principal—for an increased standard of living for all.

The chapters in this book show that uncritical optimism about the benefits of offshoring for developing countries is not warranted. Offshoring can have and, indeed, has had a very positive development effect in some developing countries. Three key cases are analyzed in different chapters of this book: Central and Eastern Europe, which has benefited greatly from offshoring in manufacturing (Kaminski); India, the great beneficiary of offshoring of IT-enabled services (Suri); and China, which has mostly benefited from offshoring in manufacturing, but increasingly also in services (Jefferson). But the experiences of these countries cannot necessarily be reproduced in other countries. In a broader analysis of offshoring and development, Abugattas as well as Paus and Shapiro argue that there is nothing automatic about a positive offshoring-development nexus, neither in the service sector (Abugattas) nor in manufacturing (Paus and Shapiro). They argue that in the absence of a certain level of key capabilities, developing countries will not be able to attract offshoring FDI, and that even if they do, spillover effects will often not develop without proactive industrial policies.

Analyses of the offshoring-development nexus often subsume offshoring under FDI more broadly and then focus on the potential benefits from FDI. That is an oversimplification, though not a critical one. While offshoring also occurs through arms-length contracts between TNCs and suppliers in developing countries, the available evidence suggests that it takes predominantly the form of FDI.[1] And it is mainly FDI and not arms-length contracts that forms the basis for positive spillovers.

Offshoring for Development: The Success Stories

India

Among developing countries, India is the great beneficiary of the growth in service offshoring. Its exports of IT-enabled services increased more than tenfold in six years, from $565 million in FY 2000 to $6.2 billion in FY 2006 (Nasscom Strategic Review 2006, cited in Suri, this volume). Suri provides an intriguing summary of the origins of IT-based offshoring in

India; how the highly educated Indian diaspora, particularly in the US, established connections back to India for their US companies and how the large supply of technically educated people enabled Indian companies to solve the problems of the Y2K millennium bug. After the Y2K success established India's credentials in the IT sector, TNCs increased IT-based service offshoring to India, first to captive units, and subsequently to Indian companies.

Suri contends that IT offshoring has been a catalyst for the economic development of India. By FY 2006, the ITES/BPO sector had generated directly 415,000 jobs and indirectly an additional 1.3 million jobs; it had also induced employment effects through the increase in consumption. Additional benefits were learning spillovers, empowerment of women (who make up about half of the BPO workforce), a boost to air travel, and the promotion of decentralized growth with the creation of ICT infrastructure and employment opportunities.

The ICT success has changed the perception of India in the world, and facilitated its move up the value chain in the IT sector. In addition, it has led to the emergence of IT-based Indian multinationals, for example, Infosys and Wipro, with offices world-wide.

New Europe

Offshoring in manufacturing in the specific context of EU expansion has been a catalyst for structural change in the new member countries of the European Union. After the collapse of the central command economies in the early 1990s, Central and Eastern European countries had a large pool of cheap, skilled labor to offer to producers from the West. At the beginning of the transition, participation in buyer-driven TNC networks (clothing and furniture) was a prominent force behind new exports, but then the driver behind growth changed to producer-driven TNC networks (especially in the automotive sector and the IT sector).

Kaminski argues that foreign firms increased output, employment, productivity, and exports, and that the integration into production-driven networks in IT products and automobile production has led to a restructuring of the industrial sector and internationally competitive industries. He contends that technological spillovers did indeed materialize, as TNCs increased domestic sourcing over time. It is difficult to determine, however, how large the spillovers to national firms have really been, since many TNC supplier firms have colocated with their clients and have become "domestic" suppliers.

The EU factor has been hugely important in the success story of New Europe. The pan-European agreement on rules of origin, which created access to a vast market for the Eastern and Central European countries, played a critical role in TNC offshoring to the East. Kaminski credits the EU-imposed restrictions on institutional and policy discretion with the new member governments' ability to create a business-friendly environment for foreign investment.

China

During the last decade, China has been the leading recipient of FDI and offshoring in manufacturing. In 2005, FDI inflows into China were $72.4 billion, which corresponds to 21.7 percent of all FDI flows into developing countries, and 7.9 percent of global FDI inflows (UNCTAD 2006, Annex Table B1). Concomitant with the huge FDI flows into China, R&D has made huge leaps as well. As a share of GDP, R&D spending has increased from 1 percent in 2000 to 1.4 percent in 2005 (Jefferson, this volume).

Such an impressive increase in such a short period of time, together with a rapid rise of TNC research institutes in China, seems to suggest that offshoring and FDI more generally did indeed have the technological spillover effects to induce a significant advancement of the host country's technological capabilities. Jefferson's analysis in this book refutes such a simple conjecture. He argues that while foreign-funded firms have substantially expanded the scope of R&D efforts in China, they have not been the key drivers behind China's growing R&D intensity. China's domestic industrial enterprises have accounted for the large majority of R&D spending and patenting activity. But, according to Jefferson, foreign investment played a significant indirect role in motivating domestic firms to increase their R&D intensity and to patent their innovations.

Common Traits of the Success Stories

Success stories are always the result of a multitude of causal factors, some of them specific to one country and others common to them all. One of the common factors in the cases of China, India, and Central/Eastern Europe has been the large supply of cheap, highly skilled and educated workers.

A second common factor is a government that, for many decades, has been very active in the development of a home grown sector and indigenous technological learning capabilities. With the possible exception of Singapore, development successes have been rooted in the expansion of national enterprises and national learning capabilities and the dynamic synergies they generated. In the Eastern and Central European countries, government promotion of domestic industry went from one extreme under central planning to the other extreme after the collapse of the former regime. It remains to be seen whether these countries will continue to be successful without strong national producers and with a preponderance of TNCs. One key factor that might enable them to do so is the large inflow of European Structural Funds (3 to 4 percent of GDP for some of the countries), which can be used wisely for development purposes, for example, improvements in infrastructure and advancements in human capital. The experience of the Celtic Tiger reflects both the critical role of EU structural funds and the challenges when the economy is dominated by transnational corporations (Paus 2005).

A third common factor, closely linked to the first two, has been the countries' ability to have FDI and offshoring move up the value chain; in India it is reflected in a focus on ever greater value added in IT-based services, in China, in the rise of foreign research centers, and in "New Europe" in the move from integration into buyer-driven networks to producer-driven networks. In all cases, wages have gone up, raising workers' living standards, while—at the same time—exerting pressures to move up the value chain.

Finally, it is very clear that offshoring/FDI is not the panacea for all development problems. The size of the economies and of the development challenges is simply too large for offshoring/FDI to work as the engine of development. But it can certainly be a handmaiden if the internal conditions are right.

Can the Success Stories Be Emulated?

Not all developing countries will necessarily be able to attract offshoring/ FDI, and even if they do, they will not automatically reap positive spillover effects. In 2001, the Gini coefficient (population-weighted) of net inflows of FDI was .7, more unequal than any measure of the distribution of world income (Sutcliffe 2004, 35). And the recipients of offshored services have been highly concentrated as well. One estimate suggests that five countries receive 84 percent of offshored services, among them India with 32 percent and China with nine percent (McKinsey 2005, cited in Abugattas, this volume).[2]

To attract FDI, from offshoring or otherwise, countries need to be able to offer key location-specific assets. These include political and economic stability, possibilities for low-cost production or special market access. In the case of IT-based services, a well-functioning telecommunications infrastructure and a burgeoning software sector are necessary preconditions for potential participation in the offshore market for back office processes and software services. Abugattas (this volume) suggests that the countries that are currently attracting the bulk of offshore services will continue to do so in the future, due to agglomeration economies and incumbent advantages, branding, as well as TNCs' imperfect information about other possible sites.

Regarding offshoring in manufacturing, the "great doubling" has significantly increased the competitive pressures on the production of all manufactured parts and products. Those pressures manifest themselves in job losses not only in today's industrialized countries—as discussed earlier—but also in today's middle-income developing countries. The doubling of the global labor force has altered the range of possibilities for those countries' new comparative advantages (Freeman, this volume; Abugattas and Paus 2006). In Latin America, for example, wages are relatively too high for countries to compete any longer in the production of unskilled labor–intensive commodities. And productivity is often relatively too low to compete successfully with more technologically advanced countries, including China and India, in the production of highly skill-intensive goods and services. As a result, Latin American countries, and others in a similar situation, face the challenge of identifying new areas for industrial advancement and new niches in which to attract FDI/offshoring.

Whether countries are able to participate in the new international division of labor is only the first question. Equally important is the question of subsequent spillovers. While there is not much evidence of widespread spillover effects from service offshoring, Abugattas (this volume) suggests that the potential for upgrading of human capital is greater, if TNC affiliates have a systemic effect on technological learning, serving as a driver for an improved education system.

The empirical studies on FDI and spillovers show very mixed results. Paus and Shapiro (this volume) argue that the FDI-spillover nexus is rooted in the interaction between the dynamics of TNCs' global value chains on the one hand, and the development of host countries' absorptive capacity for spillovers on the other. The type of FDI and the global strategies of TNCs determine the *potential* for spillovers. But the *realization* of that potential depends upon the ability of host country producers to compete in related products; it depends on the absorptive capacity of the host economy.

In sum, whether the success stories can be emulated depends on two key factors: whether developing countries have the right location-specific assets to attract offshoring, and whether they have national absorptive capabilities, an indigenous technological infrastructure and the requisite learning capabilities.

What Is To be Done?

The main issue in the policy debate is as old as the field of development economics itself. It centers on the right complementarity between state and market. On the one hand, there are those, such as Kaminski (this volume), who argue for limiting government policies to the creation of a business-friendly environment, a hallmark of the Washington Consensus propagated by the World Bank and the IMF for nearly three decades. On the other hand, there are others, such as Abugattas (this volume) and Paus and Shapiro (this volume) who argue that a business-friendly environment is not enough, and that more activist government policies are needed.

Paus and Shapiro (this volume) argue that proactive policies are becoming ever more urgent with the intensification of global competition: from targeting specific TNCs to supporting cluster formation, to expanding technical education and learning processes, to improving access to telecommunications, to aggressive support policies to develop indigenous linkage capability and integrate national firms into emerging. When devising such policies, some key points have to be kept in mind. First, international trade and investment agreements have dramatically narrowed the space for industrial policies. Policies that were used successfully in the past to enhance spillover effects from FDI, e.g., domestic content requirements for foreign investors—are no longer an option under the TRIMS Agreement. Some interventionist policies are still possible, though, under WTO rules, for example, R&D support, provision of information and active consultation, matchmaking, and cluster formations.

Second, the identification of market failures and bottlenecks and their prioritization across sectors and policy areas should not be left to the government alone. Rather, those choices need to be made in close consultation and cooperation among the relevant government institutions and domestic producers.

Third, while some policies will have to target sectors identified as strategic or most likely to succeed, other policies will be applicable to all producers. These horizontal policies are especially important in expanding the human capital base and infrastructure. With respect to the ability to attract offshored IT-enabled services, Abugattas (this volume) argues that developing countries should adopt comprehensive policy packages that address human resource development, infrastructure development (especially telecommunications infrastructure), and development of the software industry.

From the vantage point of global capital, the world may indeed be flat. But from the perspective of most developing countries, it is not a level playing field. When they do not have the requisite locational advantages or when national producers do not have the ability to compete and when technological capabilities are low, then developing countries do not have the requisite equipment to participate in the game, let alone win.

The Great Unanswered Questions:
The Quest for Maintaining Peace

In analyzing the winners and losers from offshore outsourcing, the contributors to this book highlight the key challenges facing developed and developing countries and suggest policies to address them. But important questions remain, questions for which we need to find answers, if we want to make offshoring and globalization work for more people and more countries.

First, where will agency for positive change reside? Who will bring about the advocated policy changes? How can one implement policies aimed at strengthening the bargaining power of labor, when workers have lost bargaining power in the first place? With respect to the need for activist policies in developing countries, Paus and Shapiro wonder where the political constituency is—after two decades of neoliberalism and deindustrialization in Latin America—that would exert the needed pressure to use the windfall from the current high export prices of primary products to develop national knowledge-based assets and linkage capability.

The second big question is whether a decline in the standard of living of the average person in developed countries is avoidable? Standing, Martin, and Freeman all suggest that it is not likely. Standing argues that there will be a convergence of wages and benefits between India and China and the developed countries, with much greater economic insecurity in the rich countries. Freeman sketches out a "good" and a "bad" scenario of how a transition might look like to return to the capital-labor ratio that prevailed before the "great doubling." But even the "good" transition lasts fifty years, a period during which wages and benefits will have to fall in developed countries. Martin is the only one who raises the specter of major political upheavals and maybe even wars if global capitalism cannot be tamed.

But even if policies can be implemented to generate a win-win scenario for more people and countries, the third big unanswered question is how to make continued growth—especially as it involves the catch-up of India and China—compatible with limited natural resources and sustaining the environment. Access to natural resources, from minerals to oil to water is becoming ever more critical and is already driving foreign policy in the United States, China, and other countries to a considerable extent. The latest assessment from the intergovernmental panel on climate change in early 2007 should have convinced the last doubter that human actions are indeed responsible for growing global warming.

The final question concerns the fate of today's least developed countries, many ridden by violence and wars, and many lacking viable state structures. There is no level playing field for them. It is highly unlikely that offshoring and globalization will make it possible for them to move forward. There is a desperate need for massive outside assistance, not down a deep hole, but tied to internal changes and developments, as suggested by the Blair Commission Report (Commission for Africa 2005) as well as Jeffrey Sachs (2005).

The global challenges before us are enormous.

Notes

1. Abugattas (this volume) puts the figure of captive offshoring at up to 70 percent.
2. The others are Ireland (23 percent), Canada (10 percent), and Israel (9.5 percent).

PART II
THE GREAT TRANSFORMATION: THE GLOBALIZATION OF THE LABOR MARKET

CHAPTER TWO

THE CHALLENGE OF THE GROWING GLOBALIZATION OF LABOR MARKETS TO ECONOMIC AND SOCIAL POLICY

Richard B. Freeman

Trade, global capital mobility, immigration, and the spread of computer-based information technology is creating a new global labor market that substantially impacts workers in the United States and elsewhere and will have even larger effects in the foreseeable future. When countries around the world signed the diverse global and regional trade agreements that reduced tariffs in the latter part of the twentieth century, most economists expected that economic transactions between advanced countries and developing countries would consist largely of trade in manufactured goods and raw materials. Skilled workers in advanced countries would benefit from increased trade with developing countries as the advanced countries export skill-intensive goods and services. Less-skilled workers in the developing countries would benefit from greater trade with advanced countries as the developing countries export products made by less-skilled labor. The increased demand for skilled workers in advanced countries was expected to increase inequality in those countries while the increased demand for less-skilled workers in developing countries was expected to reduce inequality in those countries. In both sets of countries, globalization was expected to spur economic growth and raise living standards broadly.

No one anticipated that the next phase of globalization would be a major expansion in traded services nor in the offshoring of high-skill jobs from advanced to developing countries. The "North-South" model that economists use to analyze the role of technology in trade posits that the advanced countries (the "North") have a monopoly on modern technological innovation through their research and development spending and university-trained workforces while the developing countries (the "South") produce standard older goods using low wage and lower-skilled workers (Krugman 1979). In this model, the United States and other advanced countries get the good jobs in high-tech industries while the developing countries get low-skill, mass production jobs in apparel, shoes, and other low-tech industries. The standard analysis of relations between advanced and developing countries paid little attention to the danger that farmers and farmworkers in developing countries would suffer from competition with the more productive modern agricultural sector in advanced countries, exacerbating income inequalities in their countries.

The digitalization of white collar work, development of modern information communication technology (ICT), huge enrollments of students in universities in developing countries, and rapid diffusion of advanced technology worldwide has produced outcomes that diverge greatly from what economists expected. In the 2000s, multinationals at the frontier of modern technology invested in R&D in China and India as well as in the United States, Japan, and Western Europe. They searched globally for highly skilled workers and began to offshore skilled service sector jobs as well as lower-skilled jobs (such as in call centers) to low-wage countries.

Some analysts are troubled over the impact of offshoring on U.S. workers (Blinder 2006; Hira & Hira 2005). Others either look upon offshoring as a boon to economies (Mankiw and Swagel 2006; Mann 2006; Farrell 2006)[1] or claim that it has virtually no effect on employment. Surveys show that many U.S. workers feel that offshoring poses a danger to their job security and prospects, even in a relatively full employment economy. On a 2004 Employment Law Alliance survey, 6 percent of workers reported that they had lost a job because their work was sent overseas while 30 percent reported that someone else they knew had lost a job due to offshoring. One of ten workers feared for his/her job security because their employer was considering sending their work to an overseas subcontractor. A 2004 Associated Press-IPSOS survey gave comparable statistics. It showed that 20 percent of Americans reported that they, a family member, or someone they know personally lost their job because it was offshored to another country. By a two to one ratio, respondents attributed sending jobs overseas to "the greed of corporate executives" as opposed to "the need for companies to compete."[2]

On the business side, the United Kingdom's Institute of Directors has given the most forthright statement about the way offshoring has extended the issue of globalization of jobs beyond traditional manufacturing concerns:

> the availability of high-speed, low-cost communications, coupled with the rise in high-level skills in developing countries (means that) offshoring has become an attractive option outside the manufacturing industry. Britain has

seen call centres and IT support move away from Britain, but now creative services such as design and advertising work are being outsourced. There is more to come. In theory, *anything that does not demand physical contact with a customer can be outsourced to anywhere on the globe* [emphasis mine]. For many UK businesses this presents new opportunities, for others it represents a serious threat. But welcome it or fear it, it is happening anyway, and we had better get used to it. (politics.co.uk 2006)

In this chapter, I view offshoring as part of a broader trend in the global economy toward a single global labor market in which workers with similar skills compete more extensively across country lines than ever before. The globalization of the labor market manifests itself not only in offshoring but also in trade, immigration, and global capital mobility. I begin by examining the three economic drivers that underlie the globalization of the labor market; I then analyze the winners and losers from this process, the implications for U.S. labor, and the challenges this process poses to social and economic policy. My principal theme is that the world has begun an epochal transition to a single global labor market in which workers around the world will compete more directly than in the past. Barring social, economic, or environmental disaster, the chief task facing policymakers in the United States and the global community will be to assure that the transition proceeds relatively smoothly.

The Three Drivers of the Globalization of Labor

There are three fundamental drivers behind the globalization of labor markets. The *first driver* is "the great doubling" of the global labor force due to the entry of China, India and the ex-Soviet Union into the global capitalist system (Freeman 2005a and 2005b). In 1980, the global economy encompassed roughly half of the world's population—the advanced OECD countries, Latin America and the Caribbean, Africa, and some other parts of Asia. It did not contain China, which suffered from the economic insanities of Mao's Cultural Revolution. It did not contain the Soviet bloc, which operated behind the Iron Curtain. It did not contain India, which sought self-sufficiency behind high tariffs and a state-planned and highly regulated economy. Approximately 960 million people worked in these economies. Population growth—largely in poorer countries—increased the number of workers employed in these economies to about 1.46 billion by 2000.

Then in the 1990s, the Soviet System imploded, with workers leading the opposition to communism in a process begun by Solidarnosc in Poland. China's Communist Party, witness to the economic and political disaster of the Cultural Revolution, chose to introduce market capitalism while maintaining its dictatorship in politics. India, which had lost economic ground compared to the rest of the world, decided to move from an autarkic state-run economy toward markets and the global trading community. These changes greatly impacted the global capitalist system. They added about 1.47 billion new workers to the global labor supply by 2000, which effectively doubled the labor supply in the global capitalist system (see table 2.1).

Few analysts expected the world to come together so suddenly in a single global economy based on capitalism and markets. During the cold war, it seemed normal for the world to be divided into competing economic systems that had only loose connections with one another. Many thought that the state-planned economies could function as well as or better than market economies. Many feared that communist dictatorships might defeat democracies. Instead, global capitalism has come to virtually every country in the world.

The *second driver* of the ongoing globalization of labor markets is the rapid expansion of higher education in developing countries. From 1970 to 2000, the number of college and university students in developing countries increased by 383 percent. This brought the share of enrollments in those countries to 69.1 percent of the world's total. By contrast, the share of university students in the United states fell from 29 percent of university enrolments worldwide in 1970 to 14 percent in 2000.[3] In the 2000s, China was at the forefront of increasing its supply of college-educated workers. From 1999 to 2005, the number of persons graduating with bachelor's degrees in China increased fivefold to four million persons. China also greatly increased the number of persons with science and engineering doctorates graduating from its universities. By 2010, China will graduate more science and engineering Ph.D.s than the United States, with Chinese graduates from U.S. universities counted as part of the U.S. total (Freeman 2006a). The quality of university education is higher in the United States than in China, but China will improve quality over time. India has produced many high-quality computer programmers and engineers. And

Table 2.1 The Great Doubling: Workers in the Global Labor Force, 2000, before and after China, India, and Ex-Soviet Bloc Join Global Economy (Millions of Economically Active Persons)

	Global	Advanced	LDC	New
2000 Before	1460	460	1000	—
2000 After	2930	460	1000	1470*

* China, 760 million; India, 440 million; Ex-Soviet, 260 million.

Source: Employment from International Labor LO data, laborsta.ilo.org/.

Indonesia, Brazil, Peru, Poland—name the country—more than doubled their university enrolments in the 1980s and 1990s.

To be sure, the United States and other advanced countries still have far more university graduates and doctorate scientists and engineers *relative* to the overall populations than China, India, or other highly populous developing countries. But while relative factor proportions matter greatly for some economic outcomes, they are unimportant to others. Multinationals that search globally for the best employees or for places to locate high-tech facilities are concerned with the number of highly educated workers, not with that number relative to the number of less-skilled workers or peasants in agriculture. To the extent that innovation and production of high-tech products depends on the absolute number of educated workers, rather than the relative number, the huge increase in university-going people in highly populous developing countries gainsays the principal assumption of the North-South model—that only advanced countries had the educated workforce necessary for innovation and production of high-tech products.

The *third driver* of the new globalization is the rapid transfer of modern technology to developing countries. As students around the world study the same modern science and technology, the increased number of students in developing countries contributes to the transfer of technological knowledge. So too does the immigration of highly educated people from developing countries to the United States and other advanced countries. These immigrants appear to maintain enough ties to their land of birth to contribute to the spread of knowledge through ethnic networks (Kerr 2006). Formal government and international programs specifically designed to transfer knowledge have also sped up the spread of technology. But it is the activities of multinational firms that have played the biggest role in bringing modern technology to developing countries. When IBM or Siemens sets up facilities in China or India, they employ the most modern technologies, shaded perhaps to make greater use of low-wage labor than they would in an advanced country. One of the key bargaining issues in joint ventures in China is the transmission of technical knowledge to the Chinese partner.

Indicative of the public recognition of the spread of technological knowledge, a 2006 Zogby poll reported that 27 percent of Americans believe the "next Bill Gates" will come from China while 13 percent expected that he or she will be Indian, compared to 21 percent who felt such a pioneer will be American.[4]

Winners . . .

Almost every major economic change produces winners and losers. The growing globalization of labor markets is no exception. There are two immediate "winners" from globalization of world labor markets: businesses that employ the workers in those countries and the modern sector workers in those countries.

Business or capital is a winner because the new entrants to the global economy brought little capital with them, so that their entry into the global economy sharply reduced the capital-labor ratio in the global capitalist system. In marginal productivity theory, the capital-labor ratio is a critical determinant of the wages paid to workers and of the rewards to capital. The lower the capital per worker, the lower will be productivity and pay; and the higher the productivity of capital and its rewards. A decline in the global capital-labor ratio shifts the balance of power in markets toward capital. Thus, an important measure of the effect of the great doubling on the global economy is its impact on the global capital-labor ratio.

Using data from the Penn World tables on yearly investments by country, I have estimated the level of capital stock country by country and added the estimated stocks into a measure of the global capital stock. Specifically for each country, I cumulated the annual investments with depreciation rates of 5 percent or 10 percent using the perpetual inventory method.[5] I made special adjustments for the Soviet Union due to the lower productivity of its capital relative to other countries. Then I divided the estimated global capital stock by the workforce data in table 2.1 to assess how the doubling of the workforce altered the global capital-labor ratio.

Figure 2.1 shows that the doubling of the global workforce reduced the ratio of capital to labor in the world economy in 1990 and 2000 to less than what it would have been had those economies remained outside the system. The reason the global capital-labor ratio fell greatly was that the new entrants to the global economy did not bring much capital with them. India had little capital because it was one of the poorest countries in the world. China was also very poor and destroyed capital during the Maoist period. The Soviet Empire was wealthier than China or India but invested disproportionately in military goods and heavy industry, much of which was outmoded or so polluting as to be worthless. But the reduction in the global capital-labor ratio does not imply a reduction in the capital-labor ratio throughout the world. If all other factors were to be constant, capital should flow to China, India, and the ex-Soviet bloc from the rest of the world, raising wages in those countries and lowering the wages of workers in other countries relative to what those wages would have been had these countries remained separated from the rest of the world economy.

In fact, during the period of the great doubling, capital earned relatively high rewards, though in many countries, the biggest increases in income have gone to top executives. Absent a definitive study of the determinants of the returns to capital and of the extent to which the high executive pay,

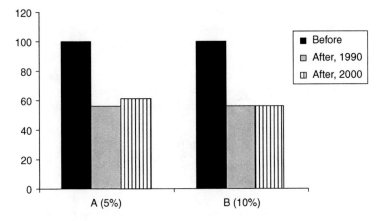

Figure 2.1   Doubling Labor Force Reduces Global K/L Ratio

Note: The A figures are based on a discount rate of 5% for transforming investment data into capital stocks. The B figures are based on a discount rate of 10%.

Source: Capital-labor ratio, calculated from Penn World Tables as described in Freeman (2005a), scaled so before is 1.00.

which is often related to company profits through stock options, reflects their ability to garner higher returns to capital, the link between the doubling of the workforce and profitability should be viewed as hypothetical. It is difficult to isolate the effect of changes in capital-labor ratios on the rewards to capital owners when so many other things are happening in the global economy: changes in technology, central bank determination of short-run interest rates, the weakening of trade unions, and changes in rates of taxation and accounting procedures. In the long run, China, India, and the ex-Soviet bloc will save and invest and contribute to the growth of the world capital stock. The World Bank estimates that China's savings rate is on the order of 40 percent, higher than the savings rate in most other countries, which will help increase global capital rapidly. Though China is much poorer than the United States, it saves about as much as the United States in absolute terms because its savings rate far exceeds the U.S. savings rate. Still, it will take three or so decades to restore the global capital-labor ratio to what it had been before China, India, and the ex-Soviet bloc entered the world economy and even longer to bring it to where it might have been absent their entry. For the foreseeable future, the United States and other countries will have to adjust to a relative shortfall of capital per worker and to the power this gives to firms in bargaining with workers.

The other big winners from the movement toward a global labor market are the workers in China and India, whose productivity has risen greatly since those countries joined the world capitalist system. Rates of economic growth have zoomed in both countries, and so too have real earnings. In China, the real earnings of urban workers more than doubled between 1990 and 2002. Poverty fell sharply despite China having a huge rise in inequality. Real wages in India also rose rapidly. Because China and India had incomes per capita below those of almost all other countries in the world, growth in their per capita income has reduced inequality of incomes worldwide.

... and losers

Workers in many of the developing countries in Latin America, Africa, and Asia have not fared so well. The entry of China and India into the world economy turned many developing countries from the low-wage competitors of advanced countries to the high-wage competitors of China and India. With the new supply of low-wage labor, firms that traditionally produced manufacturing goods in these countries can move or threaten to move facilities to lower-wage settings if workers in existing facilities do not grant concessions in wages or work conditions favorable to the firm. In 2004, for example, some employers in Central America told apparel workers that they had to work extra hours without any increase in earnings to keep business from moving to China. With wages in Central America three to four times those in China, the threat was a valid one. The location for the production of blue jeans for the U.S. market tells a similar story. Production shifted from Texas to Mexico, but with the possibility of producing with even lower wage labor in China in the mid-2000s, Mexican producers were thinking about setting up shop in China while limiting Mexican production to designer brand jeans.

As a result of the growing concentration of manufacturing jobs in China and other factors, employment in Latin America, South Africa, and in parts of Asia has been shifting since 1990 from the formal sectors traditionally associated with economic advancement to informal sectors, where work is precarious, wages and productivity low, and occupational risks and hazards great. Countries such as Peru, El Salvador, Mexico, and South Africa, among others, can no longer develop by producing generic low-wage goods and services for the global market place that the Washington Consensus[6] model of development envisaged for them.

Some of these countries benefit from Chinese growth through increased sales of natural resources; the returns from natural resource production often flow to the multinational firms that control production in the sector. Mining and related extraction industries employ relatively few workers, most of whom are less skilled. Something more is needed for the workers in these countries to avoid substantial loss or stagnation of incomes from the competition of lower-paid Chinese and Indian worker. The orthodox World Bank/IMF Washington Consensus model of development through globalization might once have worked for these countries but cannot do so anymore, leading several countries in Latin America to turn against the Consensus prescription for economic success.

What about the United States (and Other Advanced Economies)?

The entry of China, India, and the ex-Soviet bloc and the increased supply of workers in other developing countries benefit the United States and other advanced countries in several ways. Consumers can buy many goods and services at lower prices from those countries because labor costs are low. Moreover, as the Chinese, Indian, and ex-Soviet economies develop, they will increasingly demand products made in the United States and other advanced countries. In the near future, the university graduates and scientists and engineers in China, India, and elsewhere will develop new knowledge that leads to some great innovation that improves living standards worldwide. In the long run, the great doubling, the expansion of higher education to populous low-income countries, and the rapid diffusion of modern technology should create more rapid growth for the advanced countries and produce a world in which wages and incomes converge around the world.

But the transition to this economic nirvana is likely to be bumpy. The movement toward a more global labor market challenges worker well-being in the United States and other advanced countries in several ways. Trade, the offshoring of low-skilled service jobs, and immigration of low-skilled workers create downward pressures on the employment and earnings of less-skilled workers. When globalization consisted largely of increased trade in manufacturing, low-skilled workers in advanced countries could escape competition from low-wage workers overseas in the growing service sector. But as offshoring has made more services tradable, and as immigration has increased, this is no longer the case: there is competition in all labor markets. This makes it more difficult than decades earlier for the competitive market to raise pay for lower-skilled workers in the United States and other advanced countries.

The traditional policy response to the pressure that globalization places on less-skilled workers in advanced countries is to call for those workers to invest more in education. During the early 1990s U.S. debate over the NAFTA treaty with Mexico, proponents of the treaty argued that less-skilled U.S. workers would benefit from trade if only they invested more in human capital and shifted into the skill-intensive jobs likely to expand with trade. The same argument would seem to apply even more strongly to economic relations with China and India. The average worker in China and India has lower skills than the average Mexican worker. From this perspective, Chinese and Indian workers are complements rather than substitutes for American workers. Lower prices for shoes, t-shirts, and plastic toys and higher prices for semiconductors and business consulting and finance would be in the interest of all U.S. workers save perhaps for the last shoemaker or seamstress.

But the two other drivers of the trend toward globalization of the work force—spread of higher education and modern technology to low-wage countries—will reduce advanced countries' comparative advantage in high tech and the potential for education to play the deus ex machina role. In 2004, as many engineers and computer specialists troubled over the off-shoring of skilled work, Paul Samuelson reminded economists that a country with a comparative advantage in a sector can suffer economic loss when another country competes successfully in that sector (Samuelson 2004). The new competitor increases supplies, which reduce the price of those goods on world markets and the income of the original exporter. Those sectors contract and some of their workers have to shift to less desirable sectors. Some trade specialists reacted negatively to Samuelson's reminder (Bhagwati, Panagariya, and Srinivasan 2004). What he said was well known to them but irrelevant. In the real world, it would never happen.

But Samuelson has a track record of being correct, and he seems more on target than his critics. Low-income countries have increased their presence in technically advanced sectors. China has moved rapidly up the technological ladder, expanded its high-tech exports, and achieved a significant position in research in what many believe will be the next big industrial technology—nanotechnology. China's share of scientific research papers has increased greatly. India has achieved a strong position in information technology and attracts major R&D investments, particularly in Bangalore. China and India have increasing footprints in high tech because as large populous countries, they can produce as many or more highly educated scientists and engineers as advanced countries even though the bulk of their workforce is less skilled.[7]

Indicative of the change in the global labor market, multinational firms have responded to the increased supply of highly educated workers by "global sourcing" for workers. This means looking for the best candidates worldwide rather than in the advanced countries and locating facilities, including high tech R&D and production, where the supply of candidates is sufficient to get the work done at the lowest cost. Over 750 multinational firms have set up R&D facilities in China. Offshoring computer programming or moving call centers to lower-wage countries is the natural economic response to the availability of qualified labor in those countries. I have called the process of moving up the technological ladder by educating large numbers of students in science and engineering "human resource leapfrogging," since it uses human resources to leapfrog comparative advantage from low-tech to high-tech sectors. The combination of low wages and highly educated workers in large populous countries makes them formidable competitors for an advanced country.

The bottom line is that the spread of modern technology and education to China and India will undo some of the U.S. monopoly in high-tech innovation and production and place competitive pressures on U.S. wages and employment. Eventually, the wages of workers in China and India will approach those in the United States, as have the wages of European, Japanese, and to some extent Korean workers, but that is a long way off. Along with immigration, trade and the new ability to offshore skilled work will impact the labor market for educated as well as less-educated workers in the United States.

The Challenge of Transition

By bringing modern technology and business practices to most of humanity, the triumph of global capitalism promises to create the first truly global labor market. Barring social, economic, or environmental disasters, technological advances should accelerate and permit huge increases in incomes around the world that will eventually produce rough income parity among nations and, with appropriate social and economic policies, "make poverty history." But even under the most optimistic scenario, it will take decades for the global economy to absorb the huge workforces of China, India, and potentially other successful developing countries. Post World War II, it took thirty or so years for Western Europe and Japan to reach rough parity with the United States. It took Korea about fifty years to move from being one of the poorest economies in the world to the second rung of advanced economies. If the Chinese economy keeps growing rapidly and wages double every decade as in the 1990s, Chinese wages would approach levels that the United States has today in about thirty years and would approach parity with the United States in two or so decades later. India will take longer to reach U.S. levels.

How American workers fare in the transition will depend on a race between the labor market factors that improve living standards and the factors that reduce those standards. On the plus side are the likely higher rates of productivity due to more rapid scientific and technological progress created by the increased supply of highly educated workers. Also on the plus side are the lower prices of goods made by low-wage workers overseas. On the negative side are the labor market pressures from workers with similar skills to those of U.S. workers and the worsening of terms of trade and loss of comparative advantage in the high-tech industries that offer the greatest prospects for productivity advances and the most desirable jobs. Which factors win the race depends in part on the economic and labor market policies that countries, the international community, unions, and firms choose to guide the transition. I can envisage a good transition scenario and a bad transition scenario.

In the good transition, India, China, and other low-wage countries rapidly close the wage and income gap with the United States and other advanced countries. Wages converge globally because wages in the successful developing countries rise substantially, not because wages fall for competing workers in the United States or other advanced countries. Scientists, engineers, entrepreneurs from the developing countries produce new and better products for the global economy. This reduces costs of production and dominates the declining terms of trade in the advanced countries, so that living standards get better. The United States and other advanced countries retain comparative advantage in enough leading sectors or niches of sectors to remain hubs in the global development of technology. The world savings rate rises so that the global capital-labor ratio increases rapidly. The United States distributes some of its economic growth in the form of increased social services and improved social infrastructure—national health insurance, for instance—or in the form of earned income tax credits so that living standards rise even for workers whose wages are constrained by low-wage competitors during the transition.

In the bad transition, China and India develop enclave economies in which only their modern sector workers benefit from economic growth while the rural poor remain low paid and a sufficient threat to the urban workers that urban wages grow slowly. Americans maintain high consumption and low savings, dragging down the global savings and investment rate. The United States spends huge sums of money that could improve productivity and provide safety nets for workers on unnecessary wars, tax relief for millionaires and billionaires, and other nonproductive purposes. At one point citizens begin to blame globalization for economic problems and try to abort the transition and introduce trade barriers and limit the transfer of technology. Outside the United States, rising income inequalities in China, India, and other developing countries produce social disorder that creates chaos or gets suppressed by a global "super-elite" who use their wealth and power to control a mass of struggling poor. The bad scenario resembles some recalcitrant Marxist's vision of global capitalism.

Which transition is more likely?

History shows that there have been successful and unsuccessful transitions from major economic shocks in the past. Perhaps the most successful transition was the recovery of Western Europe and Japan after World War II. The United States sent capital to Europe under the Marshall Plan that helped those countries reconstruct their economies rapidly. Recovery of Europe in turn created markets for American products while rapid increases in European wages saved U.S. workers from facing low-wage competition. Similarly, the United States helped Japan develop into a market democracy with the capability of challenging the United States in many technically advanced sectors. The progress of Korea from one of the poorest economies in the world, devastated by the Korean War, to an advanced economy in about fifty years is even more remarkable since that country had never before been among the leading global economies.

For unsuccessful transitions, the most recent has been the reunification of East Germany with West Germany. The German government acted as if low-income East Germany would meld seamlessly with the wealthier capitalist West despite the legacy of nearly half a century of communism. It offered extensive welfare programs to keep workers in the East but did not raise taxes to fund a massive Marshall Plan program to rebuild the East's economy. German unions sought wage parity between East and West rather than allowing wage differences to reflect productivity differences. The result is that what had been the healthiest economy in Europe was transformed into one of the sickest, with high unemployment and sluggish growth. Closer to home, reconstruction of the U.S. South after the Civil War was an even greater failure. White-dominated southern states spent resources to suppress black citizens. They developed segregated schools and allocated most moneys on the schools for whites, in part to make sure that black youngsters could not compete in the job market with whites. They kept the human capital of blacks far below what was needed for rapid economic expansion of the South. Although in many ways the opposite of West Germany's social support of East Germany, the effect was the same: retardation of a transition to a better economy. It took over a century for the South to achieve something akin to economic parity with the rest of the country.

Conclusion

The world has entered a long transition toward a single global economy and labor market. There is much to welcome in this process, which will end with a global economy in which workers with comparable skills will be paid similar wages regardless of the country they reside in. But the transition will be long and hazardous. If the United States and other countries and international agencies adopt reasonably sensible policies, I believe that the world can achieve the good transition. To adopt reasonably sensible policies, however, policymakers will have to reorient their thinking about the dominant problem facing the world economy. The problem is not protecting business and capitalism and markets in a struggle against communist planning, the welfare state, or other government interventions that shackle economic transactions. The new problem is that movement toward a global labor market will put many workers in many countries in a more precarious position than before, with capital in the driver's seat. The overriding policy bent should therefore be more toward protecting workers than toward protecting capital. The international financial institutions and economic organizations that set much of the tone in policy discourse around the world will have to rethink their traditional emphasis on protecting capital, deregulating labor markets, and encouraging manufacturing exports to finding new economic policies for countries that cannot compete in traditional manufacturing and the bulk of whose workforce will be employed in informal sectors rather than in the formal sector. The goal should be to raise incomes and standards in the informal sector rather than to reduce the size and advantage of the formal sector.

For the United States, two broad types of domestic policies can help the country through the transition period.

The first are policies that increase our investment in knowledge to maintain comparative advantage in high-tech sectors. My studies of the relation between the number and value of stipends for graduate study and the supply of young persons entering science and engineering in the United States has led me to propose that the National Science Foundation (NSF) increase the number of graduate fellowships in science and engineering (Freeman 2006a). In addition, however, the NSF and National Institute of Health should award more research and development grants directly to young researchers rather than to senior principal investigators. This would give younger scientists and engineers the best opportunity to make fruitful innovations.

On the demand side, the federal government should reverse years of declining investments in basic research and development spending relative to GDP and increase expenditures in areas where the nation has some natural advantage for commercialization or where the economic gains to the country are likely to be exceptionally high. Energy and the environment are two prime target areas. As the country benefits most when scientific and technological knowledge leads to innovation, production, and employment in the United States, moreover, I also favor policies that increase the "stickiness" of knowledge creation to the locale in which it was developed, such as strengthening the link between universities and industries, developing research consortiums, and modernizing the patent system. At the same time, since other countries will create an increasing proportion of new knowledge, it behooves the federal government to invest in providing U.S. firms with information on research findings worldwide—for example, by translating foreign journals and offering agriculture extension type services to smaller firms to increase the likelihood that U.S. firms are the ones commercializing innovative science.

Finally, going beyond research and development spending, there is a commensurate need for increased investment in public infrastructure, particularly in the urban areas where most Americans live. One reason U.S. workers are more productive than those in other countries is that the United States has the transportation, communication, health and safety, goods and services, and legal protections of capital and labor that makes business easier to conduct. I have not examined what areas of public investment would be most productive. State and local programs may be more effective than federally funded programs, as per the infamous bridge to nowhere that one senator earmarked into federal spending.

The second set of policies is designed to prevent a repeat of the experience of the past twenty or thirty years in which nearly all of America's productivity growth ended up in the pockets of the super-wealthy. Since these policies are about the division of economic gains and losses rather than about retaining comparative advantage and raising productivity and output, they are invariably more controversial. My analyses suggest reforms in at least some and perhaps all of the following policy areas:

(1) *Strengthening the institutions that represent normal workers in their dealings with management—trade unions and other forms of worker organization.* In the updated edition of *What Workers Want* (Freeman and Rogers 2006), Rogers and I make specific proposals for unions to develop innovative strategies using modern ICT and forming organizations in local areas to support workers who cannot obtain collective bargaining contracts; and for allowing states greater leeway in enforcing and modifying the labor law governing private sector workers, ranging from placing greater penalties on firms that commit unfair labor practices to allowing workers and firms to form nonunion worker's groups within firms, if they so wish. The free-market solution to an imbalance between capital and labor is to enhance the ability of labor to take care of itself, as part owners of capital (see 3) and as an organized entity, union or nonunion, inside firms.

(2) *Increasing the basket of guaranteed, nonmarket goods and services for all citizens, irrespective of their position in the labor market.* These goods and services range from police protection to health insurance to provision of sanitation and parks and related amenities, and a commensurate increased investment in public infrastructure, particularly in the urban areas where most Americans live. Again, I favor giving states great leeway to decide on

the specifics of these expenditures, subject to some minimum floor. Public provision of additional consumption items, paid by taxes that invariably are higher for wealthier citizens, will reduce the costs of labor to firms and maintain employment and living standards even with low-wage competition in the new global economy. Public development of infrastructure, from bridges to public transportation to job training, paid by taxes that invariably are higher for wealthier citizens, will increase the productivity of firms and help their U.S. facilities compete in the global market.

(3) Greater sharing of the rewards and risk of business through increased profit-sharing and employee stock ownership; and greater share of workers in decision-making through employee involvement programs, and reforms in corporate governance that reduce the ability of management to obtain larger and larger shares of the profits of firms. If capital benefits from the globalization of the labor market, it behooves workers to increase their stake in ownership or in profits, both in their own firm but more broadly through pension funds.

(4) *Supplementing the pay of low-wage workers or families so that they can have reasonable living standards even when they are paid relatively low wages.* The notion is to "make work pay" by turning welfare support into work support. The Earned Income Tax Credit in the United States has been the most successful program in this arena. It was initially developed as a Republican alternative to the minimum wage to help low-income workers but has since won the approval of most Democrats while many Republicans have become convinced that the country benefits largely from tax cuts to the super-wealthy or subsidies to large corporations.

This is an aggressive agenda that which would both raise productivity and output and prevent further erosion of the middle class and roll back some of the huge rise in inequality that has been the major weakness in the U.S. job market. I have examined some of the policies in detail, per the references, but others are more in the nature of signposts or giving directions (Freeman 1999, 2007). I recognize that there are other policies that might accomplish some of the same goals that motivate my list, and I welcome alternatives, particularly from conservatives who also see the globalization of labor markets as a giant challenge to traditional U.S. policies. Specific policies aside, policymakers in the United States and elsewhere must avoid doing what military historians often accuse generals of doing—fighting the last war—instead of developing new strategies and policies for today's problems. What is critical is that the labor market and social policies of the next decade or so address today's big problem—assuring a good transition to a truly global labor market.

Notes

1. For a useful overview of the debate see Wikopedia, http://en.wikipedia.org/wiki/Offshoring
2. Both surveys are cited by Drezner (June 9, 2004), http://www.danieldrezner.com/archives/001355.html http://www.employmentlawalliance.com/pdf/ELA_Offshore_Outsource_Poll_ D1_5_25_04.pdf http://www.ipsos_na.com/ news/pdf/media/mr040607_1tbzzz.pdf
3. The 2000–2002 data from UNESCO, Institute of Statistics http://stats.uis. unesco.org/TableViewer/tableView.aspx?ReportId=214; Earlier data from http:// www.uis.unesco.org/en/stats/statistics/indicators/i_pages/IndGERTer.asp with some figures from Cross National Time Series Data Archive, 2004 Arthur S. Banks, http://www.databanks.sitehosting.net/www/faq.htm
4. The Zogby/463 Internet Attitudes poll, December 8, 2006, Results at http:// www.463.com/polling_results.pdf
5. OECD, http://stats.oecd.org/glossary/detail.asp?ID=2055. For a discussion of how different countries estimate their capital stock, see OECD Capital Stock Conference Canberra, March 10–14, 1997 http://www.oecd.org/document/ 63/0,2340,en_2825_500246_1876351_1_1_1_1,00.htm
6. http://en.wikipedia.org/wiki/Washington_Consensus
7. For detailed analysis of these patterns, see Freeman 2006b.

CHAPTER THREE

OFFSHORING AND LABOR RECOMMODIFICATION IN THE GLOBAL TRANSFORMATION

Guy Standing

Introduction

Offshoring is an aspect of labor market restructuring that has caught popular attention in the United States, but it has attracted nothing like as much attention in other parts of the world compared with other aspects. Offshoring is a metaphor. It is just one manifestation of *fear* that is characterizing the globalization of labor market flexibility. It goes with Perot's infamous imagery of "the great sucking sound" of Mexico.

In western Europe, the latest euphemism for the transfer of jobs to lower-cost countries is *footprint migration*, signifying the establishment of new facilities on fresh soil. This is also part of the disruptive emergence of an *international labor system*. Those firms take with them their employment cultures and often bring a minority of key workers from their corporations. Sometimes it is the corporation that adapts to local traditions, institutions, and labor regulations; sometimes, they bring pressure on local political structures to alter to accommodate their labor practices.

The global story is, essentially, that since the 1970s, the world has entered a "transformation" analogous to what Karl Polanyi had depicted as the "Great Transformation," which lasted from the nineteenth century into the middle of the twentieth (Polanyi 1944). He portrayed the first disruptive phase of that transformation (which he wrongly thought was the only one) as guided by a deliberate strategy, led by financial capital, to create a *market society* in which workers were left unprotected and subject to unbridled market forces. He recognized that a market society was unsustainable, as well as deplorable, and that policymakers and leaders would act to reembeded the economy in society, by curbing market forces and by introducing systems of social protection, income redistribution, and labor market regulation so as to moderate the worst excesses of the market system.

In the subsequent, "embedding" phase of that Great Transformation, policymakers forged the *welfare state* in its various guises, backed by Keynesian economics and a complex system of statutory labor regulations, neocorporatist collective bargaining backed by a relatively strong labor movement and progressive fiscal policy. But this system had inherent weaknesses, as documented elsewhere (Standing 2002).

The key point was that it was a systematic attempt to spread the notion of *industrial citizenship*, with a spreading array of labor-based entitlements, not *rights* but entitlements conditional on the performance of labor or the willingness to perform labor, or the state-determined perception that the person could be from excused labor, due to such contingencies as illness and incapacity or maternity or old age.

In order to position the growth of offshoring, I will argue that the era of industrial citizenship has broken down irretrievably, ultimately potentially for the better. I will summarize the global trends in labor-related insecurities, of which offshoring is a single manifestation, so far only a relatively minor one. And I will consider the nature of labor recommodification, in order to determine what policy and regulatory options are available and feasible as the progressive response.

The Age of Insecurity

To appreciate the nature of the challenge in the early years of the twenty-first century—still deep in the *disembedded* phase of the Global Transformation—one must recall what it was that was promoted in the embedded phase of Polanyi's Great Transformation. One way of seeing this is that there was a steady advance in the socioeconomic security of workers and their families.

One can identify seven forms of labor-related security, which are defined and operationalized elsewhere (ILO 2004, 2005; Standing 2002).[1] These are *income, representation, labor market, employment, job, skill,* and *work security.* As they were developed in the industrial citizenship era, these are summarized in figure 3.1, and have been refined through surveys, and a global socioeconomic security database.

In that era, advances were made in all forms of labor security, but they came at the price of producing a false paradise of *laborism*, that is, social entitlements were tied to the performance of labor, while regulations, social protection, and redistribution were based on the norm of full-time labor by a man ("the breadwinner") supporting a dependent wife ("the caregiver"). There was a tendency to promote behavioral norms that were ultimately

1. *Labor market security*: Adequate income-earning opportunities; at the macro-level, this is epitomized by a government commitment to Full Employment;

2. *Employment security*: Protection against arbitrary dismissal, regulations on hiring and firing, imposition of costs on employers for failing to adhere to rules, etc.;

3. *Job security*: Ability and opportunity to retain a niche, an occupation or "career", plus barriers to skill dilution, and opportunities for "upward" mobility in terms of status and income, etc.;

4. *Work security*: Protection against accidents and illness at work, through, e.g., safety and health regulations, limits on working time, unsociable hours, night work for women, etc., as well as compensation for mishaps;

5. *Skill reproduction security*: Good opportunity to gain and retain skills, through apprenticeships, employment training, etc., as well as opportunity to make use of competencies;

6 *Income security*: Assurance of an adequate and stable income, protection of income through, e.g., minimum wage machinery, wage indexation, comprehensive social security, progressive taxation to reduce inequality and to supplement those with low incomes, etc.;

7. *Representation security*: Possessing a collective voice in the labor market, through, e.g., independent trade unions, with a right to strike, etc.

Figure 3.1   The Seven Forms of Labor-Related Security

restrictive and stultifying. It was a prescription for dumbing down, for "job-holders" so witheringly depicted by Hannah Arendt (1957). It also produced labor rigidities and thus rising labor costs. That was sustainable in a world consisting of a closed-economy model, in which international trade took place primarily between countries with similar levels of labor security and thus cost structures, and an international division of labor that was based on an arrangement where "underdeveloped" countries produced primary goods while "developed" countries produced manufactured goods and services. Once the world began to become an open economy system, there was no way the old laborist model could be sustained.

In itself, the demise of the laborist model should be welcomed. There was no Golden Age, even though old social democrats harp on about it.[2] But what was ushered in with the reforms of the 1970s onward—epitomized by the experimental madness of Pinochet in Chile, and followed on in a grander scale with Reaganism and Thatcherism, and supported by the

World Bank and IMF elsewhere—was a rupture that has spread economic insecurity everywhere.

That rupture can be presented in several ways. First, it can be seen as a *disembedded* phase of a new transformation. All such phases are characterised by the growth of inequalities and insecurities as commercial elites that dominate policy development and the state push remorselessly toward the creation of a *market society*. In this respect, we are clearly at a sensitive point in history. The last time such a concerted drive toward a market society was unleashed, in the nineteenth century, the end result was fascism and bolshevikism, before the welfare state emerged from the ashes of the first of those madnesses. One must hope that the dangers of current developments will be learned before we lurch into another phase of sharply curbed freedoms and dehumanizing authoritarianism.

It might seem a long way from that fear to the labor market restructuring that is taking place. It is not. What this great transformation is leading toward is an international labor market, whereas Polanyi's transformation was about the emergence of national labor markets. So far, the model that has emerged under the rubric of flexibility and "neoliberalism" has been about the destruction or erosion of all the institutions and policies of national labor markets that had ameliorated the inequalities and insecurities. The changes profoundly altered the nature and distribution of economic insecurity.

Indeed, this is the first time in human history when we are being presented with a global model based on the premise that "insecurity is good for you." We are urged to participate in *the risk society*. But, whereas in the embedded phase of welfare state capitalism, capital was allowed to receive higher income than labor in return for bearing most of the risks and insecurity, while labor was rewarded with greater security, now capital is provided with greater economic returns and is increasingly protected against risk and insecurity, while labor is expected to bear much more of the risk and receive lower income and is also expected to deal with systemic insecurity.

Globally, there has been a regrowth in all seven forms of labor insecurity. Perhaps the defining feature of labor reforms in the past two decades is the systematic attempt in all parts of the world to make labor relations more *flexible* by weakening workers' entrenched entitlements and by removing or lowering those forms of social income that are relatively fixed. *Flexibility* is one of the defining euphemisms of our age. So is *labor market deregulation*. But there is no such thing as labor market deregulation. This has been a period of labor market reregulation. There has never been a period in history when more regulations have been passed into law around the world. A defining feature of the regulatory drive has been its anticollective character, with more restraints placed on worker organizations and more efforts made to encourage contractual individualization.

The world is playing a game called *beggar-my-neighbor-flexibility*. This has been going on with a process of *social policy dumping* and *fiscal policy dumping*. Everywhere you go you will find earnest ministers of labor or social welfare, and their even more earnest advisers, wondering how they can make their labor market more flexible and competitive than the wonderfully flexible system they imagine is "over there."

Offshoring is part of this process. But it is just one means by which flexibility, economic insecurity, and labor force fragmentation are being extended. It must be seen as part of a globalizing labor chain. Seeing it as a single phenomenon would be analytically and politically mistaken. Whereas the first phase of Polanyi's Great Transformation involved the forging of national labor markets, through the mass migration of labor power into the new urban centers of mass production, this transformation is about the painful emergence of an international labor market, involving the mobility of capital to where labor can be supplied most cheaply. The main trend in what is the first phase of a Global Transformation is best described as labor recommodification.

The Era of Labor Recommodification

In the last transformation, the most relevant change of the first "disembedding" phase was the development of national labor markets in which labor became a commodity, to be bought and sold, without capacity to resist exploitative and oppressive working conditions, or the receipt of low and irregular wages. Outwork and subcontracting were common, and the great feature was the mix of labor migration into the urban industrial areas and *labor circulation*, as workers moved to and from emerging labor markets. But all this came at a high and growing cost, of deprivation and tensions among the working population, and restricted productivity. In order to sustain social stability and economic growth, the state had to respond by ushering in social reforms that had the effect of reducing the commodity character of labor relationships.

This is often described as decommodification, in that, participation in the labor market was more protected and income was made less dependent on the amount of labor performed. But, as argued elsewhere, this was really a *fictitious decommodification*, since although the main changes involved a shift from monetary to nonmonetary compensation, workers' welfare was still made dependent on the performance of labor (Standing, forthcoming).

In any case, since the mid-1970s, there has been a process of labor recommodification around the world, which can best be captured by considering what is happening to the structure of incomes.

Social Income

It may be useful to depict what has happened in the "disembedding" phase of globalization by means of the concept of *social income*. Obviously, in any but the most primitive society, everyone has some source of income, or else he/she dies.[3] The total may be inadequate or grotesquely large, but to survive they must have something. There are various sources, and the composition determines not just the level but also the security of a person's income.[4]

Basically, although many of the elements might be nonexistent, any individual in any society has up to six sources of income, which together constitute the person's social income. This may be defined as follows:

$$SI = SP + W + CB + EB + SB + PB$$

where SI is the individual's total social income, SP is self-production (whether self-consumed, bartered or sold), W is the money wage or income received from work, CB is the value of benefits or support provided by the family, kin, or the local community, EB is the amount of benefits provided by the enterprise in which the person might be working, SB is the value of state benefits, in terms of insurance benefits or other transfers, including subsidies paid directly to workers or through firms to them, and the value of social services, and PB is private income benefits, gained through investment, including private social protection.

The relevance of the decomposition of social income is that the prevailing pattern of remuneration indicates the degree to which a person is subject to labor market forces. Thus, one can assess the degree to which the person's labor is commodified and the extent to which he or she is commodified. To give the simplest example, if W were a very large share of SI the degree of commodification would be much greater than if W were zero or a small part of the person's total income.

In an era of decommodification, W would shrink as a share of SI, whereas in an era of (re-)commodification it would grow. One would also expect that in the former, those elements of SI that were relatively secure, as a result of institutional interventions or legislation, would be eroded, whereas those that were insecure and conditional on the performance of labor could be expected to grow in relative terms.

Dismantling Social Income

In the era of globalization, there has been a strong shift back to money wages. There have been many pressures inducing this. But four changes stand out.

First, there has been a steady cutback in enterprise benefits (EB) via *explicit* and *implicit disentitlement*. The former has come about through a mix of concession bargaining and legislative changes that have allowed firms to abandon or reduce nonwage benefits, such as pensions, healthcare, and worker subsidies of various kinds. The latter has come about by moving workers from statuses under which they had entitlement to such benefits to statuses in which they do not. All sorts of ruses have been used to achieve the latter.

Second, there has been a shift from universal and insurance-based state benefits, in which workers and employers make contributions in return for contingency transfers, to selective, means-tested benefits. Within that decline, there has been a shift to discretionary and directional transfers. Besides the increase in worker income insecurity, these changes also weaken *social solidarity*. Indeed, the decline in workers' collective voice has been both instrumental in the dismantling of social income and the result of it.

Third, there has been a trend toward the use of *labor subsidies*, effectively monetary supplements to top up low wages, which represent a subsidy to capital. The classic case is the Earned Income Tax Credit in the United States, but all industrialized countries have moved in that direction. These are surely a trade distortion, since they effectively subsidize relatively unskilled labor and thus artificially increase the competitiveness of import-substituting industries, such as garment production. One may predict that the issue of labor subsidies will come up before the World Trade Organization sooner or later.

Fourth, there has been the issue of increased necessity for workers to rely on informal support systems, covered by the term CB in the identity. In effect, people have to find such support because of the removal of EB and SB. This relates to offshoring and the restructuring of labor markets, because it means that many forms of labor have to be subsidized by supportive transfers from family members or communities. Where there are such networks, workers can receive such support, undercutting those living where community systems have been eroded.

In any case, the restructuring of social income is central to the global growth of economic insecurity. As such, it might be of interest to see how the United States has been faring in terms of the extent and pattern of such insecurity.

Economic Insecurity in the United States: A Comparative Perspective

This phase of the transformation has led to a growth of labor-related insecurity. To examine the trends, we developed a global database for over

120 countries. The methodology, explained elsewhere, is as follows. First, we identify *input* indicators of the forms of security, that is, proxy measures of government commitments on the main dimensions of that form of security, epitomized by ratification of international conventions. Second, we identify *process* indicators, that is, measures of mechanisms to put those commitments into practice. Third, we identify *outcome* indicators, that is, measures of how well actual experience has been in that area. To give an example, an input indicator of work security would be ratification of occupational health and safety conventions, a process indicator would be the existence of a labor inspectorate to ensure that safety laws are put into effect, while an outcome indicator would be the accident rate in manufacturing and mining.

Several of each type of indicator are combined into indices, and these are combined into security indices, using the methodology of the UNDP's Human Development Index. In each case, the outcome subindex is given double the weight of the input and process subindices. Normalizing the resultant indices, we combine them into a composite *Economic Security Index*, which we can estimate for countries that together cover over 80 percent of the world's population. Not all countries have all the data on all forms of security. For the overall index, however, we have data for 90 countries.

The United States does not emerge with as high a ranking as some would wish, nor does its position correspond to what it would be if there was a straight correlation with national income per capita. Table 3.1 shows the positions on each form of security for the countries for which there were

Table 3.1 Economic Security Index: The United States in Comparative Perspective

	U.S. ranking	Number of comparison countries	Main reasons behind U.S. ranking
Labor market security	16	94	low input values
Employment security	30	99	poor input and process
Job security	22	94	strong process
Skill security	12	139	high outcome
Work security	29	95	poor input
Representation security	41	99	poor outcome
Income security	23	96	low process
Overall economic security index	25	90	

Source: ILO (2004).

complete data, with the final column indicating the most revealing feature of the U.S. index by comparison with the average for rich industrialized countries.

There are surprises in the international patterns and points to bear in mind in reflecting on desirable responses to the insecurities surrounding such phenomena as outsourcing and external flexibility. The United States comes out badly, relatively speaking, because its governments have subscribed much less to international labor standards than other countries and have relatively ineffectual institutional machinery to put them into effect. The United States does not do too badly in terms of employment security, contrary to its image of a hire-and-fire culture. But it provides lower employment protection than other rich countries. So, it would be dubious to blame excessive employment protection for large-scale offshoring.

The United States scores relatively badly in the forms of economic security that we regard as the *metasecurities*, namely income and representation security. It is the combination of basic income security and voice that gives full freedom.[5] If a person has basic income security, he or she can make choices rationally and adapt to pressure to change more easily. But if the person lacks voice, individually and collectively, he or she will be vulnerable to loss of income, status, and other forms of security. This is why we gave double weight to income and representation security in the Economic Security Index.

The United States does badly in terms of worker's voice, which not only reflects low unionization. An outside observer may join Americans in wishing it were otherwise, as we share some of the disadvantages. But it is a reality that seems unlikely to go away.

The United States also provides a relatively low degree of income security. This in part reflects the high level of income inequality, in part the selective and partial array of state benefits. Unfortunately, we know that low income security weakens representation security and vice versa. That combination is a breeding ground for labor *fragmentation*.

American workers are by no means alone. Americans and their west European counterparts, and even many counterparts in middle-income countries, are constantly told that unless they make concessions, their jobs will go abroad. Their concessions, and those their governments have made on their behalf, have weakened *income* security more than other forms of security, although they have weakened those as well.

Offshoring is one instrument of fear. So is the process, currently sweeping continental western Europe, of creating *fragmented workforces*, consisting of privileged insiders, with access to a wide range of benefits and forms of security, surrounded by a motley assembly of "contingent" workers, some working in the same premises, some working locally in other places, some in other parts of the country, and some "overseas."

In such circumstances, social solidarity is hard to imagine. Typically, those in one labor status have little in common with those in another. The issue epitomising the contrast between unified and fragmented workforces is *social insurance*, or *mutuality*. Social insurance principles were central to the evolution of the welfare state. No country had a full insurance system, and the Bismarckian and Beveridge models differed. However, it was the norm that drove the laborist agenda and that united social democratic thinking for fifty years on both sides of the Atlantic and in many parts of the world, including most of the decolonizing regions. That has broken down.

Offshoring as Metaphor

Labor outsourcing, or whatever it was called in earlier times, becomes prominent in times of resistance to economic restructuring. It is partly a reflection of resistance by workers to the loss and threats of losing a set of preestablished entitlements and hard-won freedoms. It is also a means of accelerating change through inducing concessions.

Today's transformation is about the emergence of an international labor market. At the heart of it is a huge movement of workers, involving migration to and from all parts of the world for the first time in human history. While globalization has involved a liberalization of markets in goods and capital, barriers have been erected to the movement of relatively unskilled workers, while inducements have been introduced to encourage skilled labor migration. Unashamedly, this has been designed to benefit the rich countries, above all the United States.

Offshoring is helping in the global redivision of labor. It involves several levels of workers—the highly-paid, educated IT specialist, the clerical "call center" type, and the relatively "unskilled" worker, usually a woman, required to do assembly labor, typically in Export Processing Zones. Each suffers from some insecurity and each has some advantages for those doing the work.

Surveying the available estimates of the extent of offshore outsourcing shows that, in most countries, the numbers seem to be too small to have had much impact. The McKinsey Global Institute estimates that the number of offshore service workers will rise from 1.5 million in 2003 to 4.1 million in 2008. According to the MGI, about 4.6 million Americans start work with a new employer every month in the year, and while this means that many face a period of concern about their chances of obtaining another job, the extent of labor turnover merely shows how limited offshoring has been so far (McKinsey Global Institute 2005). The WTO has taken the same view, stating that *"the impact of offshoring services jobs is far stronger in the popular perception than on actual production, employment and trade patterns"* (WTO

2005 and Williams 2005). As of 2005, the estimated $45 billion of off-shored IT services accounted for less than 10 percent of world exports of business services, while the two countries playing the biggest role in off-shoring, the United States and the United Kingdom, were also by far the biggest net exporters.

Trade unions have led the opposition to offshoring. But some are planning for the trend rather than fighting it. For example, in 2005, Computer Sciences Corporation, one of the world's largest IT service providers, agreed with Amicus, a U.K. union, to plow some of its savings from moving tasks offshore into retraining those whose jobs were threatened in the United Kingdom. That has not been the only such deal.

Offshoring of jobs is still at the stage of anecdotal claims and counter-claims. It is surely underestimated, in the sense that transfers of jobs mostly take place at the margin, through boardroom decisions or through adjustments in the direction of investment. The actual numbers claimed are only part of the emerging challenge. It is the *ex ante* anticipation of shifts that imparts a fear and insecurity among workers, which makes them more amenable to make concessions in the workplace, to take lower pay, to accept the loss of entrenched benefits, and so on.

The fact that firms can offshore alters the bargaining position of workers and employers. It puts an onus on all concerned to find ways of making labor more dignifying and to finding ways of limiting "free riders," those who may benefit in the short-term by paying lower wages or benefits and worsening working conditions.

Commentators who concentrate on the amount of offshoring, dismissing it as having limited significance, miss the point that it is because off-shoring is *potentially* vast that a few swallows do indeed mark the summer's arrival. Or to alter the metaphor: the fear of the "sucking sound" induces workers and their representatives, including government agencies, to accept that they must lose various enterprise and state benefits, or give up employment security and accept more flexible labor relations and payment systems.

If that is the main effect, then the significance would not be how large offshoring was but how easy it would be to practice it and how many concessions could be forced on workers by its threat. Making people fearful may be a clever device for inducing people to accept a lower standard of social income.

Given the huge differences in labor costs, even net of any remaining productivity differences, between the United States and the new industrial workshops of the world, notably India and China, one should rather wonder why outsourcing is so modest. Given the huge changes in labor policies taking place in those countries, one can predict a rapid increase in the next decade. Here one should recall the concept of social income. In China, the recent shift away from enterprise benefits to state benefits has been one of the least discussed trends that will profoundly affect the global labor market in the next decade.

This leads to a hypothesis. It is that *social policy dumping* in rich industrialized countries is being matched by the pace of *regulatory reform* in the energized workshop countries. It is wrong to have an image of a "race to the bottom," in which wages and benefits will fall to those currently received by workers in India or China. But there is a high probability of a *convergence*, which will imply moves away from what had been established as "best practice" employment relations in affluent countries toward a much lower level of economic security. To state this is not being fatalistic or pessimistic. It is rather to suggest that an alternative strategy is required rather urgently.

What Policies Are Needed?

We are faced with the prospect of a global labor market characterized by multiple forms of labor flexibility and economic insecurity stretching into the future. Progressive thinking should take that as a given, rather than expect much gain in trying to restore the trappings of *industrial citizenship*. The interesting question is whether or not there are ways to overcome the adverse trends associated with that reality. It would be atavistic to try to recreate the system of *industrial citizenship* that characterized the three decades following the end of World War II.

In thinking about responses to an open economy world, in which labor offshoring is merely an integral part, we must remember another outsourcing that is even more significant, the *offshoring of capital*. Much of this is done to avoid or evade corporate taxation. Numerous companies have moved their headquarters and/or subsidiaries to tax havens. From there they can indulge in sophisticated transfer pricing so as to disguise profits. This has led to the convenient argument that capital cannot be taxed heavily, or perhaps not at all, because its potential mobility is so high that (higher) taxes will merely lead to a mass offshoring of capital and jobs.

Along with other forms of social dumping, governments are indulging in a beggar-my-neighbor process of *tax dumping*, producing a situation in which not only are taxes on capital falling (while taxes on labor are rising relatively, and often in absolute terms as well), but also *subsidies* to capital are rising (to attract or retain foreign investment) while subsidies to workers and their families are falling. Since capital is deemed the more mobile factor, corporate tax rates are declining, and financial experts are predicting a "race to the bottom," with tax havens bidding down rates from over 30 percent a few years ago to below 10 percent in many countries now.[6] This has fuelled government budget deficits, which have provided political justification for cutting social transfers and social services. It is a recipe for chronic inequality that is greater than can be conveyed by conventional income statistics, since the nonmonetary elements of social income are becoming more unequally spread, with some groups losing on most counts and some gaining on most.

Let us consider the dilemma from the perspective of offshoring. In rich countries, short of raising artificial drawbridges and shrinking into a protectionist fortress, which is an unrealistic populist response, one can envisage a continuing trend to offshoring, more in-migration (with more reverse flows of remittances) and more irregular migration.[7] With the decline in agricultural, industrial, and service jobs, other forms of work will come into focus in those countries, so there should be no worry about people having no work to do. But given the way labor markets work, wages and enterprise benefits will fall in countries where they have been most advanced, under pressure from opportunities to employ workers at much lower wages in developing countries. Because capital wants more wage flexibility, EB will shrink by more than W, and W may rise if part of the shrinking EB is converted into monetary payments.

Meanwhile, liberalization has doubled the global labor supply, with millions of Chinese and Indian workers coming at a price much lower than what is being paid in industrialized countries. For instance, the cost of employing a car worker in Germany or the United States is about fifty times what it costs in China. If equilibration were to occur, Chinese wages would have to rise dramatically and/or U.S. wages would have to fall substantially. But labor productivity is rising faster in China than in the United States or Germany. So, labor cost differentials can be expected to widen even more.

In such circumstances, there is little prospect of real wages or workers' social income rising in the United States in sectors affected by international competition. Already, the functional distribution of income has widened, and in the globalization era there is a high probability that it will continue to do so. Capital's share of GNP will rise relative to labor's share. That is weakening workers' bargaining position everywhere, particularly in rich countries.

The lesson of this painful reality must be learned quickly. If policymakers wish to reduce income inequality they must do so by redistributing capital income, not by trying to raise real wages. The latter would be counterproductive and would merely accelerate the transfer of jobs to low-wage economies.

There should be two primary concerns—the need to find ways of responding to the chasm of inequality, and the need to determine which forms of socioeconomic security are crucial. As far as the second is concerned, the metasecurities are *income security* and *representation security*.

On income security, recall the main trends. Inequality arises increasingly from a shift in the functional distribution of income, from labor to capital. Workers have weakened bargaining power, while capital can be as mobile as it wishes, inducing governments to lower corporate taxes and provide capital with an increasing array of subsidies. One may wish for stronger bargaining power for workers, but the prospect is unlikely. More realistically, the growing inequality must be combated by other methods, including opportunities for profit-sharing, both individual and collective.

In other words, as people move to a lifestyle of *portfolio working*, a desirable response would be a social income system based on *portfolio incomes*. Imagine if most people had multiple sources of income to go with multiple forms of work, including care work, and various forms of community work.

If redistribution is to occur—and it is inconceivable that societies could tolerate a steadily growing functional inequality without such adverse consequences as to threaten political stability—then innovative fiscal policies will have to be considered and implemented.

Two policies stand out. The first is a basic income, as a right of citizenship. This would help in the Painian objective of enabling all citizens to share in the wealth generated by past generations and technological advances.[8] It would provide the basic security needed to encourage workers to accept more flexibility, and the labor-related insecurities that go with that. And it would overcome the worst forms of poverty trap and unemployment trap, which go with means-tested selective benefits.

A guaranteed basic income would provide the essence of *full freedom*, which progressives and libertarians claim they wish to see. It would advance Isaiah Berlin's two liberties, by reducing the control over workers, and by enabling them to make more rational choices about the way they organize their work and life.

Given governments' desire for light statutory regulation, for fear of capital going elsewhere, workers will have to rely much more on bargaining. They can only do that if they have some basic security. A basic income would also help in the fight against insidious state paternalism and social engineering, whereby policymakers are trying to steer the poor and unemployed to behave in ways they wish them to behave. Progressives should be profoundly uncomfortable about that and should welcome policies that would counter the paternalistic twitch.

A basic income would be a modest monthly amount, not enough to enable a person to live in comfort, but enough to give modest subsistence in extremis. As such, it would not undermine the desire to work and be creative. It would give meaning to the *right* to work. However, it should be accompanied by mechanisms to redistribute capital income that do not undermine investment, entrepreneurial risk-taking, or labor incentives. Finding the mechanism with those properties is a major challenge.

Thus the second redistributive instrument flows from the same desire to usher in lifestyles of multiple activities (combining various forms of work, with varying intensity) coupled with multiple sources of income. There is no intrinsic reason for workers to be sharply distinguished from "shareholders," or "managers" from "workers." These are social constructs. Having multiple sources of income would reduce the risk to which individuals are exposed. For this, besides a guaranteed basic income, the only way by which capital income could be redistributed is through collective and individual *profit sharing*, something like the original design of the Swedish wage-earner funds. To make that redistributive—and satisfy the Rawlsian Security Difference Principle enunciated elsewhere—such funds should involve some profit being put into social investment funds, for sharing out with outworkers and citizens outside the labor market, and for investing in social infrastructure.[9]

Economic security requires equally strong voice representation for all groups in society. In the laborist era, representation security was supposedly achieved within a model involving trade unions, tripartism, and labor law, all presuming a norm of direct "standard" employment in a workplace away from home. In the globalization era, unions have gone into deep decline, tripartism has largely gone, and labor law has been quietly reformed to make it more an instrument of labor control and competitiveness than of worker protection.

In the globalization era, *labor law* has become anachronistic, since it mainly protects those in standard employment, not the growing number of people whose activity lies outside its mandate, including those millions doing care work, voluntary community work or freelance or distance work. The growth of outsourcing accelerates that trend.

Consider what is happening in the three largest countries. In the United States, labor law is being reinterpreted by the Supreme Court and the National Labor Relations Board (NLRB). Notions of *employer* and *employee* are becoming more anachronistic. We will see many more corporate HQs delegating their employment function to subsidiaries, which will outsource to contracting suppliers, who will subcontract to agencies, middlemen, and contract workers. In such circumstances, notions of responsibility for working conditions and remuneration blur. U.S. labor laws are being adjusted to suit the desires of capital, in that the growing numbers of "contingent workers" are being denied legal rights gained for those in standard employment. For instance, both the Supreme Court and NLRB have ruled that more workers are not to be counted as "employees" since they do not pass the common "agency" and "master-servant" test, or what is called the "right to control" test.[10] Many more will find themselves outside the legal definition of "employee" and thus beyond entitlement to labor rights. And those in standard employment will make concessions in order to limit outsourcing and other forms of nonstandard labor.

Meanwhile, labor law reform in the world's emerging industrial workshops is setting the pattern. In India, the second National Commission on Labour (NCL) produced a report in 2002 in which it proposed a radical overhaul to make labour law an instrument of national competitiveness and flexibility, rather than one of worker protection. If its recommendations were to become law, rather than merely the actual trend anyhow, the space for offshoring jobs from the United States and elsewhere would accelerate. The NCL proposed a narrowing of the definition of a worker protected by labor law and, crucially for its implication for outsourcing to India, it proposed that those earning more than a certain amount would not be considered ordinary "workmen," a label that is necessary to be covered by labor law. The thrust of Indian reform is to reassert the duty to labor, with renewed emphasis on worker "responsibilities."

In China, recent labor reform has been geared to the creation of a flexible labor market, a far cry from the *danwei*, the workplace-based system that meant a high EB relative to W. The 1994 Labor Law formalized individual contracts and promoted labor administration institutions to regulate labor markets, including compulsory arbitration and mediation. The government has drafted new reforms to regulate labor, with more emphasis on workers' duties and responsibilities. It may reduce the incidence of extreme abuses, but labor law is being constructed as an instrument of *proletarianization*. And, contrary to the public posturing by the American Chamber of Commerce, the reforms will make it more attractive for multinationals to shift production and employment to China, since it will create a predictable, regulated labor market.

Whether in China, India, or the United States, labor law is geared to the standard employment relationship and is changing from being a means of labor protection to one of enhancing competitiveness. As such, it is strengthening various forms of inequality and insecurity. In that context, there are two possible routes to reform.

One is to extend the standard employment relationship to give protections to near-standard groups. Thus, agency workers and temps could be given the same entitlements as full-time workers, with part-time workers entitled to similar pro-rata benefits. This tack might cut the exploitation and oppression of migrants and agency workers and help curb the use of illegal migrants. To give teeth to this strategy, governments should expand the size and powers of their labor inspectorates. One could envisage this being a route to limit exploitation of workers in outsourced arrangements. But it would still leave the dominant standard employment model intact.

And it would fail the Rawlsian Security Difference Principle, in that the most insecure would still be unprotected.

An alternative tack is to create a *core* or floor of basic rights for everybody doing *all* types of work. This starts from the position that there is nothing sacrosanct about the so-called standard employment relationship, which represents a form of dependency and a way of dividing workers into "bread-winners" and "caregivers." If the standard is eroding, and the first tack were followed, then there would still be erosion, favoring a convergence toward a model of precariousness and labor recommodification.

In brief, labor law reform should surely not stretch the standard dualism but replace the premises on which it was based. This can come only from building a universal floor of social and economic rights. Labor law must be phased out, not further refined; it should become part of common law, covered by contract law, for example. Labor law has existed to protect *labor*, which has meant the *standard employment relationship*, accepting the "right to be managed", in a position of subordination. But in the globalization era, not even the quid pro quo of decent protection in return for the supply of effort is accepted. Labor markets are denying more people even that much. In those circumstances, and with the growing legitimacy of diverse forms of work that are not labor, having a body of labor law separate from common law does not make sense. For example, all people doing all forms of work should have an equal right to *freedom of association* and *freedom to bargain collectively*. This is not the case at the moment. The fact that labor law is becoming more dualistic and more an instrument of labor control makes the development of independent voice even more important.

So, we come to voice. Some observers place hope in *external monitoring*, seeing this as a way of inducing multinationals to stay clear of sweatshops and other forms of exploitative outsourcing (Fung, O'Rourke and Sabel 2001). In the new areas of labor supply, with weak unions and ineffectual labor protection, there have been attempts by U.S.-based NGOs to moni-tor the links in labor chains, with occasional naming-and-shaming suc-cesses. These may do little more than hinder the emergence of a more effective strategy. This is not to belittle those initiatives. But these cannot be an alternative to comprehensive *regulation* and *representation* by the workers themselves. What is required is a new form of *agency*, with institutions of collective and individual representation being overhauled.

Two innovative models, one in India and the other in the United States, are harbingers of forms of collective organization needed for flexible labor markets in which more are working at a distance from formal worksites. In India, the Self-Employed Women's Association (SEWA) has mushroomed into an organization of over a million women outworkers, giving street-vendors, beedi workers, garment workers, construction workers, wastepaper pickers, tobacco workers, and others an organizational base, awareness of their rights and social entitlements, access to microcredit, childcare arrangements, and much more. The SEWA model is being emulated elsewhere. It offers work-related services for women in flexible, informal labor, and as such provides basic security.

For several decades, the trade unions refused to recognize SEWA, claiming it was not a union, in that the people it represented were not workers in the standard definition of that term, and as such its members were not covered by India's labor law. Most of its members do not have employment contracts. They are deemed to be providing services. And SEWA is undoubtedly a *social movement*, with objectives not encompassed by collective bargaining or workplace representation. It provides its members with literacy courses, with microcredit, banking facilities, social protection schemes, and access to cooperative childcare. The unions frowned. It was not until 2006, after years of lobbying, that the international trade union confederation, then the ICFTU, finally allowed SEWA to join. Oh, those wonderfully progressive laborists.

The SEWA model is spreading, along with other hybrid bodies giving voice to those in indirect or casual labor relationships—or deemed to be "providing services"—that are at the end of the labor chain, in which outsourcing and offshoring fit. It is just one part of the *associational revolution* taking place in response to globalization and the collapse of the laborist model.

In the United States, several types of organizations have emerged. One is the Freelancers' Union, in New York State. Like SEWA, it emerged as a means of giving social services to workers in flexible, precarious labor situations, or in outsourced jobs. Its founder, Sara Horowitz, recognized that informalized workers, those working as "self-employed" contractors, as home workers or on short-term contracts, lack access to social benefits that are essential for a decent life. So, it negotiated a collective health insurance for members. Originally, it called itself the Portable Benefits Network, since it offered members benefits such as assistance in education and healthcare. Its latest initiative is to provide something like a 401(K) defined-contribution retirement-savings account as one of a menu of services its members can purchase. The union is a means of filling the gaps left by the erosion of enterprise and state-based social protection.

Part of the needed reorganization of voice concerns institutional *governance*, so as to give work higher priority in social policymaking and policy evaluation. Among feasible institutions are national councils for work and negotiated compacts between workers' bodies, employers, and governments. Here too, old models are unlikely to suffice. Fortunately, there is an *associational revolution* taking place, with thousands of new forms of civil society groups trying to come to terms with the new order. Many of these may be flawed, but they reflect a continuing desire for voice.

Those who fear their jobs being offshored, or who fear their communities are about to be blighted by an outflow of jobs to distant places, should reflect on the adage that we are as weak or strong as the weakest link in the labor chain. Traditionally, the labor battalions in rich countries, most notably the AFL-CIO, made public pronouncements in support of "the international labor movement," but they acted in their narrow nationalistic interest. There have been exceptions. But the legacy of the AFL-CIO of George Meany and Lane Kirkland included fragmented, pacified workers' movements in parts of the world where outsourcing is booming.

The challenge before us is to give assistance to the weakest in the global labor chain. If their income security and their voice were strengthened, we all would stand to gain. Offshoring is a reminder to recall the rallying cry of workers throughout the ages.

Notes

1. I first defined the seven forms in the 1980s, and find the framework useful for analyzing labor market dynamics and for developing a framework of labor and social statistics, through Enterprise Labor Flexibility and Security Surveys (ELFS) and People's Security Surveys, so far conducted in 20 countries.
2. For instance, Full Employment was a myth, since it left out a large number of women, who were a labor reserve, outside the measured labor force.
3. Even in the most rudimentary society, people have access to land with which to produce or acquire food, or receive gifts and support from those who do.
4. Of course, some groups receive less *income* than they *earn*, not because of taxes but because intermediaries control access and deduct some of it, so concealing their true poverty. Women, in particular, are often impoverished in this manner. If you wished to increase their income security, a primary objective should be to break the *control* mechanisms. Distinctions between gross and net incomes are as relevant for workers as for businesses, yet rarely do income statistics or labor market analyses take that into account.
5. For those wishing to see a fuller rationale for this claim, see Standing, 2002, or G. Standing (ed.), *Promoting Income Security as a Right* (London, Anthem Press, 2005).
6. Switzerland has rates as low as 6% that can be "negotiated" with foreign firms. Specialists predict that corporate tax will virtually disappear in the global economy, while the tax burden is passed onto workers. V. Houlder, "Europe's tax rivalry keeps multinationals on the move", *Financial Times*, Jan. 19, 2007.
7. Countries are already competing for skilled migrants and skilled return migrants.
8. For arguments in favour of a basic income, and a review of criticisms, see G. Standing, "Why Trade Unions Should Favour a Basic Income", *Transfer*, April 2005; idem, "Why basic income is needed for a right to work", *Rutgers Journal of Law and Urban Policy*, Vol. 2, No.1, Fall 2005, 91–102.

9. On these, see Standing, 2002, and my paper in E.O. Wright (ed.), *Redesigning Distribution* (London, Verso, 2006).
10. Outsourcing of services results in those doing the work being called "independent contractors", often putting them outside the sphere of the standard "master-servant" rule.

PART III
THE IMPACT OF OFFSHORING AND GLOBALIZATION IN DEVELOPED COUNTRIES

CHAPTER FOUR

GLOBALIZATION OF SERVICES: FRIEND OR FOE?

Catherine L. Mann

Globalization of services is underway: Is it to be welcomed or despised? What is at the root of the changes sweeping through the white-collar workforce in the United States, and to a lesser extent abroad as well? What might be the implications for metrics of economic performance, such as productivity growth, income, and employment? More broadly, this new globalization of business and professional services as enabled by networked information technology (IT) features dramatic change for workers, businesses, and policymakers. Businesses are already implementing change by altering what activities and jobs they expand in the United States and which ones they expand abroad. Workers must respond to these rapid changes, and they are responding. Is there also a rationale for policymakers to change?

This chapter investigates these questions considering the central role that information and communications technologies (ICT) play to alter the production of business and professional services and to enable these services to be traded across borders. The analysis quantifies the role of ICT to bolster total factor productivity growth in the United States, thus increasing the potential performance of the economy, but also widening the gap in employment and wage outcomes for workers according to their training, skills, and the sectors in which they work. To the extent that this gap implies worker-job mismatches, the potential economic performance of the economy will not be reached. Public policy to promote skill augmentation to better match workers with evolving job demands allows the economy and its participants to reach their potential.

ICT and the Globalization of Services

Some services have been traded across borders for years and centuries—shipping is a service that has been around since the Vikings and Polynesians. Business and professional services (BPS) on the other hand, such as accounting and advertising, architecture and engineering, legal services and management consulting, have been termed "nontraded" in economic language. For reasons ranging from culture to regulation, these services have tended to be idiosyncratic and delivered with buyer and seller in close proximity. In addition, these services have tended to be functionally integrated within the firm's other productive activities. The introduction of IT and communications networks has increased the standardization of some activities—for example, mortgage-application scoring or call-center support—and thus reduced the importance of proximity, especially when activities can be unbundled from within the firm.

International trade in a wide range of business and professional services is an important part of the U.S. and global economic landscape. For the United States, the share of BPS in services exports (imports) was around 14 (9) percent in 2005. In the narrower category of IT services, global spending rose about 10 percent per year over the decade 1993 to 2003, to exceed $500 billion in 2003, only one-half of which was spending by the U.S. communications networks, which are key to the globalization of services; that is, both sides of the trading relationship need to have the information technology and be able to access the network cost effectively. Global spending on communications was $1.2 trillion in 2003, of which U.S. spending was less than 40 percent.[1]

Increased application of information technology to many service activities means a very rapid pace of change in the ability to fragment production based on standardized elements. Robust international communications networks both in the United States and abroad imply that this now fragmented production can be done at a low-cost location with cost-effective communications. Thus there are very strong synergies between technological change and global sourcing: the two of them go hand and hand.

Globalization of business and professional services based on the application of information technology still is relatively recent; so data to quantify the impact on overall economic performance are hard to come by. It is possible, however, to quantify the impact of the globalization of IT hardware on overall economic performance. The methodology used in this narrower topic suggests an approach to analyzing the broader issue.

Research makes clear that investment and economy-wide diffusion of networked information technology can generate substantial macroeconomic gains, especially in terms of productivity growth. IT products and service activities have three key characteristics—price and income elasticity, and network externalities—that make these products and activities different from, say, food, clothes, cars, or oil. These key characteristics mean that globalization will play out differently.[2]

The most important characteristic of information technology and of service activities more generally is that they exhibit income and price elasticity of investment and demand. With regard to income elasticity, as a country grows, the demand for IT diffuses throughout more sectors in the economy. Hence the income elasticity of demand for IT is estimated to be greater than one. With respect to services, as a country's income grows and as it moves through the stages of development, the demand for services grows as well and more than proportionally to the rise in GDP. With regard to price elasticity, as the price of IT products falls, investment demand rises more than proportionately. So too for services in general; as prices fall, people tend to buy disproportionately more.

A third characteristic of IT—network externalities—adds to the other two to enhance IT's role as a special economic driver.[3] The concept of network externalities is based on the principle that the value of IT increases with the square of the number of participants in the network (Metcalfe's Law). Empirical research supports the notion that the value of IT is dramatically greater if a firm's suppliers and customers both also have and use IT products that are interoperable through a communications network.

Because services in general and IT in particular both have an elasticity of price and of income greater than one, globalization-induced price declines play out differently for producers, consumers, and workers compared to how globalization affects demand for products where demand is not elastic (for items such as food, clothes, or oil). In short, elastic prices and income for IT and services ensure that globalization is not a zero-sum game: As globalization reduces the price of IT products and services activities, the overall market size expands more than one-for-one, thus creating new activities, new firms, cross-border trade, and higher overall employment in the United States and abroad.

Previous research leaves no doubt that economies can experience significant macroeconomic gains from the production and, more importantly, diffusion and use of information technology by many sectors throughout the economy. For the United States, more than half of the gain in productivity growth, from the mid-1990s to the recent 2000s, has come from the use of IT.[4] Enhanced productivity growth comes through four channels. First, IT investment leads to capital deepening and faster labor productivity growth. Second, network effects and transactions spillovers between enterprises that use IT raise the productivity of these enterprises. Third, information technology together with changing workplace practices within firms enhance total factor productivity growth. And fourth, international technology transfer and global engagement raise productivity growth by weeding out lagging firms.

If IT is such an important economic driver of productivity, would not global sourcing of some IT products impede continued macroeconomic success? In fact, the globalization of IT, as measured by investment in new production facilities at home and abroad as well as international trade in IT products, leads to lower prices of these products. My research suggests that prices of some key IT products are 10–30 percent lower than they would have been if no globalization of IT had taken place. Recalling the price-elastic nature of these products, the lower price implies more than proportional investment in the economy, and overall greater productivity and GDP growth than would have been the case in the absence of globalization of the sector. Adding up the gain to the U.S. economy of the globalization of IT, we find that U.S. GDP was some $250 billion higher over the 1995 to 2000 period than it would have been had there been no globalization of IT hardware.[5]

Leaders and Laggards in Diffusion of IT and Productivity Growth

The macroeconomic analysis masks significant disparity in IT use across sectors of the economy. Large sectors of the U.S. economy have not yet fully integrated IT into their business operations, even as other sectors have led the way in investing in IT. Figure 4.1 shows the relationship between IT intensity (IT capital per worker) and contributions to aggregate productivity growth in the United States by sector, along with the size of the sectors in terms of GDP.[6]

The upward slope of the trend line is consistent with the finding derived from macroeconomic time series data—that investment in IT is positively related to productivity growth and macroeconomic performance. But there is substantial diversity underlying this macroeconomic performance. Understanding why some sectors have led in the investment and use of IT while other sectors have lagged may point to the future role for deeper globalization of IT, particularly IT software and services, with implications for the U.S. economy as we go forward.

A first observation is that among manufacturing sectors, electronics is a leader in terms of IT investment and above-average contribution to productivity growth (which is why this sector was the focus for the first stage of research on IT and productivity growth). But it is a relatively small sector in terms of GDP. There are other high-productivity manufacturing sectors, but when they are all added up, "above average manufacturing" accounts for only about 12 percent of GDP. In contrast, the leading services activities account for 35 percent of GDP.[7] Therefore, the rapid acceleration of U.S.

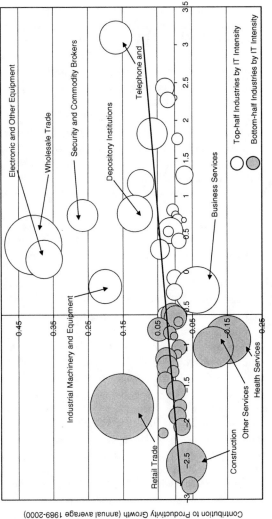

(Size of bubbles indicate share of GDP By Individual Sector in 2000)

IT Intensity of Sector (IT Capital per Worker, rank average 1989-2001)

○ Top-half Industries by IT Intensity
● Bottom-half Industries by IT Intensity

Contribution to Productivity Growth (annual average 1989-2000)

Electronic and Other Equipment

Wholesale Trade

Security and Commodity Brokers

Depository Institutions

Telephone and

Industrial Machinery and Equipment

Business Services

Retail Trade

Construction

Other Services

Health Services

Figure 4.1 Leaders and Laggards in IT Intensity and Productivity Growth

Source: Economic and Statistics Administration, Digital Economy 2002 Table A.4.4, Digital Economy 2003, Table 4.C.1.

productivity growth has come more from productivity-enhancing IT use in the services arena rather than from manufacturing.[8]

Which sectors lead in terms of IT investment and contribution to productivity growth? Wholesale trade, securities and commodity brokers, depository institutions, and communications are all sectors where networked IT has played a particularly important role in linking customers and suppliers in the industry. Retailing is the only notable example of a large service sector that, over all firms, did not use IT particularly intensively across the board and yet experienced above-average productivity growth. On the other hand, although the sector as a whole does not appear to use IT particularly intensively, research shows that much of the productivity gain in retailing comes from more productive establishments replacing less productive ones, and IT is an important factor underpinning the success of the more productive establishments (Foster, Haltiwanger, and Krizan, 2002). IT use by Wal-Mart's supply chain, specifically its IT-based backward linkages to its suppliers, is consistent with both network externalities as well as with the productivity contribution.

And as for the laggards, health services and construction stand out for being large in GDP terms and low in terms of IT capital per worker, and for being below average in their contribution to productivity growth. In addition, there is the highly heterogeneous group of "other services," which among other activities includes engineering, accounting, research, and management services.

Exactly why some service activities have led in the use of IT while others have lagged remains a fertile area for research. There are several nonexclusive hypotheses, including those related to the information content of the activities of the sector, the degree to which firms in the sector were already organized in or around networks, the population of small and medium-sized enterprises in the sector, the extent of sector-specific regulation, and exposure to international market forces.

With regard to the nature of the sector's activities, research by Frank Levy and Richard Murname (2004) finds that industries intensive in business processes and jobs characterized by routines and explicit rules have invested the most in IT, thus changing the mix of tasks between those done by people and those done by technology. IT-intensive industries then increase their demand for labor with skills such as judgment, problem-solving, and communications and reduce their demand for workers who perform the routine tasks that follow explicit rules. In fact, Wilson (2004) suggests that these routine tasks can increasingly be done by IT itself using various software programs.

With regard to the second hypothesis on the role of pre-Internet networks, it may be that the sectors that have led in IT intensity and in contribution to

GDP growth already exchanged information over telecommunications networks before the Internet and IT made this interchange even more integral to the activity of the sectors. For example, in the financial system, interbank payment systems and automated teller machine networks created both forward and backward linkages within and among firms and customers well before the advent of Internet technology.[9] Similarly, telecommunications firms were well positioned, with networks in place, to add new services based on IT investments. Lower-cost supply-chain logistics and improved management of supply-chain information were at the heart of just-in-time inventory management systems and rapid package delivery systems that contributed to improvements in productivity in some manufacturing sectors and wholesale trade (Gereffi 2001).

With regard to the third hypothesis, the two large lagging sectors—health services and construction—are also those with a high population of small and medium-sized enterprises. These firms have tended not to invest in IT to the same extent as larger firms and their IT intensity per worker is substantially lower. Whether IT is too expensive or too hard to use remains an area for further exploration.

In addition, culture and regulatory constraints may affect the incorporation of IT by the lagging sectors. For example, in health services, privacy and regulatory issues are quite important for software and services design and implementation. Moreover, there are no IT hardware, software, and services packages that are common to the disparate entities that are part of the sector (doctors' offices, pharmacies, hospitals). Professional licensure, particularly when it varies from U.S. state to state, may be important for construction and for engineering services as well. Such fragmentation could increase the costs of producing IT applications appropriate for these sectors and thus reduce IT investment and use by firms in these sectors. Finally, legacy issues of existing training, information management systems, and technology equipment complicate integration and the type of business transformation and networks that are the hallmark of productivity growth in the leading sectors.

The fourth hypothesis relates international engagement, investment in IT, and its contribution to productivity growth. Although more analysis is needed on the causal relationships (Mann 2006), the services that were at the heart of productivity gains are also services that run a balance of trade surplus, most notably financial services, but also business and professional services (accounting, management consulting), legal computer and information services; and research, development, and testing services (figure 4.2). There appears to be a correlation between the use of information technology, the transformation of the workplace associated with that investment, and global comparative advantage as revealed by trade.

(thousands of dollars)

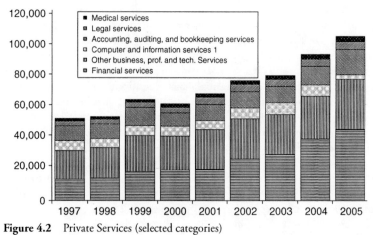

Figure 4.2 Private Services (selected categories)

Source: Bureau of Economic Analysis, U.S. International Services Cross-Border Trade, Table 1.

Globalization of IT and Implications for Labor

Detailed data on occupations in IT-related fields point to how technological change and globalization together may affect jobs and wages in the U.S. labor market in general. The diffusion of IT throughout the economy implies that IT occupations exist economy-wide, not just in the IT sector; indeed more than two-thirds of workers employed in IT occupations work outside the IT sector. This implies that the generalized economic business cycle may have an accentuated impact on IT workers, in part because the business cycle is being driven more by the technology-investment cycle, most notably by the dot-com boom and bust. Data suggest that theretofore, employment of engineers and computer programmers was less cyclical than for most workers in the economy. But now, particularly following the dot-com boom and bust, the unemployment rate dynamics for these professions look much more similar to those of the economy as a whole.

Technological change and globalization within the IT sectors also appears to affect high and low-wage technology-related workers in different ways (table 4.1). Low-wage workers who use IT appear to be particularly hurt by the combined effect of technology and international trade. These occupations that in general pay about $26,500 (below the average U.S. income) include telemarketers, data entry workers, word processors, and office machine operators. More than one-third of the people employed in

Table 4.1 U.S. Technology-Related Occupations, 1999–May 2005

Occupations	1999	May–05	Total change	Percent change	Annual wage May 2005 ($US)	Annual real wage change, 1999–May 2005 (%)
Call-center type occupations						
Telemarketers	485,650	400,860	−84,790	−17.5	23,500	−1.1
Telephone operators	50,820	29,290	−21,530	−42.4	31,030	−0.2
Low-wage technology workers						
Switchboard operators, including answering service	248,570	194,980	−53,590	−21.6	23,020	−0.1
Computer operators	198,500	129,160	−69,340	−34.9	33,580	0.5
Data entry keyers	520,220	296,700	−223,520	−43.0	24,910	0.3
Word processors and typists	271,310	153,580	−117,730	−43.4	30,140	1.4
Desktop publishers	37,040	29,910	−7,130	−19.2	34,770	−1.0
Electrical and electronic equipment assemblers	387,430	207,270	−180,160	−46.5	27,150	1.5
Semiconductor processors	42,110	44,720	2,610	6.2	32,870	0.5
Total call-center and low-wage tech. workers	**2,241,650**	**1,486,470**	**−755,180**	**−33.7**	**26,446**	**0.2**
Mid-level IT workers- computer support specialists	462,840	499,860	37,020	8.0	43,380	−1.3
High-wage technology workers						
Computer and information scientists, research	26,280	25,890	−390	−1.5	94,030	4.3
Computer programmers	528,600	389,090	−139,510	−26.4	67,400	1.1

Continued

Table 4.1 Continued

Occupations	1999	May–05	Total change	Percent change	Annual wage May 2005 ($US)	Annual real wage change, 1999–May 2005 (%)
Computer software engineers, applications	287,600	455,980	168,380	58.5	79,540	0.8
Computer software engineers, systems software	209,030	320,720	111,690	53.4	84,310	2.0
Computer systems analysts	428,210	492,120	63,910	14.9	70,430	1.0
Database administrators	101,460	99,380	–2,080	–2.1	65,590	1.6
Network and computer systems administrators	204,680	270,330	65,650	32.1	63,210	1.8
Network systems and data communications analysts	98,330	185,190	86,860	88.3	64,970	0.0
Computer hardware engineers	60,420	78,580	18,160	30.1	87,170	2.5
Electrical engineers	149,210	144,920	–4,290	–2.9	76,060	1.3
Electronics engineers, except computer	106,830	130,050	23,220	21.7	79,990	1.8
Total high-wage tech. workers	**2,200,650**	**2,592,250**	**391,600**	**17.8**	**73,504**	**1.6**
Comparable; production workers in manufacturing				**–24.5**		
Comparable; total private CES employment				**2.5**		

Source: Bureau of Labor Statistics CES Data, 1999, 2000, 2001, 2002, May 2003, November 2003, May 2004, November 2004, and May 2005 National Occupational Employment and Wage Estimates.

these occupations in 1999 were not employed in these occupations in May 2005.[10] On the other hand, jobs held by high-skilled, judgment-oriented, analytical, and problem-solving IT workers such as applications and system software engineers and database administrators (earning $73,500 on average) increased about 17 percent.

The data also reveal the rising skill bar against which domestic and foreign workers compete in the global marketplace. Between 1999 and May 2005, the number of 'programming' jobs paying on average $67,400 fell by more than 25 percent. Whether these programmers graduated to become system engineers or whether their jobs were off-shored is not known. It is clear that coding, which is slang for what programmers do, is a Levy and Murname–type activity that can be digitized and produced wherever it is most cost-effective. That is, computer programmers who are not analysts, not information managers, not network administrators, not application programmers who work on specific customer needs face technology-enhanced globalization risk of job loss. If they are coders, and a design is specified, coding can be done anywhere.

More generally, what we see in the IT arena is a microcosm for what may happen in business and professional services in the U.S. economy in the future. There is a wage-employment disparity and a skill disparity that is growing wider in the U.S. economy. The high-skill workers are doing better both in terms of wages and in terms of employment prospects. The low-skill workers are doing worse on both counts. And, even as there is a range of increasingly higher skills in global play, there is also an expanding market for workers with those skills, both at home and abroad. This question is: do U.S. workers face impediments as they compete for the next rung up on the skill ladder?

A Role for Public Policy

What is skill today? If we could identify "skill," then maybe educational institutions and public policy advocates could alter curricula and offer incentives to speak to and support what skill is today. Levy and Murname (2004) describe "skill" using the words judgment, problem solving, communications, tacit knowledge, sector-specific knowledge. Additional requirements might include current technical skills, team-work skills, flexibility, and ability to undertake learning on an ongoing basis. Skill today is a broad collection of learned and acquired attributes.

Not everybody is in college now or going into high school now; that is, a lot of people are in the labor force right now. So a policy focusing on skill-attributes must address not just K-12-16, but also incumbent workers. A sizeable fraction of the 136 million workers in the labor force face the challenge of what is skill today. Jensen and Kletzer (2005) suggest that 14 percent of the labor force may be in tradable occupations. Blinder (2006) implies that a quarter to one-third of the work force may be in tradable occupations. In either case, the numbers are large.

Is there a role for policymakers to ensure that the incumbent labor force can deal with both the challenges of technological change and globalization? First, we need to address the cost of adjustment (which other researchers have addressed), including healthcare and pension portability. Technological change and globalization means there will be permanently displaced workers, such as call center workers. Their jobs are gone, either to India or replaced by menu-systems or voice-activated computers. For them, transition policies are critical, including, for example, wage insurance or training credits as described by Rosen and Kletzer (2005).

A specific approach to the skill-depreciation and demand for skill-augmentation that faces incumbent workers is the "human-capital" investment tax credit. This initiative focuses on incumbent workers in the prime of their earning career who are in the position of having their skills effectively degraded by technological change and globalization, including the new availability (through cost-effective communications and IT) of educated workers from around the world (Richard Freeman, this volume). In many cases, this incumbent workforce went to school five years ago, seven years ago, fifteen years ago, and their skills were current then. But, because of technological change and the expansion of the global labor force, their skills are not current anymore.

A human-capital investment tax credit recognizes three realities in the marketplace for skills: free riders, incomplete information, and societal spillovers. First, firms that train their own workers face the disincentive of poaching by firms that do not train; so they do not train enough. Second, incomplete information about career prospects not only dissuades students from entering the career pipeline but also makes it difficult for incumbent workers to choose advanced training. Third, an investment tax credit recognizes the spillover benefits for the economy as a whole of having a better match between job demand and supply of skills.

These textbook market imperfections are the rationale for the R&D tax credit and the investment tax credit for IT capital investment. Given the importance of skills for competition and globalization in the twenty-first century, a human-capital investment tax credit offered to individuals through firms and implemented by educational institutions has merit.

Altruism is not the only reason why we want to keep people in the prime of their career earning at their maximum capability. Workers who are 40 to 60 years old are, in an intergenerational sense, at the center of growing prosperity, or not, for the United States: They fund social security for the old and support educational attainment for the young. It is crucial that this age-group of workers maximizes its earnings in the labor force, but they face an environment with rapidly changing skill demands. The human-capital investment tax credit can work with the incumbent skilled workers to enhance their capacity to compete in a changing world.

What is the benefit? This type of investment tax credit could be a centerpiece to support our labor force in terms of intergenerational enhancing of productivity and prosperity of the U.S. economy. It supports the next wave of productivity growth from the globalization of services. It creates and maintains an internationally competitive knowledge economy that is founded on its people, our assets.

Conclusion

As IT allows more service activities to become fragmented and globalized, a larger segment of the economy will have global opportunities and face global competition, which raises the stakes for firms, workers, and the U.S. economy. Maximizing the benefits of technological innovation and transformation, which go hand-in-hand with deeper globalization, is key to ensuring the continued positive impact of IT on the U.S. economy. But so too is ensuring that the benefits of those innovations are more widely obtainable and shared. Therefore, a new policy agenda and compact around workforce preparation and participation, in conjunction with a business community actively engaged in innovation and transformation, are needed.

Agile businesses will respond to technology-enhanced global opportunities and challenges, and workers are feeling the effects. Innovations not implemented because resources cannot adjust forfeit economic potential. Policymakers must show leadership and respond proactively to the new environment of technology-enhanced global change.

Notes

1. Data in this paragraph from World Information Technology and Services Alliance (WITSA), as presented in Mann and Kirkegaard (2006, 14, Table 2.1).
2. See van Ark, Inklaar, and McGuckin (2003); Stiroh (2002); Kirkegaard and Baily (2004), OECD (2003); Wilson (2004), Mun and Nadiri (2002); Atrostic and Nguyen (2005).
3. See Mann and Kirkegaard (2006, 5–10) for more discussion.
4. Van Ark, Inklaar, and McGuckin (2003) calculate IT's contribution at sixty percent. Economics and Statistics Administration (2002, 36) calculates it at seventy percent.
5. For calculations, see Mann (2003). Bivens (2005) calls into question this calculation. But his reassessment assumes that the rate of return to IT investment is

the same as for all other investment in the economy. Wilson (2004) shows that the rate of return to IT investment is about 5 times that for other types of capital in the economy. For more discussion of the rate of return to IT investment, see also the presentation in Mann and Kirkegaard (2006, 8–9).

6. Analysis by the Economics and Statistics Administration (2002) for the *Digital Economy 2002* report for the US Department of Commerce developed sector-level measures of IT investment, productivity contributions to U.S. growth, inflation, and other important indicators.

7. The balance to 50 percent of GDP is leading sectors in mining.

8. Research already cited from Mun and Nadiri (2002) confirm this finding. In addition, researchers from Europe (including van Ark, Inklaar, and McGuckin 2003) have noted that the disparity in productivity performance between Europe and the United States is due more to productivity performance in services than in manufacturing.

9. This is consistent with the research cited in Atrostic and Nguyen (2005). See also Morisi (1996).

10. The period of 1999 to May 2005 is the window for which these detailed data are available.

CHAPTER FIVE

DYNAMIC GAINS FROM U.S. SERVICES OFFSHORING: A CRITICAL VIEW

William Milberg, Melissa Mahoney,
Markus Schneider, and Rudi von Arnim*

The explosion over the past ten years of U.S. imports of information technology (IT) and IT-enabled services has been a clear boon to the economies of India, China, Singapore, the Philippines, and a number of other developing countries. But there is a considerable debate about the welfare effects of offshoring for the United States. International trade economists generally agree that in the short run the surge in offshoring has brought efficiency gains, but it has not been beneficial to U.S. welfare overall because of inadequate assistance to displaced workers. Accordingly, most economists support an expansion of Trade Adjustment Assistance (TAA)—which currently only covers manufacturing—and a wage insurance plan funded by a tax on employers.

Some economists calculate, however, that over time there are significant gains to the U.S. economy from services offshoring. These longer-term gains, it is typically claimed, are not rooted in traditional free trade theory, but in a model of economic growth in which lower input costs lead to greater investment demand, which in turn brings higher productivity, output, and employment. In this chapter we question the extent to which this growth dynamic has operated in the case of services offshoring. While the cost savings from services offshoring are potentially great, to date these savings have contributed to a historic rise in the share of profits in U.S. national income. But the expected effects for business investment—integral to achieving the dynamic gains from offshoring—have not materialized.

While the globalization of services has in many cases lowered their cost to business, there is no clear indication that this has led to increased demand for these services overall. The cost savings to U.S. firms from services offshoring revert to firms' profits, and the question of the long-term economic effects then hinges on the extent to which these additional profits are invested in productivity-enhancing and employment-generating activities. As predicted by many of the studies of offshoring, profit shares in the most affected sectors are higher than they would normally be at this stage of the business cycle. But the evidence is that firms are raising dividend payments, buying back their own shares, and undertaking mergers and acquisitions at higher than historical rates, and spending on investment goods and services at lower rates.

Instead of relying on faith in the private sector's dynamism, policymakers should work creatively to raise the chances for the positive growth dynamic to unfold. We oppose tariffs or other forms of protection that would stifle the process and focus on ways to share the benefits of offshoring more equitably and to encourage the dynamic aspects of the process to promote economic growth. We identify three levels at which policy intervention could be effective. At the first level is support for the direct "losers" from services offshoring, that is, workers who lose their jobs and those who get reemployed at lower pay. At the second level are incentives for firms to reinvest profits at a higher rate, including tax incentives for R&D, rescinding tax cuts on dividend income, complementary public investment, and a monetary policy focused on keeping interest rates low. At the third level are broad policies to enhance innovation by making health insurance and old age pensions portable and more fully provided by the government. These policies enhance innovation because they remove the disincentives for workers to resist change in an environment where change, investment, and foreign trade are integral to the innovation process. Moreover, to the extent that taxes to support these programs are progressive, these programs spread the gains from globalization much more equally across the American society than they have been until now.

Services Offshoring and Jobs

The rise in services offshoring has been driven to a great extent by technology: With the unimagined expansion in capacity of the Internet and telecommunications, today any information that can be digitized can be used and manipulated anywhere in the world. The level of services imports is still not very high compared to imports of manufactured goods or exports of services, but services imports have been growing more rapidly than exports for over ten years.

Table 5.1 shows the growth in U.S. imports and exports of private services for the period 1986–2005. The overall balance on services has deteriorated slightly over the period, with some specific private services showing considerable import growth. The trade balance in "Other Private Services"

Table 5.1 Private Services Trade by Type, 1986:Q1–2006:Q3

	Trade balance 2006 (Q1–Q3), US$ million	Export growth* 1986–2006 (%)	Import growth* 1986–2006 (%)
Total private services	65,331	8.3	7.9
Travel	9,240	7.3	5.0
Passenger fares	−4,146	6.8	6.9
Other transportation	−13,206	5.8	6.6
Royalties and license fees	26,479	10.7	15.4
Other private services**	46,964	9.4	11.5
Education	7,441	7.3	12.2
Financial services	19,746	12.0	8.6
Insurance services	−18,393	9.5	15.1
Telecommunications	535	5.1	1.5
Business, professional, and technical services	20,915	11.2	13.3
Other unaffiliated services	9,665	5.4	8.3

* Export and import growth are calculated as annual compound growth rates.

** The OPS aggregate includes intrafirm and arm's length transactions; OPS categories show only arm's length trade.

Source: BEA Balance of Payments and author's calculations.

and its component "Business, Professional and Technical (BPT) Services" remained in surplus despite more rapid growth in imports. The trade balance worsened significantly in certain subcategories of BPS, including financial services and telecommunications services. However, the share of these services in total services imports remains small. We should note that a number of studies conclude that the official statistics understate the level of offshoring activity, perhaps because so much of it is occurring on an intrafirm basis.[1]

Even the official figures show a very rapid growth of BPT services imports from selected Asian countries, in particular India, China, and Singapore. From 1992 to 2005, U.S. imports of professional and technical services grew at an annual rate of 12.3 percent, with compound growth of 19.3 percent from China, 17.7 percent from Singapore, and 33.5 percent from India.[2]

As many analysts have noted, services offshoring is different from offshoring in manufacturing because it includes many higher-skill jobs, including accountants, programmers, designers, architects, medical diagnosticians, and financial and statistical analysts. With continual improvement in information and communications technology, there is likely to be a rapid broadening of the scope of services subject to international trade.

Blinder (2005, 18) estimates that "the share of current U.S. jobs that will be susceptible to offshoring in the electronic future is two to three times what it is today." And it is likely that this susceptibility will continue to cut across high-skill and low-skill occupations.[3] Given the size and growth of the pool of educated workers in East Asia, South Asia, and Eastern Europe, there is clearly plenty of room for growth in these imports, even in higher-skill sectors. According to Richard Freeman (2005c), "The huge number of highly educated workers in India and China threatens to undo the traditional pattern of trade between advanced and less developed countries."[4]

According to our own calculations, nonmanufacturing employment was 1.2 million lower as the result of a change in trade patterns between 1998 and 2003, almost the same decline in jobs as embodied in trade in manufactured goods over the same period.[5] These represent a small proportion of the overall U.S. labor force, but given the expected continued high growth in services imports and the problem of underreporting, it may turn out that the controversial McCarthy (2004) projection of 3.3 million jobs lost over fifteen years is on the low side. The key, over the long run, lies in the business response to the cost savings from offshoring, and the offsetting employment gains that increased investment can generate.

Offshoring and Economic Welfare

From the perspective of the standard theory of international trade, the fragmentation of production, including the offshoring of intermediate services, constitutes a deepening of the division of labor that enhances the gains from trade beyond those achieved when trade is limited to final goods and services. According to Arndt and Kierzkowski (2001, pp. 2, 6):

> spatial dispersion of production allows the factor intensity of each component, rather than the average factor intensity of the end product, to determine the location of its production. The international division of labor now matches factor intensities of components with factor abundance of locations . . . [E]xtending specialization to the level of components is generally welfare-enhancing.

Heroism in the Static Context

Behind this rosy picture, however, are a number of heroic assumptions. Four in particular stand out: First, there is no international capital or labor mobility. Second, the trade balance will automatically adjust over time to zero. Third, there is always full employment. And fourth, winners can potentially compensate losers and still be better off than before.

If we relax these assumptions, then we can consider the possibility that services offshoring can create unemployment in the United States and lead to a worsening of the balance of trade. In fact, the first three assumptions are closely connected. When capital is internationally mobile, then it will move to where production costs are lowest. That is, absolute advantage will play some role in determining the location of production.[6] A trade imbalance can be associated with net employment gains or losses in a particular country. In other words, if an expansion of imports does not automatically generate an equivalent expansion of exports, then job losses can result.

Even orthodox trade theory shows that trade liberalization brings about both winners and losers. Free trade is best because of the *potential* for the winners to compensate the losers and still remain better off than before liberalization. This is the fourth assumption. Many have expressed doubts about the merits of this assumption when in fact compensation rarely occurs.[7]

To these doubts about the benefits of services offshoring, Paul Samuelson (2004) has added the issue of a possible deterioration in the terms of trade as the result of low-cost import competition in affected services. In a prominent response to Samuelson's skeptical essay, Bhagwati, Panagaryi, and Srinivasan (2004) claim that Samuelson's point is irrelevant since services offshoring is about the creation of newly traded services such as call centers and radiology reports rather than services already traded. While Bhagwati et al. are right to criticize Samuelson on the issue of newly tradable services, they by no means refute his claim that offshoring of services can have negative welfare effects in the United States. And even they conclude that overall benefits from offshoring require the compensation of displaced workers or the ability of displaced workers to find other jobs with the same pay, an issue on which there is at best mixed evidence.[8]

The large and growing overhang of unemployed labor in developing countries means that, in a world where absolute cost competitiveness plays a role in determining the pattern of trade, the United States will face continual pressure to raise imports. The traditional U.S. strategy of abandoning lower value-added varieties and upgrading to higher value-added sectors and protected niches will provide only temporary relief, since a considerable and growing share of the labor overhang in developing countries is relatively high-skilled. The risk is that losers from this trend will cut across the full spectrum of the U.S. labor force, and winners will be those with an ownership stake in companies that are able to raise share values through innovation in new products and in marketing, through peripheral financial activity or through cost-cutting from offshoring itself. We return to this larger picture of corporate performance after we consider the dynamic case for offshoring.

Faith in the Dynamic Context

While economists cite the famous Ricardian principle of comparative advantage to show the benefits of offshoring to all countries, the view that services offshoring will benefit the U.S. economy overall hinges on another argument found in Ricardo—his theory of economic growth and especially of the link between international trade and domestic investment.[9] In Ricardo's view, the importance of trade liberalization was its impact on the profit rate. He saw England's protection of the farm sector as responsible for keeping the price of food high, and, as a consequence, pushing up the real wage. Relatively cheap food imports would lower the real wage paid by employers and thus raise their rate of profit. A higher profit rate would induce a more rapid rate of investment, which in turn would generate a higher rate of economic growth.[10]

The dynamic Ricardian scheme is depicted in figure 5.1. Offshoring of service inputs reduces production costs and raises profit margins. The additional profits provide retained earnings that can support an expansion of business investment. A further incentive for investment demand is provided by the decline in the cost of inputs (now produced abroad). These investments lead to productivity growth, which generates higher levels of income and employment.

A similar dynamic is implied in much of the applied work on the effects of offshoring on the U.S. economy, for example, in the commonly cited research on IT hardware offshoring by Catherine Mann (2003, 2007) and Mann with Kierkegaard (2006). The positive outcome is the result of capital deepening that comes from increased business purchases of IT hardware in response to the price reduction from cheap imports. Mann (2003) estimates that U.S. imports of IT hardware between 1995 and 2002 accounted for 20 percent of the observed decline in IT hardware prices and as a result raised U.S. real GDP by 0.3 percentage points over what it would have been otherwise.

Mann's estimate has been lauded by many as proof of the positive long-term effects of offshoring and has been criticized by others for overstating

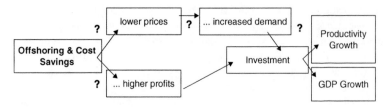

Figure 5.1   U.S. Offshoring and Economic Growth

the share of IT capital income in total national income and thus for over-stating the implications for GDP growth.[11] In any case, her study shows that the strongest case for services offshoring is not found in the static efficiency gains identified in the traditional theory of international trade, but in the dynamic process of capital deepening that can occur when the off-shored good is an input to production. The higher capital intensity of production following the price decline leads to higher productivity and output.

Profits and Reinvestment

We argue that the same positive dynamic that Mann finds in the case of IT hardware is less likely to be operative in the case of services offshoring. The price declines in semiconductors and the explosion in computing power and IT throughout the 1990s brought about tremendous increases in demand, as not only businesses, but also private households and the gov-ernment installed these technologies and upgraded them more often. Offshored business services, on the other hand, involve tasks common to the business process before the rise of IT, which allows these tasks to be undertaken abroad. But even with dramatic cost savings and potential price decreases, it is not clear what the demand response will be per unit of output of final goods and services.[12] Thus the price declines from off-shoring of services may bring an increase in profits without the same pro-portional rise in business spending, which can happen if expectations of future returns on domestic investment are too low. Moreover, economies of scale are not as evident in services as in manufacturing, so the incre-mental investment may not provide the same productivity boost in services as it has in manufacturing.[13] The dynamic Ricardian model that was apparently operative in the case of IT hardware is more questionable in the case of services. Question marks remain at a number of links in the dynamic scheme, as indicated in figure 5.1. A further question mark could be added at the end, concerning the quality of new jobs created by the dynamic process. There is considerable debate over the adequacy of the reemployment rate and the replacement wage (that is, the wage workers earn on average in a new job) for workers who lose their job from import competition.[14]

Of course, higher profits can also be passed through to higher wages or lower consumer prices, but neither appears to have been the dominant trend in the recent period. Most evidence shows that average earnings of workers have stagnated at the same time that increased offshoring has weakened these labor markets, both directly, by raising the number of job seekers, and indirectly, by diminishing wage demands when the threat of offshoring is credible. And there is little evidence of relative price dampening in service-intensive sectors, as service sector prices have increased more than the GDP deflator since 2000. The point is that the beneficial dynamic from a skewed distribution of the static gains from offshoring is undermined if profit reinvestment does not follow the cost-saving trade.

The structural changes taking place in some categories of services trade with certain regions are too small to be held accountable for the large increase in the level of undistributed profits in the U.S. corporate sector over the past five years. Still, offshoring has contributed to higher margins. Services offshoring has expanded most rapidly during a period when corporate profits have reached a historic high, and the share of profits in national income is higher than at any time since 1969.

These aggregate trends in the profit share are reflected in studies at the firm and industry levels. Firm level surveys find that services offshoring reduces costs to the firm by around 40 percent for the offshored activity.[15] Dossani and Kenney (2003, 7) report that a 40 percent cost saving represents the hurdle rate of return on services offshoring—that is, the minimum cost saving from such sourcing shifts. A number of large firms they surveyed reported savings considerably higher than that. The share of profits in value added in a number of IT services sectors fell as the dot.com bubble burst in the late 1990s and has since rebounded dramatically, in some cases beyond the level enjoyed in the 1990s boom. The profit share in Computer System Design and Information and Professional, Scientific, and Technical Services has almost attained the levels of the mid-1990s (figure 5.2). The Information and Data Processing sector has experienced a rise in its profit share to a level above that enjoyed in the boom period.

For the period 2000–2003, we calculated a strong positive correlation between profit share growth and the growth in offshoring in services. Controlling for changes in other variables that affect the profit share (including the sectoral employment share, capital intensity, and labor productivity), we found that on average a 10 percent increase in offshoring is associated with a 1.34 percent increase in the sectoral profit share. Services offshoring and their threat are certainly a contributing factor in the unprecedented rise in profits and the profit share, even in comparison with other business cycle recoveries.[16]

The increase in profits and profit shares—both economy-wide and in many services sectors—has not been met by an expected rise in business investment. While profits rise procyclically, investment usually rises at an even higher rate in the upturn, so that the ratio of profits to investment normally falls as the economy moves toward the cycle peak. This has not been the case in the latest recovery, as the ratio of profits to investment in

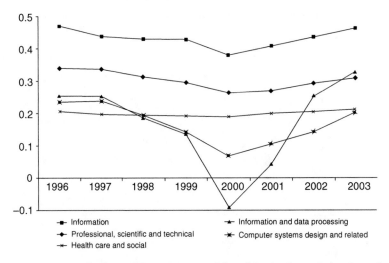

Figure 5.2 Profit Share of Gross Output in Selected Service Sector Industries and Subindustries, 1996–2003

Source: Author's calculations from U.S. Bureau of Economic Analysis, Annual Industry Accounts: Gross-Domestic-Product (GDP)-by-industry Data. See also http://www.bea.gov/bea/dn2.gdpbyind_data. htm. U.S. Bureau of Economic Analysis Annual Input-Output Tables. Last updated on November 15, 2005. http://bea.gov/bea/dn2/i-o_annual.htm.

the corporate sector has risen dramatically since 2000 and to a level higher than in previous recoveries (figure 5.3).

One implication of the pattern shown in figure 5.3 is that the liquidity of the corporate sector is considerably higher than usual. Dividend payments rose to nearly $577 billion in 2005, up almost 7 percent from 2004. Relative to national income, dividend payments were 5.3 percent in 2005, compared to 3.9 percent in 1995 and 2.6 percent in 1985.[17] These figures indicate a long-term trend that reflects many factors unrelated to offshoring. But given the contribution of offshoring to corporate profits, there is the likelihood of a connection. Merger and acquisition activity has surged since 2002 and soared to $1.23 trillion in the first three quarters of 2006, representing a year-on-year increase of 30 percent (Thompson Financial 2006). *The Financial Times* reports that the most recent M&Aactivity pushed this cyclical peak past the Internet bubble (Saigol and Politi 2006). Finally, corporations are buying back stock at an unprecedented rate; $164 billion in the first half of 2005, almost double the amount in the same period in 2004 (Aeppel 2005). Over the past two years, and for the first time since the mid-1960s, the corporate sector is a net lender to the rest of the economy.[18]

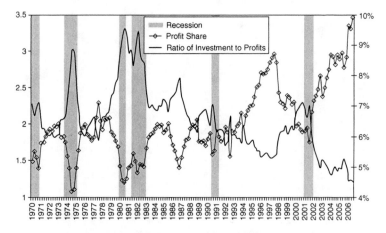

Figure 5.3 Profits and Investment, 1970:I–2006:III

Source: U.S. BEA and author's calculations.

Note: Profit Share (right hand scale) is the share of corporate profits after tax with IVA and CCAdj in national income. The bold series (left hand scale) shows nonresidential private fixed investment relative to corporate profits. Recessions as defined by NBER.

Another possible use of cash flow is for investment abroad. But relative to domestic investment, foreign direct investment, especially the net out-flow of foreign direct investment, is very small, averaging 2.9 percent of total investment over the period 1990–2006.[19] This is above levels in the 1970s (1.6 percent) and the 1980s (2.2 percent), but still not high enough to explain the use of funds by non-financial corporations.[20]

Policy Responses

Offshoring is a sensible strategy for firms seeking to cut costs and raise profit by focusing on core competencies. But unregulated private markets will not always meet social demands. In this case, there is no clear evidence that the investment response to cost savings from services offshoring and the productivity and employment growth that should result have material-ized at the levels required for the hypothetical dynamic gains from off-shoring to be realized. Are there policies that could stimulate such a positive growth dynamic? Tariffs on services imports are not a viable strat-egy for promoting gains from trade and for overcoming the long-term employment problems associated with import competition in services. Tariffs would hurt developing countries and, since the services are inputs to production in the United States, would also hurt U.S. firms that import such lower-cost services. A similar effect would result from a large and rapid U.S. dollar devaluation, something many economists have called for in response to the ballooning of the U.S. current account deficit. While some targeted devaluation is appropriate and appears to have occurred in the last quarter of 2006, a large and rapid dollar devaluation would be disruptive and, like a tariff, hurt U.S. trading partners—especially those holding large amounts of dollar reserves. This might trigger a large interest rate increase in the United States, depressing investment, economic growth, and job creation.

Rather than adopting protectionist tariffs or beggar-thy-neighbor devaluation policies, the United States should move to raise competitiveness by sharing the burden of adjustment between firms and workers and encouraging productive reinvestment of the cost savings from offshoring. We identify three levels of policy reform.

Level 1: Adjustment Assistance to Compensate Losers

The expansion of TAA to raise benefit levels and the duration of benefits and, most importantly, to expand coverage to the service sector is a crucial first step in sharing the benefits from offshoring in a more equitable fashion. Although the 2002 Trade Act expanded eligibility and funding, it does not include service sectors except very indirectly. And despite its expanded funding, the actual outlays remain very small, as do the number of workers covered. In 2004, TAA covered 148,000 workers, up from 100,000 in 2000.[21] Far less people participated in the training component of TAA assistance. Proposed legislation by senators Baucus and Coleman goes some distance in remedying the problem and should be passed immediately.[22]

Wage insurance would further protect the losers from offshoring, especially if premiums are paid by employers and if it does not substitute for existing unemployment benefits. The small wage insurance component of the current TAA program is inadequate and covers only manufacturing. The idea behind wage insurance is to provide a wage subsidy to those workers who lose their jobs for reasons beyond their control (from trade or other factors) and find new jobs at lower pay. The plan thus addresses an important problem of adjustment, namely that reemployment often comes at a lower wage. We agree with McKinsey Global Institute (2003) that employers can and should cover the cost of the insurance premium out of their savings from offshoring. Brainard and Litan (2005) put the total cost of an insurance plan that covers 50 percent of lost wages (with a maximum annual benefit of $10,000 for two years) at $3.5 billion or $25 per worker per year. They note (2005, 2) that "this is a small price to help displaced

American workers get back to work more quickly, seek opportunities in new sectors and gain more valuable reskilling through on-the-job training." For slightly higher premiums, even more of the wage-loss gap could be covered.

Level 2: Subsidies and Taxes to Spur Profit Reinvestment

The second level of policies is aimed at raising the elasticity of investment with respect to profits. Here we support two types of incentives, one using tax policy, the other using public investment to "crowd in" private business spending. On the tax side, we support expanding the coverage of investment tax credits, increased tax credit for R&D investment, and accelerated depreciation. These instruments are not unproblematic. The great risk of such business incentives is that they simply become a loophole rather than a spur to employment, innovation, and productivity growth. Accelerated depreciation schemes are particularly prone to such abuse. One way to avoid this is to include employment requirements for eligibility. Also, these programs should be implemented at the national level to avoid interstate competition.

The 2003 tax act lowered the top tax rate on corporate stock dividends from 35 percent to 15 percent and reduced the top capital gains tax rate from 20 percent to 15 percent. In 2006, Congress passed a two-year extension (until 2010) of these lower rates. Many analysts have noted that these tax changes are regressive and redistribute income in favor of wealthier Americans.[23] The changes also reduce the incentive for profit reinvestment. A reversal of the tax reduction would create greater incentive for firms to retain and reinvest rather than distribute and push firms to raise funds through capital markets. Thus the case for reinstating past tax levels on dividend income and capital gains is based both on equity and efficiency considerations, since it will encourage new investment expenditure out of corporate profits, promoting the productivity and employment growth that will also provide a more equitable distribution of income gains.

Nonetheless, investment is more responsive to overall conditions of demand in the economy than it is to small tax advantages. Thus any system of expanded investment tax incentives should be undertaken in conjunction with an expansionary macroeconomic policy, including targeted public investment and a monetary policy focused on low interest rates. Infrastructure investment, in transportation, communications, and Internet access can induce private investment. Also, public investment in research and in the training of more high-skill workers can promote profitable business investment. Federal spending on R&D as a share of GDP has fallen since the early 1990s and has focused excessively on defense rather than on sectors that would spur domestic economic activity, such as energy.

Level 3: Portable Benefits for Increased Efficiency and Equity

Ideally, the regulatory environment and the system of providing social protection in the United States would promote innovation and productivity growth, facilitate rapid adjustment to changing patterns of international competitive advantage and, at the same time, spread the burden of such adjustment across the economy. The existing social contract in the United States works neither for corporations nor for workers. Corporations suffer from high costs of health insurance and pensions to the point where these costs have become a primary reason for offshoring. And workers lose all benefits when they lose a job, and in many cases must work with no benefits other than a wage or salary. Thus, at this third level of policy reform, we propose a reformulation of the way social protection is provided and financed. Health insurance, old-age pensions, child care, and other needs should be provided at some minimum level irrespective of job or job status—employed or not. Such portable benefits would ease the burden of adjustment for those displaced by technological innovation or trade.

The costs of such a comprehensive and portable program must be shared more broadly across the economy, with an emphasis on sharing more equally the benefits from globalization, thus easing the burden of adjustment for those hurt in the process. Madrick and Milberg (2006) offer a broad sketch of such a plan and show how it can be financed with modest increases in personal taxes, payroll taxes, and corporate taxes. It is time to rethink the relation between government and the private sector in this era of globalization. As the wealthiest nation in the world, the United States is in a position to redefine the social contract in a way that compensates globalization's losers and encourages a positive profit-investment dynamic.

There is a growing recognition of the economic divide between haves and have nots across the globe and within the United States. Economists have tended to focus on wage differences between skilled and unskilled workers. In this chapter we have argued that this focus has veiled a deeper divide emerging in the United States between profit and wage income. To date, neither the Republican nor Democratic parties have shown a willingness to address the problem. Growing discontent among losers could easily translate into efforts to slow or halt the globalization process or to place the entire cost of adjustment on business.[24] If a new social compact of the sort we have outlined is to emerge, it will require not just labor union pressure, but also a progressive business view that acknowledges the need to manage globalization more fairly in order to sustain the gains from globalization over the long term. The great burdens on the private sector of rising health care costs and pension obligations may bring the business community around to this view sooner rather than later.

Conclusion

The benefits of offshoring of services to the economies of India, China, and some other East Asian and Eastern European countries are significant and are likely to increase. Income growth in those countries also drives U.S. exports, offsetting job losses from offshoring. Services offshoring has not yet reached levels that constitute a serious labor market disruption in the United States, but affected workers have not been adequately compensated and its dampening effect on wages is hard to quantify. The rate of growth of services offshoring is high and the potential for expansion is great, so the fears of American workers at all levels of skill and training are not misplaced.

At the same time, the cost savings from offshoring are considerable, and offshoring has corresponded with historic highs in the profit share of national income. Despite the profit increases, rates of investment have not grown accordingly. As services offshoring increases, neither the heroic assumptions of static trade theory nor the faith in the dynamic of profit reinvestment give us much confidence that the long-run positive effects articulated by Bhagwati, Mann, and others will be realized.

A more realistic approach would consider that expanded trade in intermediate services is likely to create unemployment and income inequality but has the possibility of generating gains in productivity and economic growth that can more than offset the negatives. We propose policies at three levels. First, we support the expansion of the benefits (level and duration) and coverage of TAA and its wage insurance to include services workers, with insurance premiums paid by corporations. Second, we advocate tax credits to promote investment, and the reversal of tax reductions on capital income, especially dividends. We also support public spending on infrastructure and technology to "crowd in" private investment. Third, we urge a broad reform of health insurance, pensions, and unemployment insurance, providing a minimum level of such benefits and making them portable across jobs. This approach pushes the policy discussion forward to the issues of how to make the economy more flexible without reducing the well-being of those adversely affected by offshoring.

Finally, adjustment to economic change is easiest and less costly to society when economic growth is more rapid. When aggregate demand is rising rapidly, the labor market effects of offshoring are more likely to be absorbed elsewhere in the economy. This simply brings out the importance of a pro-growth adjustment to the U.S. international payments imbalance rather than a deflationary policy of trade protectionism and large dollar devaluation.

Notes

* The authors are grateful to Eva Paus, Richard Freeman, and Lance Taylor for comments and to the Schwartz Center for Economic Policy Analysis for financial support. This paper is a revised and extended version of our SCEPA Policy Note (Mahoney et al., 2006).

1. NASSCOM data on Indian software exports to the U.S. are 5 to 10 times those reported in official U.S. government data on imports. For suggestions on how to improve services trade data, see Sturgeon (2006) and GAO (2004).
2. BEA, International services trade statistics, http://www.bea.gov/bea/di/intlserv.htm, Table 5b and author's calculation.
3. Lohr (2006), for example, summarizes a recent report for the National Academies on the expected rapid expansion of offshoring of corporate R&D activity, especially to India and China.
4. Predictions vary on the magnitude of expansion in the scope of services trade. In addition to Blinder (2005), see Jensen and Kletzer (2005) and Bardhan and Kroll (2003).
5. Our calculations are contained in Milberg and Schneider (2007). Groshen, Hobijn and McConnell (2005) report very similar results. Note that these figures include changes in final and intermediate goods trade.
6. See Jones (2000) for a formal model.
7. Even Paul Samuelson (2004, 115), the founder of the modern theory of free trade, expressed doubt, writing: "Should noneconomists accept this as cogent rebuttal if there is not evidence that compensating fiscal transfers have been made or will be made? Marie Antoinette said, 'Let them eat cake.' But history records no transfer of sugar and flour to her peasant subjects."
   Responding to the many criticisms he received following the publication of this article, Samuelson (2005, 243) added that "None of my chastening pals expressed concern about globalization's effects on greater inequality in a modern age when transfers from winners to losers do trend politically downward in present-day democracies." Although they are staunch free traders, Bhagwati, Panagariya, and Srivivasan (2004) do support an expansion of U.S. Trade Adjustment Assistance to compensate losers from trade—an implicit recognition, however, that offshoring has brought potential, not actual, improvement.
8. Moreover, Bhagwati, Panagariya, and Srivivasan take up only a part of the problem. They rule out consideration of intra-firm trade, that is, trade within multinational corporations. Intra-firm trade accounts for a large share of trade in goods and a growing share of services trade. If the issue of the welfare effects of offshoring on the labor market hinges on the degree of import competition, then all imports must be included in the analysis. Moreover, intra-firm trade presumes prior foreign direct investment, the capital movement that is problematic for the standard trade theory. MGI (2003), for example, includes profit repatriated from offshore service providers as part of U.S. gains from offshoring.
9. The original statement is Ricardo (1815).
10. Today we do not assume a subsistence real wage and thus the decline in input prices should lower final goods and services prices and thus raise the real wage, ceteris paribus. This is a potentially important aspect of the offshoring question,

but it has not been at the heart of the discussion of the gains from offshoring, which has instead focused on investment and productivity responses to the lower input prices on the one hand and lower nominal wages on the other.

11. For praise, see, for example, Bhagwati, Panagariya, and Srivivasan (2004). For a critique, see Bivens (2005).

12. There is scant research on price elasticities of demand in services, especially business services. One recent study of household demand for all services suggests that services demand is rather price inelastic, but elastic in some types of services. See Gardes and Starzec (2004, 25 and Table A1).

13. See Blinder (2005) for a discussion of Baumol's disease in the context of the rise of services offshoring.

14. For details, see the discussion of the "Kletzer effect" in Milberg (forthcoming).

15. See McKinsey Global Institute (2003).

16. The estimated profit share equation includes controls for all the variables typically used in such a model. See Milberg and von Arnim (2006) for more detailed discussion of the econometric model and estimation results. Note that for manufacturing sectors in this period the correlation is small and negative, presumably because offshoring in manufacturing had already reached very high levels by 2000.

17. Source: BEA and author's calculations.

18. Flow of Funds, Board of Governors of the Federal Reserve System. Barbosa-Filho et al. (2005) report net borrowing cycles by major sectors for the U.S. economy post–World War II. The business sector's net borrowing—investment expenditures less undistributed profit income—turned negative only occasionally and briefly and appears to be at all time high levels since the late 1960s. Bivens and Weller (2006) attribute this cash position of corporations to a longer-term change in corporate governance. Bates, Lemmon and Linck (2006) find the cash-to-assets ratio of U.S. firms to be at a historic high and attribute this to risk, that is an increase in the volatility of cash flow. Hedging this risk requires more cash holdings relative to the value of assets.

19. While these figures are small relative to domestic investment, they do not invalidate the finding by Harrison and Macmillan (2006) that increased U.S. foreign direct investment in low-income countries reduces U.S. employment.

20. Another possibility is that investment is simply lagging behind its usual cyclical pattern. Two often-cited possible factors in such an investment lag are (a) the overhang of IT investment resulting from the bust after the dot.com boom and (b) the effects of higher productivity growth in the late 1990's that lowered investment needs for a given amount of output growth. With the U.S. economy headed into another slowdown—suggested by several indicators—it does not appear, that there will be a return to the pattern seen in previous cycles.

21. See http://www.doleta.gov/tradeact/

22. The Trade Act of 2002 grants the U.S. president the so-called Fast Track Promotion Authority—the right to introduce a trade agreement to an "up or down" vote in Congress, that is without amendments possible. This power was granted along with extensions to the Trade Adjustment Assistance program. However, the current TAA program does not cover services workers. Senators Baucus and Coleman have proposed legislation to do so, but the bill did not reach the floor in the last Congress. Baucus and Coleman will reintroduce the

bill in the session starting in 2007. See http://www.taacoalition.com for more information.

23. See, for example, Friedman and Richards (2006).

24. See, for example, the "Agenda for Shared Prosperity" promoted by the Economic Policy Institute at http://www.sharedprosperity.org/.

Chapter Six

Bargaining Power, Distributional Equity and the Challenge of Offshoring

*James Burke and Gerald Epstein**

Introduction

Offshoring, like globalization generally, is not inherently good or bad. Its effects will strongly depend on the overall national and international context within which it occurs. Here we focus on three aspects of the overall context that are especially important in determining the impact of offshoring: the state of both national and global aggregate demand (AD), the nature of domestic and international tax rules, and the nature of domestic and international coordination of policies. These three factors have a significant impact on the effects of offshoring and related phenomena on the economy, in particular on their effects on wages, inequality, and the level of unemployment and underemployment.

There are many channels through which these factors ultimately affect the distributional and overall macroeconomic effects of offshoring, but here we focus on two major mechanisms: (1) their impact through the *bargaining channel* and (2) their impact through the *social investment channel*. By bargaining channel, we mean the impact of offshoring on the bargaining power of workers and governments relative to corporations. And by the *social investment channel*, we mean the impact of offshoring on the ability of governments to provide social goods such as infrastructure, education, and health benefits. We argue that it is not only the level and growth rate of offshoring that can affect its distributional and macroeconomic impacts, but that the *threat of offshoring* can have potent affects as well.[1]

When offshoring occurs in a context of high levels of aggregate demand, and adequate tax levels and effective rules that allow governments to coordinate, then it may indeed have a positive impact on nations and communities. On the other hand, when it occurs in a context of low levels of aggregate demand and destructive economic and political competition in the absence of effective rules, then offshoring can have a significant negative impact on workers in both home and host countries. These problems reduce citizens' bargaining power, making it difficult for the majority of them to gain from offshoring and they undermine the ability of governments to provide the social investments that would enhance the ability of these countries to compete successfully in the global economy.

Economists must confront the resulting bargaining and social investment problems directly, if policies to reduce the distributional and macroeconomic costs of offshoring and related phenomena are going to be implemented. The need for an increase in the bargaining power of workers and citizens to demand ameliorative policies and a larger capacity of governments to provide such policies must be part of any serious discussion of these issues. Up to now, however, most economists have ignored these issues.

The Impact of Offshoring on Employment in the United States

In this section we examine the scope and employment impact of offshoring in U.S. manufacturing. Empirical evidence supports the idea that offshoring has had a negative impact on employment in U.S. manufacturing. Our findings provide evidence that offshoring has distributional implications through the bargaining channel, and, moreover, that aggregate demand can have an important impact on the direction and strength of those implications.

The increase in offshoring together with the negative employment impact in U.S. manufacturing provides the needed context for understanding the importance of the *bargaining channel* between workers and firms that we return to in the following sections of this chapter.

The growing literature on the impact of offshoring on employment and wages in the United States has not generated a consensus. The prima facie evidence would suggest that increased expansion of Multinational Corporations (MNC) abroad has a negative impact on U.S. domestic employment. For example, between 1977 and 1999, U.S. MNCs reduced U.S. domestic employment in manufacturing by 3 million, while expanding employment in low-income countries (Burke and Epstein 2002, Harrison and McMillan 2006, 4). Yet, a number of recent studies suggest that U.S. MNCs create more domestic employment, when they invest abroad.[2]

Harrison and McMillan (2006) argue that the inconsistency among these different studies is mostly resolved, when one distinguishes between MNC activities in low-income countries and in high-income countries. For

MNCs with affiliates in low-income countries, the contraction in U.S. manufacturing employment has been accompanied by an increase in employment in foreign affiliates abroad. Harrison and McMillan (2006, 35) also find a big employment impact of U.S. MNC investment abroad.[3] A 10 percent increase in the capital stock in high or low-income affiliates is associated with a decline in U.S. employment of between .1 and 1.8 percent. And since the capital stock in affiliates has increased by over 100 percent between 1982 and 1999, "this diversion of investment towards affiliates resulted in a decline of up to 18 percent in U.S. manufacturing employment" (Harrison and McMillan 2006, 35).

Other authors have estimated the impact of offshoring on U.S. employment in manufacturing by using the ratio of imported intermediate goods relative to total intermediate input purchases as an indicator of offshoring activity in an industrial sector (e.g., Feenstra and Hanson 1999, Campa and Goldberg 1997). When goods produced abroad replace intermediate stages of production at home, the flow of imports of intermediate goods increases across country borders. Tracking the share of imports in total purchases of intermediate manufacturing goods allows us to detect changes in the scope of offshoring in U.S. manufacturing over time.[4]

Feenstra and Hanson (1999) find that imported intermediate goods increased from 5.3 percent of total intermediate purchases for U.S. manufacturing industries in 1972 to 7.3 percent in 1979 and 12.1 percent in 1990. Using a narrower measure of intermediate goods, Campa and Goldberg (1997) find that imported inputs have increased from 4.1 percent of total intermediate goods in 1975 to 6.2 percent in 1985 and 8.2 percent in 1995 for U.S. manufacturing industries.

Our own research (Burke and Epstein 2006) shows that the share of imported intermediate inputs in total intermediate inputs is much higher. Between 1987 and 2003, the share of imported inputs in the whole manufacturing sector rose from 12.4 to 22.7 percent. Our results also indicate that the growth rate of the imported input share accelerated during this period. Of the total increase of 10.4 percentage points in the import share of inputs, the period 1987–1992 accounts for 1.5 percentage points, the period 1992–1997 accounts for 3.8 percentage points, and the latest six-year period, 1997–2003, accounts for 5.0 percentage points. We found an acceleration of the growth of the imported input share in 13 of the 19 manufacturing industry groups.

Since we are interested in the links between offshoring and industry employment at home, we also examined which industries *produce* these intermediate inputs, rather than, as before, which industries *use* them. The reason for this is simple: we expect the demand for production and workers to be linked to the extent to which the intermediate goods a particular industry *produces* are displaced by imported inputs. We found that for every industry group and for the manufacturing sector as a whole, the share of imports in total inputs produced has risen over the time period. For all manufacturing, the share of imported inputs rose from 19.1 percent in 1998 to 22.8 percent in 2003.

Following a more gradual downward trend since the late 1970s, employment in U.S. manufacturing fell by 3 million jobs, 18 percent, between 1998 and 2003 to reach its lowest level in over half a century. Our research suggests that the increase in offshoring has contributed to that decline. Table 6.1 shows data on employment declines as well as the import ratio of intermediate goods produced by the nineteen industry groups that make up the manufacturing sector for the period 1998–2003. Employment fell in all nineteen industry groups during this time span, although the rates of employment decline varied greatly across industries. The apparel and leather products group—an industry that lost over half of its employment in the period 1998–2003—appears to have been the most affected by off-shoring, with the ratio of imported inputs in total inputs produced by the group reaching over 60 percent.

The statistical results in Burke and Epstein (2006) support a link between offshoring and employment losses. Changes in demand, techno-logical processes, trade, and offshoring are each associated with changes in manufacturing industry employment in expected ways. Increases in off-shoring are shown to have a modest effect in reducing employment in manufacturing industries, while a decline in domestic and foreign demand corresponds to large decreases in employment over the period. As we will discuss in detail below, these results suggest that measures to expand aggre-gate demand at home and abroad can play an important role in ameliorat-ing the negative employment impact of offshoring in manufacturing.

A newer phenomenon of increasing concern, but also of less clear dimensions, is the rise of services offshoring. There is enormous uncertainty about the current extent of services offshoring and its future potential (see, e.g., Abugattas in this volume). But several authors have made compelling arguments that it is likely to become much more widespread over the next ten to twenty years than it is today. Alan Blinder (2005) argues that "imper-sonal services" will become increasingly tradable, placing higher paid U.S., European, and Japanese workers in direct competition with much lower paid workers in developing countries, especially those who are able to com-municate in Western languages. These pressures will increasingly put jobs and wages at risk in the richer countries and will require significant labor market adjustments and interventions by governments, especially in the area of education and social safety nets.

Table 6.1 Employment Change and Import Ratio of Produced Inputs, 1998–2003

Industry	Employment Change, thousands, 1998–2003	Employment Change, 1998–2003 (%)	Import Share of Inputs, 2003 (%)	Import Share of Inputs Change, 1998–2003(%)
Apparel and leather and allied products	−342.9	−50.30	64.00	9.70
Textile mills and textile product mills	−211.7	−33.60	23.00	8.00
Computer and electronic products	−474.3	−26.40	39.40	3.10
Primary metals	−166.5	−26.30	21.30	0.60
Machinery	−357.1	−24.00	29.40	3.80
Electrical equipment, appliances, and components	−140.2	−23.80	34.70	9.60
Other transportation equipment	−160.5	−19.90	19.90	0.30
Paper products	−115.8	−18.70	12.10	1.10
Printing and related support activities	−151.6	−18.40	3.50	1.20
Petroleum and coal products	−21.3	−16.10	13.00	3.80
Fabricated metal products	−261.3	−15.10	12.50	3.00
Plastics and rubber products	−135.1	−14.40	12.20	2.00
Motor vehicles, bodies and trailers, and parts	−177.2	−13.60	35.40	8.70
Furniture and related products	−81.8	−12.60	25.00	9.90
Wood products	−74.6	−12.10	16.60	2.50
Miscellaneous manufacturing	−73.5	−10.10	35.50	3.30
Chemical products	−97.8	−9.90	23.40	6.10
Nonmetallic mineral products	−47.8	−8.90	16.50	3.90
Food and beverage and tobacco products	−61.3	−3.50	7.70	1.80

Source: Authors' calculations.

Bargaining, Coordination, and the Impact of Offshoring

The previous discussion suggests that offshoring has been increasing, that it has had a significant negative impact on manufacturing employment and that, in the service sector, there are reasons to believe that a significant number of workers will be affected negatively in the future.

In discussions of these issues, it is common now to blithely note that there will be "winners" and "losers" from international trade. To do so is seen as a major advance over earlier discussions that claimed that everyone is a winner from international trade. However, identifying the potentially negative impact of offshoring as "only" a distributional problem within an overall context of increased efficiency and productivity fundamentally underestimates the potential social costs. The deep and long-lasting individual costs associated with layoffs are much larger than commonly understood, even when workers are reemployed at similar wages (Uchitelle 2006). But, as a number of economists have shown (e.g., Kletzer 2002), former U.S. manufacturing workers typically are reemployed at significantly lower wages.

In light of this, are we really sure that offshoring increases the size of the economic pie? As Keynes stressed in his discussion of unemployment, involuntary job loss is not only a personal and distributional problem: it also represents a fundamental loss to community and society. This is true even in the event that job loss is temporary. And, in fact, the dislocations associated with broad structural changes are permanent and have much greater costs in terms of obsolescence of skills and disruption of community. Of course, not all change, even change that has costs, is on balance bad. But, as Uchitelle effectively points out, economists have been lax in trying to estimate these costs and seriously balance them against the true (as opposed to theoretical) benefits of more open trade regimes.

What can be done to counteract these distributional and social costs? Most economists reject out of hand any discussion of interference with the market processes of expanding trade. These economists are then typically left with a number of non–trade related policy suggestions. The first and most hopeful argument is that the profits made from those industries and sectors that benefit from expanded trade will be reinvested and create more jobs, thus absorbing into high-paying jobs workers who were laid off due to offshoring and changes in trade patterns. But Milberg et al. (this volume) show that in the United States increases in profits and the profit share have not led to commensurate increases in investment in recent years. Along with the evidence from Kletzer (2002) and others cited above, this suggests that the optimistic scenario is not generally prevailing.

A second possible response to the distributional and social costs associated with offshoring losses is investment in education and retraining to allow workers to find jobs more easily in the expanding sectors. Currently the resources devoted to such retraining are woefully inadequate (e.g., Kletzer and Rosen 2005). Between 1974 and 2002, approximately 25 million workers were eligible for Trade Adjustment Assistance, the major U.S. government policy for workers loosing their jobs due to international trade. And of these workers, only 2.5 million actually received assistance, mostly income assistance for up to 52 weeks beyond that available due to unemployment insurance, training, and job search help. The income maintenance was on average only $200 per week, less than half the average weekly pay in the jobs that had been lost (Kletzer and Rosen 2005, 317). It is widely understood that this program, and subsequent similar programs, such as those created with the North American Free Trade Agreement (NAFTA), are completely inadequate. Yet there is little political support for a dramatic increase in resources, probably largely due to the lack of political power wielded by those who directly suffer from changing trade patterns. Only when the political power of these individuals and their communities is increased, is it likely that serious and adequate support will be forthcoming.

A more general argument favors better education as a mechanism for enhancing the ability of U.S. workers to compete in the global economy (e.g., Friedman 2005). Blinder (2005) doubts that typical formulations of the education solution will work as suggested, as future offshoring will not be based on education but on the degree to which jobs require personal interface. Still, most observers believe that more and better education is one of the key ways to reduce the social costs from globalization for U.S. workers. Another, related proposal is enhanced investment in infrastructure so that the United States is a more attractive and productive site for production and trade.

But even if these policies were helpful, these potential solutions are likely to fail because they are undermined by the very processes of offshoring and globalization themselves. Offshoring industries gain more profits but do not reinvest them domestically because globalization enhances the after-tax profitability of investment abroad rather than at home. However, these profits cannot be captured in the form of taxes to be reinvested at home because globalization allows the firms to evade or politically undermine tax enforcement; workers are not able to get sufficient adjustment assistance because their political power has been lowered relative to firms who can play off one jurisdiction against the other in the competition for investment; and education and infrastructure cannot be adequately funded because of the loss in tax revenue due, at least in part, to offshoring and globalization. In short, globalization precludes the very solutions required to compensate for its negative impacts. This is the fundamental conundrum of offshoring that economists have not confronted adequately.

Capital Mobility and the Weakening of Sovereign Taxing Powers

Economists have long known that increased international capital mobility might result in a reduction of nations' ability to tax corporations and other mobile factors of production (Avi-Yonah 1998, Wilson 1999). If corporate taxes fell, governments would have to raise taxes on others less able to avoid these taxes, or cut expenditures or some combination of the two.

Despite the theoretical presumption of such impacts, empirical work, until recently, has found mixed evidence of a corporate tax race to the bottom. Some economists have suggested that agglomeration effects—that is, the desire of corporations to invest in locations with high levels of social and physical infrastructure and to be near other firms—allows "core countries" to attract foreign direct investment (FDI) even if they maintain high corporate tax rates.[5] In this case, the race to the bottom could be attenuated or play out differently in different countries. Still, the most recent studies show that corporate tax rates have indeed fallen, as capital mobility has risen. In the OECD countries the rates fell from 40 percent in 1981 to around 28 percent in 2001. The variability across countries in corporate tax rates declined as well (Garretsen and Peeters 2006, 9).[6] Hines (2005) shows that between 1982 and 1999 the decline in effective tax rates on U.S. MNCs was even larger that the decrease in the statutory corporate tax rates in OECD countries (see table 6.2).

It is likely that these declines are at least partly due to tax competition among countries, as they vie for more FDI. Numerous studies have shown that FDI responds to lower tax rates, thereby fueling this tax competition. De Mooij and Ederveen (2003, 5) find that the "mean value of the tax rate elasticity . . . is around −3.3, i.e., a 1% reduction in the host-country tax rate raises foreign direct investment in that country by 3.3%." Of course,

Table 6.2 Statutory and Effective Corporate Tax Rates (%)

	1982	1999
Statutory corporate tax rates:		
Average, weighted by GDP	45.9	32.9
Unweighted average	41.3	32
Effective corporate tax on U.S. multinationals:		
Average weighted by GDP	42.6	26.2
Unweighted world average	36.5	23.9

Note: The table presents information for matched samples of 68 countries in 1982 and 1999 with respect to statutory rates and 45 countries with respect to average effective corporate tax rates.

Source: Hines (2005, 29).

this tax competition afflicts not only nation states, but also states, provinces, and regions within countries, as we discuss more fully below.

The decline in capital tax rates has also been promoted by capital exporting countries through changes in their tax and regulatory policies. Altshuler and Grubert (2005) describe U.S. tax policy changes that have contributed to enormous losses in tax revenue due to offshore tax avoidance. In 1997, the United States Treasury issued regulations that greatly simplified the use of more aggressive tax planning strategies. These allow, among other things, for the United States and a partner country to cooperate in allowing corporations to shift income to a third country, such as a tax haven, to avoid paying corporate taxes. Altshuler and Grubert (2005, 6) find that in 2002, for example, MNCs saved about $7 billion in taxes from these more aggressive tax-planning activities, which is about 4 percent of FDI income and 15 percent of total host country tax burdens. They also report that during the period 1992–1998 countries that had seen a decline in their shares of U.S. FDI lowered their tax rates to attract more investment (traditional tax competition).

Recently, changes in U.S. tax laws have further increased the incentives for MNCs to offshore, and they are likely to drive the effective corporate tax rates even lower. The so-called American Jobs Creation Act, signed into law in October 2004, further reduces the tax burden on the foreign income of multinational firms (Clausing 2005, 5), resulting both in increased incentives for U.S. MNCs to offshore and in lowering corporate income tax revenue in the long run.

Companies use a variety of strategies to reduce their tax liabilities, including accounting changes to shift profits to low-tax areas and transfer pricing that involves setting prices for buying and selling inputs within the MNC so as to declare high profits in low-tax areas. Evidently, U.S. MNCs are very effective at this practice. Clausing (2005) compares the *real* and *accounting* activities of U.S. MNCs in 2002. There is practically no overlap between the top ten locations of U.S. MNCs by their employment and the top ten locations by reported income. The reason is not hard to find: the average effective tax rate is 31 percent in the top ten locations by employment and 17 percent in the top 10 locations by reported income (see table 6.3).

The use of offshore tax havens by individuals has gone up tremendously as well. Guttentag and Avi-Yonah (2006) estimate that the use of offshore tax havens by individuals cost the U.S. treasury between $40 billion and $70 billion each year. The IRS further estimates that corporate offshore tax evasion in 2001 totaled about $30 billion (Levin 2006). But *The Citizens for Tax Justice* estimate that the annual loss of tax revenue is $255 billion (Spencer 2005).

Table 6.3   Top Employment and Top Income Countries Reported by U.S. Multinational Companies, 2002

Top employment countries	Effective tax rate* (%)	Top income countries	Effective tax rate* (%)
United Kingdom	31	Ireland	8
Canada	26	Bermuda	2
Mexico	37	Netherlands	9
Germany	27	United Kingdom	31
France	34	Canada	26
Brazil	>100	Luxembourg	1
China	17	Switzerland	4
Australia	29	Japan	39
Japan	39	Mexico	37
Italy	41	Singapore	11
Average**	31	Average	1

* Effective tax rates are calculated as foreign taxes paid by U.S. affiliate firms in a given country relative to net (pre-tax) income.
** The average is calculated without Brazil's rate, which is greater than 100% due to highly idiosyncratic factors.

Source: Clausing (2005).

Aggregate Demand

A second self-reinforcing problem associated with the current version of globalization is the lack of *domestic* aggregate demand. This problem has many deep and complex causes that have been discussed in detail in the literature (e.g., Crotty, Epstein and Kelly 1998, Pollin 2003, Crotty 2005, Baker, Epstein and Pollin 1998). Among the key causes of this problem are the common neoliberal trifecta of fiscal austerity, antiinflation monetary policy, and export-led trade policy. In combination, these policies export to other countries the responsibility for generating aggregate demand, while at the same time putting enormous downward pressure on domestic wages and costs. In the current environment, the United States has become the aggregate demand generator of last resort and this has put enormous pressure on domestic wages and employment in the United States. Freeman (this volume) stresses the importance of the doubling of the global labor force. The lack of widespread aggregate demand and the related focus on export-led growth means that increasing numbers of workers in the global economy are placed in increasing competition with each other. Hence, the forces we describe here intensify the negative impact this doubling has on employment, wages, and bargaining power for workers around the globe.

It is worth exploring a little further some of the elements of this negative aggregate demand picture. One of the factors that has worsened the *global* aggregate demand picture has been the increased focus on inflation targeting and other antiinflation monetary policies, promoted by the IMF and many economists (Epstein, 2005). These policies represent a change from earlier central banking practice in much of the world that focused in a more balanced way on promoting employment and limiting inflation. A second factor is the promotion of export-led growth as a standard strategy embedded in bilateral trade agreements, IMF structural adjustment, poverty reduction strategy papers, and other mechanisms of neoliberal global governance (Rodrik 2006b). These policies result in high levels of international labor market competition in a context of relatively slow global aggregate demand.

Coordination Problems

An additional factor reducing global aggregate demand in the current environment stems from the reduction in national capital controls and the accompanying lack of global regulation of destructive speculative global financial flows. In addition to generating financial crises that lead to recessions and broader crises, these factors have led to an unprecedented buildup of foreign exchange reserves among developing countries, undertaken to self-ensure against sudden outflows of foreign or domestic capital. This enormous hording of reserves likely creates a significant drag on global aggregate demand. If there were national and/or global controls on unstable financial flows, then countries would not have to hold these excessive, costly reserves and could spend the reserves, thereby increasing global aggregate demand (e.g., Epstein, Grabel, and Jomo 2005, Rodrik 2006b).

Bargaining Power

All of these factors—tax competition, insufficient aggregate demand, and coordination problems—have contributed to a dramatic decline in the bargaining power of labor in the United States and some other wealthy countries, especially in the context of the doubling of the global labor force. In the United States, the decline in the bargaining power of workers has been exacerbated by political changes, including changes in laws that have made it more difficult to unionize, the decline in the real minimum wage, and increased foreign competition in manufactured goods (e.g., Pollin 2003, Bronfenbrenner 2000, Brown 2004, Faux 2006). This decline in bargaining power has greatly reduced the ability of U.S. workers to either reap sufficient benefits from globalization, including offshoring, or to change the laws and regulations in such a way that they could be protected from the negative impacts of these changes.

Globalization has affected wages and tax rates through *threat effects* as well as actual changes in the quantities of employment, goods, and investment moving across borders. Bronfenbrenner (2000) shows how the threat by employers to move jobs abroad increases the likelihood of failed contract negotiations for workers and failed unionization drives. Burke and Epstein (2002) review literature that shows the powerful impact of threats by firms not to locate in particular locations on the tax rates and subsidies offered by governments attempting to attract or retain jobs.

Altering the Political Dynamics

In order to alter the dynamics in such a way that workers and citizens share the benefits from globalization in general and offshoring in particular, there must be an increase in the bargaining power of the losers from these processes. Below we sketch some examples of policies that could be implemented to help shift more bargaining power toward the losers from globalization and offshoring. Comprehensive discussions of these policy changes are far beyond what we can provide here; these examples are simply meant to provide a general idea of the types of policies that we have in mind.

Taxation

Tax reform to generate more revenue, to reduce artificial incentives for offshoring, and to reduce the bargaining advantage of corporations relative to workers and the majority of citizens needs to occur at a number of levels: changes in laws, improvements in enforcement, and improvements in tax coordination.

Changes in Tax Laws

There has been much discussion of altering the corporate income tax, including the suggestion of eliminating it altogether on the grounds that a corporate income tax cannot be maintained in a world of high capital mobility.[7] With the right enforcement and tax coordination (see below), however, corporate taxes can be maintained and can help to maintain the integrity of the personal income tax.[8] Some reforms could, in principle, raise significantly more revenue and reduce or even eliminate the tax incentives currently in place for offshoring. Among the most important reforms is the elimination of deferral of U.S. taxation on unrepatriated income earned in low-tax countries. Under current U.S. corporate tax law, MNCs—for the most part—do not have to pay income tax on profits earned in foreign affiliates until they repatriate the profits to the United

States. With some exceptions, this allows firms to accumulate income off-shore free of U.S. income tax. This increases the value of reporting profits in low-tax jurisdictions. A complete elimination of deferral would bring the U.S. tax system closer to the ideal of capital export neutrality, as there would no longer be a tax incentive to earn income in low-tax countries or to shift profits to such locations (Clausing 2005, 26). Some have suggested combining this policy with a reduction in the statutory tax rate to reduce the incentive for evasion, including the increasingly popular practice of corporate inversion, where U.S.-based companies choose to move their headquarters to locations with low tax rates.

Tax Coordination
More coordination among tax jurisdictions is needed to address the challenges of the race to the bottom competition, that is, to reduce the pressures for excessive reductions in tax rates or increases in subsidies. This coordination is often necessary at the international as well as the domestic level. Below we discuss efforts to share information to improve enforcement. Here, it is important to note the efforts to harmonize tax rates in the European Union, for example. Such efforts should be extended to larger groups of countries. Vito Tanzi (1995) has proposed an international tax authority to strengthen international coordination of tax rates and enforcement significantly. Undoubtedly, there are many practical objections to such a scheme, but serious consideration is warranted, given the seriousness of the tax problems facing many countries around the world as a result of globalization.

Problems of tax competition arise not only at the national level. In the United States, there is a "war among the states" to attract investment from both domestic and foreign capitalists. In a recent survey, Timothy Bartik (2004, 11) concludes that many incentives currently offered in the United States have costs that exceed benefits, often costing upward of $140,000 per job created in terms of lost revenue. Among the proposals to eliminate wasteful interstate competition for investment is a ban on such competition among the fifty states in the United States (Holmes 1995). Short of outlawing such incentives, other proposals include making the incentives transparent (now it is often impossible for the public to know which subsidies are being given and under what conditions); performance requirements to hire a certain number of workers, including local workers; claw-back provisions so that the subsidies must be returned if the conditions are not met; and the creation of an overall budget constraint to limit the number of incentives. A particularly important feature of a reformed incentive structure would be to focus the hiring on the unemployed, thereby increasing labor demand for the unemployed or underemployed at the local level (Bartik 2004, 32).

Enforcement

On the enforcement front, Avi-Yonah (2006, 2) describes the challenge succinctly: "Simply put, we have the technology which enables people to conduct their affairs without regard to national borders and without transparency, while restricting tax collectors to geographic borders . . . " He recommends a number of steps to address offshore tax abuses, including an increase in IRS enforcement to close the international tax gap; more bilateral information exchange, in particular the adoption of the new OECD exchange of information rules that makes exchange of information on civil as well as criminal tax liabilities mandatory, does not require dual criminality or suspicion of a crime other than tax evasion, and overrides bank secrecy provisions of domestic laws; and the imposition of sanctions on noncooperating tax havens, including denying portfolio interest exemption to countries that do not provide adequate exchange of information.

Aggregate Demand

A great deal of research has suggested policy reforms that could take place at international, regional, and national levels to reverse the common focus of fiscal and monetary policy on austerity and inflation reduction, and to reduce the international financial instability that leads to demand-reducing crises or policies to avoid crises, such as the promotion of export-led growth and the accumulation of resulting hard-currency reserves.

In the United States, central bank policy should take seriously the Humphrey Hawkins bill, which requires the Federal Reserve to maintain both full employment and price stability. Abroad, countries should strongly consider abandoning inflation-targeting approaches to central bank policy and adopt policies that promote other domestic goals such as more employment generation, higher investment rates, or more stable and competitive exchange rates, along with moderate inflation rates.[9] Both domestic and international reforms need to be implemented to reduce the costly and contractionary policies of excessive foreign exchange accumulation occurring in many developing countries. The implementation of domestic capital controls, and capital management techniques in general, can reduce the unstable inflows and outflows of capital that have contributed to the need to accumulate more reserves (Epstein, Grabel, and Jomo 2005; Grabel 2005).

A variety of reforms should be considered at the international level to reduce excessive, procyclical, and short-term speculation. These could include, for example, a so-called Tobin Tax—a small tax on all foreign exchange transactions. At a regional level, reserve pooling schemes could be created to allow more reinvestment of reserves into local development projects that could help domestically oriented industries and generate more employment.

Getting There from Here:
Bargaining Power and Economic Reform

Bargaining Power

Enhancing the bargaining power of workers and citizens vis-à-vis mobile corporations will be necessary to bring about long-lasting reforms in domestic and international institutions and policies to insure that benefits from global integration are more widely shared. Tax changes such as the ones described above can preserve government revenue that can be used to improve infrastructure and the educational qualifications of U.S. workers so that they can better compete for high-quality jobs and pay. Policies to increase aggregate demand can enhance workers' incomes. Bernstein and Baker (2003), for example, find that during the boom of the later Clinton years, reductions in unemployment had a significant impact on the ability of workers to bargain for higher wages, particularly for those at the low levels of the wage ladder. More generally, extensive empirical work on the wage-curve in different countries suggests that reductions in local unemployment rates have a significant positive impact on real wages, presumably at least partly through the bargaining channel (Blanchflower and Oswald 2005).[10]

Other policies that increase the bargaining power of workers include increases in minimum wages and living wages (Pollin 2003; Pollin et al. forthcoming). Other possible labor market policies would include ways to pre-identify industries and provide trade adjustment assistance to all workers laid off in these industries, independent of whether unemployment was due to international trade, and extend wage insurance programs to help workers recoup lost wages if they are laid off and cannot find a job that pays as much as their previous job (Kletzer and Rosen 2005). Bernstein (2006) proposes more public employment programs to provide employment, skill training, and needed infrastructure. All of these programs would directly increase the income or reduce the instability of income for workers. And they would indirectly enhance workers' bargaining power, making it more likely that they can push back against corporations both at the bargaining table and in the political sphere.

A Paradox

A fundamental paradox in this argument will not have escaped most readers. We need changes in policies and institutions to give workers and citizens the bargaining power that will induce governments to govern offshoring and capital mobility so that there will be widely shared benefits; but only when citizens and workers have more bargaining power will these policy changes actually come about. This is the proverbial chicken and egg problem, or the "you can't get there from here" conundrum. What is to be done?

Threat Effects in Reverse

One way to answer this question is to look at how such changes occurred in the recent past. Kletzer and Rosen (2005) report, for example, that laws to implement and improve Trade Adjustment Assistance have only been passed when the president was trying to get Congress to pass a trade deal. The threat by Congress *not* to pass the trade agreement leads supporters of trade agreements to make concessions on more labor-friendly policies. This experience suggests the key: threats to refuse to pursue future agreements or even to reverse previous agreements on trade such as the WTO agreement, bilateral trade agreements, and NAFTA could bring about significant changes along the lines we have described, if these threats are credible.[11]

More specifically, proponents of a more efficient and equitable approach to offshoring and globalization more generally in the United States. should support a moratorium on all future trade and investment agreements until solutions are implemented to the taxation, social investment, and aggregate demand problems we have identified. In short, the presumption should be that globalization should *not* be allowed to undermine the bargaining power of citizens or the social investments of society. And until globalization can proceed without doing so, future movement in that direction should be reduced.

Recently, the consensus among U.S. elites in favor of more trade agreements has been showing signs of cracking. The 2006 congressional elections, which elected trade policy critics such as Sherrod Brown (Brown 2004) to the Senate, reflects this sagging consensus. Supporters of more trade liberalization decry this shift in sentiment. They maintain that trade liberalization is better for society as a whole, and we can make the outcomes fair by having the winners simply compensate the losers.

But, in our view, this is an illusion. In a world where allocation, distribution, and power are as inextricably linked as they are in the areas of trade and offshoring, the separation of these policies into neat, separate piles called "allocation" and "distribution" will simply not work. Economists can convince themselves that they can talk about the efficiency of offshoring and then, as an afterthought, describe a redistributional package. But if the new political economy has taught us anything, it is that this artificial separation is wishful thinking at best, and it, more likely, contains a heavy dose of self-delusion. A healthy skepticism about the merits of more trade liberalization, and threats to reverse these trade agreements, is a good exercise in our democracy, if it is accompanied by realistic, well thought-out policies to allow us to capture the benefits of more trade and offshoring, and to use those benefits to reinvest into our society, making sure that the benefits are widely shared.

Notes

* Many thanks to Eva Paus for her many helpful comments and suggestions. The authors also thank Arjun Jayadev, Minsik Choi, Derek Weener and Elissa Braunstein for help. The Political Economy Research Institute (PERI) provided research support. All errors are ours, of course.

1. See Crotty, Epstein and Kelly (1998), Rodrik (1997), and Burke and Epstein (2002) for elaborations of these arguments with respect to globalization generally and foreign direct investment in particular.
2. See Harrison and McMillan (2006) for a recent review; see also, for example, Mankiw and Swagel (2006).
3. This is consistent with earlier work by James Burke (1997).
4. A basic assumption of this method is that the import share of the commodity when it is used as an intermediate good in each particular industry is the same as the import share of the commodity in the economy as a whole as calculated from the I/O accounts.
5. See Garretsen and Peeters (2006) for a recent review.
6. Garretsen and Peeters (2006). There are many measures of corporate tax rates used in the literature: statutory tax rates, effective marginal tax rates, and average effective tax rates. Garretsen and Peeters use average effective corporate tax rates. Using statistical analysis, they also find that the decline in corporate tax rates is associated with increases in capital mobility, though so-called agglomeration effects attenuate the negative impacts, allowing large countries more leeway in maintaining higher corporate tax rates if they choose to do so.
7. See, for example, Clausing (2005) for a discussion.
8. In the absence of a corporation income tax, wealthy individuals can shift income to corporations and thereby avoid the personal income tax as well (Clausing, 2005).
9. See Epstein, (2005) and Pollin et al. (2006) for an application of this approach to the case of South Africa.
10. Blanchflower and Oswald (2005) report that a large number of studies from different countries, including the United States suggest that the elasticity of real wages with respect to the unemployment rate is approximately 0.1, implying that a doubling of the unemployment rate is associated with a ten percent decline in the level of real wages (1).
11. Crotty and Epstein (1996) argued in a different context that capital controls, or the threat of imposing them, could be helpful, or even necessary to convince firms to pursue more socially desirable behaviors, such as paying more taxes, increasing domestic investment, and generating more employment. As long as firms knew they always had an exit strategy, then it would be difficult for the government to gain the bargaining power necessary to win concessions from firms.

CHAPTER SEVEN

SOCIAL CONTRACTS UNDER SIEGE: NATIONAL RESPONSES TO GLOBALIZED AND EUROPEANIZED PRODUCTION IN EUROPE

Vivien A. Schmidt

"Offshoring," "delocalization," going south or east: whatever the words, the issue of jobs moving not just out of firm or out of town but out of country and out of continent due to the forces of globalization is not new. What is new is that offshore outsourcing has been affecting not just manufacturing but also, and increasingly, services. This has been a cause for concern because the rise in services has long been seen as compensating for the decline in manufacturing. In Europe, moreover, enlargement to Eastern Europe combined with the Single Market liberalization program, in particular with regard to the recent attempt to liberalize services, adds pressures of Europeanization to globalization, as jobs move eastward in the EU as much as out of the EU. To worries about nearshore outsourcing resulting from Europeanization, however, have also come those about nearshore insourcing, as workers move in from Eastern Europe while jobs move out.

But although offshoring has become a matter of general concern in Europe, public responses vary greatly. These depend not just on the amount of offshoring to Asia and nearshoring to Eastern Europe but also on how countries' work and welfare systems cushion the effects of such outsourcing and on how national publics have come to perceive globalization and Europeanization in general and offshoring in particular. Winners and losers vary with the type of welfare state: social-democratic, liberal, and conservative welfare states. But national publics' perceptions of who is winning or losing are also influenced by national leaders' legitimizing ideas and discourses about globalization and Europeanization. This is illustrated using a range of West European countries, including Britain, Ireland, France, Germany, the Netherlands, Sweden, and Italy.

Offshoring in Perspective

The media blitz across Europe on the threats to jobs from offshore and nearshore outsourcing has been phenomenal, with headlines blaring in particular about major corporations from automotive manufacturing to financial services firing thousands of workers in Europe to hire others in East Asia or Eastern Europe. The news has also been replete with stories about West European workers losing jobs to East European immigrants or being blackmailed into reducing wages and increasing working hours in order to keep firms from offshoring their jobs. And yet, if one looks behind the headlines to the statistics, offshoring has not—at least as yet—had much overall impact on jobs. Losses in industry have largely been counterbalanced by gains in services, and losses in certain service sectors have been replaced by gains in others. Estimates vary greatly, but most suggest that overall job losses due to offshore outsourcing are negligible in comparison with overall employment in the EU (Kirkegaard 2005) as well as in individual countries such as Germany, France, and even the United Kingdom (Barysch 2006; Aubert and Sillard 2005; UK National Statistics 2005). Moreover, FDI outflows have been more than compensated by FDI inflows, with European companies investing in other West European countries even more than in Eastern Europe, Asia, or the United States (UNCTAD 2005a).

These general statistics suggest that adapting to offshoring, the latest manifestation of globalization, has not been a disaster for employment in Europe. However, the statistics do not tell us anything about the losers from globalization. These are the people who have felt the impact of globalization on their wages, which have not progressed at nearly the same pace as in the past, and on the quality of jobs, as more secure, higher-paid manufacturing jobs are exchanged for more temporary or part-time, lower-paid service jobs. These are the people who sit at the lower end of the wage scale, as wage inequalities rise in terms of differentials in pay between highest and lowest-paid jobs, and who find themselves less protected by the traditional welfare state, as benefits and services are "rationalized." Finally, these are also mostly the people who suffer from the "new social risks" related to unemployment, incomplete work histories, and lack of skills, who are disproportionately young, female, and/or immigrants, as opposed to the traditional workforce, which continues to be mainly affected by the "old social risks" linked to old age, ill health, or job loss, for which the welfare state was originally constructed.

In addition to the problems affecting certain segments of the labor force across Europe, offshoring also has differential effects on European member-states' economies. Some European countries have experienced much more offshoring than others. But interestingly, public responses have been highly varied and are not closely correlated with a country's higher (or lower) level of offshoring. As we shall see below, the public in one of the countries hardest hit by global offshoring and European nearshoring of manufacturing and service jobs, Britain, has until recently been much less concerned about it than publics in countries so far less affected, such as France. Moreover, although European insourcing of workers has become an issue even in Britain, it has been a much bigger issue in France, despite the fact that such insourcing is much lower. Other big countries remain somewhere in between these extremes. The public in Germany has been gloomy on the topic of nearshoring of manufacturing and insourcing of East Europeans, but not nearly as much as the French. Until very recently, Italy has been much more enthusiastically pro-global and pro-European despite suffering from a greater economic slowdown. Furthermore, small states where one might have expected significant concern about offshoring—whether because of great vulnerability to changes in foreign direct investment, as in Ireland, or because of the dominance of large internationalized firms, as in the Netherlands or Sweden—are nevertheless highly pro-global. The puzzle, then, is: Why such varied public responses?

The answers lie not only in economics—with inhabitants of the country "winners," those experiencing comparatively higher levels of economic growth and lower levels of unemployment, such as Britain, Ireland, and Sweden, generally less concerned than inhabitants of the country "losers," which have been in the economic doldrums with higher levels of unemployment, such as France, Germany, and Italy, or underemployment, such as the Netherlands. They also have to do with countries' differing systems of welfare and work, in particular with whether their social policies have cushioned the effects of offshoring and nearshoring on the "losers" through welfare benefits and services and whether their labor policies have helped create more "winners" through job creation and labor market activation programs.

European countries divide into three basic "families" of welfare states: the "liberal" welfare states of Anglo-Saxon countries such as Britain and Ireland, which offer the lowest levels of benefits and services and in which the major risk is poverty; the "social-democratic" welfare states of Scandinavian countries such as Sweden, which provide the highest level of benefits and services and for which the main issue is sustainability; and the conservative welfare states of Continental and Mediterranean Europe, including France, Germany, the Netherlands, and Italy, which provide reasonably high levels of benefits but low levels of services, and for which the primary problem is unemployment or underemployment. These systems have not only had very different ways of dealing with the "old social risks," they have also developed different policy responses to the "new social risks," sometimes differing even within the same families of welfare states.

But although economics combined with work and welfare systems may go a long way toward explaining public reactions toward offshoring, in particular in a country such as Sweden, where a highly generous welfare state and extensive labor market activation policies together allay most public concern, they do not fully account for them. They do not explain why, for example, national publics in liberal welfare states such as Britain or Ireland seem comparatively unconcerned about offshoring, given the lack of job security and the risk of poverty, or why national publics in some conservative welfare states appear very worried about it, as in France, and in others much less so, such as Italy.

The answer here lies in national legitimating discourses about globalization and Europeanization, that is, the way in which national leaders have spoken to the question of who wins and who loses with regard to these outside pressures. Public attitudes in Britain and Ireland toward offshoring owe much to the strong and unified pro-globalization discourses of the "third-way" developed since the late 1990s, with Europeanization playing a supporting role. French public attitudes, in contrast, cannot be understood without taking note of the increasingly strong and unified antiglobalization discourse since the mid-1980s, with Europeanization originally cast as a shield against globalization rather than as the conduit some see it as today. German public attitudes have a lot to do with the long-standing residual but unified pro-global discourse that has only recently become contested. The Italians' attitudes result from a default unquestioningly pro-global and pro-European discourse as the only answer to the incapacity of the state. The responses of Swedish and Dutch publics are also related to the long-standing unified pro-global discourses of small states with open economies in a global environment.

Economic effects alone, in short, do not serve as predictors of public attitudes toward offshoring. This is because such attitudes are additionally linked not only to the coping mechanisms of national work and welfare institutions but also to national ideas and discourse about globalization and Europeanization. In what follows, I demonstrate this by first examining the ways in which systems of work and welfare have been reformed (or not) in response to the challenges of globalization and Europeanization in general and offshoring in particular. I then explore the "social construction of reality," that is, the ways in which national leaders' ideas and discourse have (or have not) served to legitimate reforms to systems of work and welfare in order to meet the challenges of globalization and Europeanization.

Challenges to Work and Welfare Systems

The central problem with regard to offshoring is not the loss of jobs per se but how workers are affected by it and whether national systems of work and welfare manage to moderate its effects. And this in turn is related to the ways in which national governments have (or have not) adjusted their systems of work and welfare to meet the competitive challenges posed by globalization and Europeanization more generally.

Reforms Responding to the "Old" and "New" Social Risks

Work and welfare reforms have been of two different kinds: those focused on the "old" social risks and those targeting the "new" social risks. The old social risks are mainly those for which the postwar welfare state was designed, including pension systems, disability schemes, and health care for those who found themselves too old or incapacitated to work, as well as unemployment schemes for those who found themselves out of work. Reforms have involved belt-tightening in benefit programs, whether by reducing the recourse to early retirement, the number of people on disability, or the generosity of unemployment compensation; by cutting costs in social services, often by increasing the marketization of public services; and by diminishing the size of pensions, increasing the years of contribution, or partially privatizing them. Work reforms have primarily involved attempts to increase flexibility in labor markets by easing rules for hiring and firing, promoting part-time and temporary jobs, and decentralizing bargaining on wages and work conditions to sectoral and firm levels.

The reforms targeted toward the old social risks disproportionately affect the older workers and the "insiders" who have benefited from the *status quo ante* of the postwar welfare state. The reforms that focused on the new social risks disproportionately affect those who benefit the least from the postwar welfare state: the "outsiders" who tend to be younger, female, or immigrant, who may be without work, without skills, or on welfare, although it can also affect older workers who have lost their jobs. The new risk reforms are largely focused on work-related issues and emphasize "equality of opportunity" rather than the "equality of results," or redistribution, which was at the heart of the social policies related to the "old" risks. These new risk reforms encompass primarily labor activation policies such as education, training, and jobseeker aid. But they are also linked to welfare, whether through welfare-to-work programs for the young and the long-term unemployed or through child-care services (and to a lesser extent elderly care) for women, to free them up for work (Taylor-Gooby 2004).

All of these new risk reforms tend to cushion the effects of offshoring for those at the lowest end of the job hierarchy, since they are focused on improving skills and finding jobs for those who are most vulnerable when lower-skilled manufacturing or service jobs are offshored or nearshored. The reforms related to the new social risks sometimes join with the labor market flexibility reforms for old social risks, by promoting *flexicurity* for part-time and temporary jobs through benefits and services at the same level as full-time jobs or close to it, with pension top-ups for those with incomplete work histories.

European Countries' Diverse Responses in Welfare and Work

European countries' reforms of their systems of welfare and work have been highly diverse, with some having adjusted more than others with regard to the old social risks, and some having done more than others to address the new social risks. These reforms are best examined by considering countries in terms of their trajectories of development within one of three postwar constellations of welfare states: traditionally liberal, Anglo-Saxon welfare states such as Britain and Ireland; social-democratic, Scandinavian welfare states such as Sweden; or conservative welfare states such as Germany, France, and the Netherlands or Italy (Esping-Andersen 1990; Scharpf and Schmidt 2000).

Welfare

Liberal welfare states in Anglo-Saxon countries such as Britain and Ireland—where the postwar welfare state was characterized by a comparatively low level of state-provided benefits and services and an emphasis on individual responsibility—have all moved toward an even more liberal, leaner welfare state. Benefit levels are still low, the emphasis on individual responsibility is even greater, and poverty is now the main challenge, largely because social transfers do not bring the poverty level down as much as in the two other, more generous welfare systems (Rhodes 2000).

By contrast, social-democratic welfare states in Scandinavian countries such as Sweden and Denmark—where the postwar welfare state was characterized by a very high level of state-provided benefits and services and a premium on equality and universality of service provision—have remained true to the social-democratic model. They continue to respect values of equality and universality of provision and to maintain a high level of generosity despite cuts in benefits and the introduction of user fees. Their main challenge has been how to sustain the welfare state at such a high level (Benner and Vad 2000).

Finally, conservative welfare states in Continental countries such as Germany, the Netherlands, and France, as well as in Mediterranean countries such as Italy—where the postwar welfare state was characterized by reasonably generous, state-provided benefits differentiated by status and gender and a lower level of services provided by intermediary groups (if not left to the family)—have reformed their model to varying degrees in different ways. But all have retained their reasonably high level of generosity in benefits even as they have introduced some degree of individual recourse through pension reform. Their main challenge has been how to reform social protection systems to reflect changing gender roles and patterns of work while overcoming the problems of unemployment that stem from much greater labor-market rigidities than in liberal or social-democratic welfare states (Manow and Seils 2000; Ferrera and Gualmini 2004; Hemerijck, Visser, and Unger 2000).

Work

The changes in welfare systems have also been accompanied by changes in work regimes. In the labor markets, liberal Britain and Ireland as well as social-democratic Sweden have developed much higher levels of flexibility than conservative Germany, France, and Italy. But whereas in liberal Britain and Ireland, such flexibility stems mainly from much higher percentages of part-time and temporary employment and much easier hiring and firing rules than in conservative welfare states, in social-democratic Sweden it comes from more effective labor-market activation policies that emphasize state-sponsored retraining of laid-off workers and strong job-search support. Moreover, social-democratic Sweden also ensures much greater welfare security, or *flexicurity*, than the liberal welfare states, with regular benefits for those in part-time or temporary jobs, mostly in well-paid public sector services. With regard to *flexicurity*, however, social-democratic Denmark's system works even better than does that of Sweden. This is because it has even greater labor market flexibility than Britain in terms of its extremely easy hiring and firing at the same time that it also has as generous unemployment insurance as Sweden, if not better, along with equally strong state-sponsored retraining and job-search support. By contrast, in liberal Britain, part-time and temporary employment is mainly in low-paid private sector jobs with no benefits, little if any unemployment insurance, and little if any state-sponsored retraining.

The lack of labor market flexibility in conservative welfare states is typically blamed for their higher levels of unemployment over the long term. The main problem for these countries is that rigid employment protection rules make employers less likely to hire for fear that they cannot fire, which in turn makes the move into the services industry generally harder. The comparative paucity of part-time and temporary jobs has also made it harder for women to move into the workforce. This has only been compounded by the relative lack of affordable private or public day care services for women with children (with the exception of France's public services).

The one major exception with regard to overall labor market flexibility has been the Netherlands (which has therefore occasionally been classified with social-democratic welfare states, e.g., Sapir 2005). The Netherlands has the highest part-time employment as a proportion of total employment in the EU, 35 percent in 2004, in contrast to the United Kingdom's 24 percent, Germany's and Ireland's 19 to 20 percent, and France's, Italy's, and Sweden's 13 to 15 percent. But although the Dutch as a result do not suffer from the unemployment that afflicts most conservative welfare states, they risk underemployment, as evidenced by the comparatively low number of annual hours worked per person, 1357, in contrast to France's and Germany's average of 1442, Sweden's and Italy's 1585, and the United Kingdom's and Ireland's average of 1656 (OECD 2005a). Unlike the United Kingdom, however, the large proportion of part-time and temporary work does not put workers at risk of poverty because the Netherlands, like Sweden, has *flexicurity*.

Labor market reforms in conservative welfare states other than the Netherlands have done little to solve the problems of unemployment. They have tended to leave core employment areas alone while making changes on the margins, by creating fixed-term contracts for new jobs, special youth employment programs, and the like (Kirkegaard 2005). Although recent EU legislation has pushed for greater benefits tied to these jobs, to ensure some level of pension contribution and access to services, it does nothing for job security over the long term. Moreover, these kinds of temporary jobs—often called "defined term contracts" as opposed to "undefined term contracts"— can be self-perpetuating. They can also lead to two-track employment systems, where core workers are protected while increasing numbers of younger and/or newly hired, less skilled, previously laid-off workers, and immigrants, have more precarious employment, less likelihood for advancement, and fewer benefits. These are the people affected by the new "social risks" (Taylor-Gooby 2005). And they are also most likely to become the real losers with regard to offshoring, in particular in the service industries.

The massive protests in response to the French government's initiative on youth employment, the CPE (first employment contract), in late

March 2006—which was to extend to two years the six-month contracts in which businesses could dismiss young employees without cause—are clear evidence of public concern with the increasing *précarité* or precariousness of employment for the young. The bifurcation of the labor market into insiders with jobs and job security and outsiders with no jobs and no security is a problem not just for France but for most conservative welfare states as well. In Spain, there are unofficial estimates that over 30 percent of workers are in temporary or part-time employment; the figure in Italy is not much lower.

Countries in which unemployment insurance rather than employment protection rules cover the bulk of the workforce do not suffer as much from the problems of labor market bifurcation or from high unemployment. These include liberal Anglo-Saxon welfare states and social-democratic Scandinavian welfare states, plus the Netherlands (Sapir 2005). But lower unemployment does not guard against other problems—in particular the constant need to improve skills and to ensure that workers find jobs. The social-democratic welfare states of Scandinavian countries score well in this area too, given high spending on training as well as strong labor market activation policies. Not so in liberal welfare states. Whereas the United Kingdom spent 0.14 percent of GDP on training in 2002–2003 and Ireland 0.20 percent in 2003, Sweden spent close to four times the British amount, 0.61 percent of GDP in 2002, as did the Netherlands, at 0.62 percent in 2003, while Germany spent close to three times as much as the British, at 0.40 percent in 2003, and France twice, at 0.31 percent in 2003. Only Italy was on a par with Ireland, at 0.23 percent in 2003 (OECD 2005a). In the United Kingdom, those most in need of retraining because they are in the lower-paid service jobs that are currently being offshored in increasing numbers, and for which reemployment rates are also somewhat lower (UK National Statistics 2005) are also least likely to get that retraining, given the generally low spending on retraining programs by employers. Public sector programs such as the "New Deal" for youth employment, which was subsequently extended to single mothers and the long-term unemployed, have helped some, but they are not extensive enough to make a great difference. And these low-skilled workers are therefore most at risk from poverty, given the United Kingdom's low levels of benefits.

The Social Construction of Reality:
Why Discourse Matters

Change is never easy, especially if it challenges long-established ideas and deep-seated values, let alone entrenched interests. The reform of systems of welfare and work undertaken by most European countries in the 1990s in response to the challenges of globalization and Europeanization has been especially difficult, since this was coming on top of reforms to macroeconomic policies beginning in the mid-1970s and to microeconomic policies in the mid-1980s (Scharpf 2000). The presence of legitimating public discourses has often facilitated such reform efforts. These require not only convincing cognitive arguments about the necessity of reform but also persuasive normative arguments about its appropriateness. And such arguments are most effective if they occur both in the "coordinative" discourse among policy actors, to facilitate agreement on policies and in the "communicative" discourse between political leaders and the general public, to legitimate reform (Schmidt 2000, 2002 Ch. 5). The absence of such discourses helps explain why reforms failed, if they got off the ground in the first place. The ways in which these discourses connected to ideas about globalization and Europeanization in turn help explain public responses to offshore and nearshore outsourcing.

Offshoring has been a matter of concern to publics in all European countries. Evidence of such concern can be seen not only in the responses of national governments but also in that of the EU, which recently established a €500m ($650m) Globalization Adjustment Fund to alleviate the impact of globalization. It kicks in, offering job counseling, training and other help, when one thousand or more workers in a given firm or industry lose their jobs as a result of "structural changes in world trade patterns" (Galax 2007).

Public concern about globalization varies across EU member-states. When Europeans were asked in a recent poll (European Commission, question QD6) what came to mind when they heard the word globalization, the "delocalization" of some companies to countries where labor is cheaper came first, sometimes followed by new opportunities for national companies, other times by increased competition for national companies or increased foreign investment in the country. Significantly, the only countries in which majorities associated globalization with delocalization were publics in conservative welfare states such as France (59 percent) and Germany (51 percent). In liberal Britain, by contrast, only slightly over a third (36 percent) of respondents associated globalization with delocalization, while in Ireland it was just under a third (31 percent). Interestingly enough, in social democratic Sweden, respondents were far more worried about delocalization (49 percent) than in quasi-social-democratic Netherlands (13 percent), where respondents were the least worried of our sample. Conservative Italy is perhaps the most anomalous case, though, since only 26 percent worried about delocalization, despite significant economic problems and little reform. Europeanization is another matter, however, given growing concerns about nearshoring of jobs and "insourcing" of East European workers. In a 2005 Eurobarometer poll (eb 64.fr 2005), when West Europeans generally were asked what they feared most in a list of issues related to European integration, the transfer of jobs to other member-states where production is cheaper came out on top, with close to two in three Europeans worried about this (73 percent).

In Britain, the public's positive take on globalization and its seemingly low concern with offshoring may seem surprising, especially since British workers are more exposed to offshoring than the other countries considered. Economic dynamism has a lot to do with the seeming lack of concern of the general public, as does the low unemployment rate. But Britain's traditionally ungenerous welfare state and low level of support for training could nevertheless be expected to give some pause, especially for those most exposed to offshoring. Yet it took the "inshoring" of 300,000 workers instead of the expected 30,000 for the British government to decide that the doors would be closed to the Bulgarians and Romanians when they came into the EU in 2007. Even this large influx of workers did not produce the backlash that it did in Ireland, though, where concerns focused on Estonians taking Irish seamen's jobs on ferryboats and on East Europeans more generally flooding the construction industry.

The British public's general acceptance of globalization and offshoring has much to do with a public discourse that since Tony Blair came to power in 1997 has been focused on legitimizing globalization and in highlighting the policy responses to the new social risks associated with it. Globalization itself has consistently been portrayed as circumscribing the parameters of political and economic choice, for the domestic arena as well as for Europe (Hay and Smith 2005) because Europe, as Blair insisted in his speech on its future, "must be global or fail" (Oxford University, February 2, 2006). Globalization, moreover, has been central to New Labour's justification of the necessity of work and welfare reform, both as the reason for government policies to keep wages and social benefits down and as the rationale for promoting greater flexibility in the labor markets (Hay 1999; Hay and Smith 2005). The discourse of the "third way" served to legitimate such reform by arguing that government policies would "promote opportunity instead of dependence" through positive actions (i.e., workfare) rather than negative actions focused on limiting benefits and services (like the conservatives in previous governments), and by providing "not a hammock" (like "Old" Labor) "but a trampoline," not "a hand out but a hand up" (Schmidt 2000, 2002 Ch. 6). More recently, the explicitly "third way" discourse has been replaced by similarly legitimating arguments centered around adopting Swedish labor market activation policies and creating an "Anglo-social" model of welfare state.

The Irish public's pro-globalization stance (leaving aside East European insourcing) is less surprising than that of the British, given that globalization through foreign direct investment—not to mention Europeanization through the structural funds—has helped fuel the country's extraordinary growth in the past decades. Globalization has been presented as the reason for Ireland's "tigerdom" and continues to be presented that way, even through the country's recent economic slowdown (especially since the country still has the highest growth rate in Western Europe). Ireland has also had the equivalent of a "third way" discourse on the reform of work and welfare linked to globalization (Hay and Smith 2005). Much like the United Kingdom, moreover, globalization has been presented as a nonnegotiable constraint, to ensure wage restraint and to reinforce the corporatist cooperation between labor, management, and government that began in the late 1980s. Europeanization, by contrast, has always been described in much more glowing terms than in the United Kingdom, as the reason why Ireland has gotten to where it is today, despite the growing constraints, in particular with regard to the European Monetary Union.

Sweden and the Netherlands have also been very positive about globalization, but with a different and much longer history of a pro-global discourse and policy. This is mainly because, unlike the long poor and economically dependent Ireland or the bigger and long-global United Kingdom, these small states prospered in the postwar period as open economies in which cooperative, corporatist labor relations were underpinned either, as in the Netherlands, by an egalitarian, reasonably generous, conservative welfare state or, as in Sweden, by an egalitarian, highly generous social-democratic welfare state (Katzenstein 1985). As a result, globalization, represented by outside competitive forces, has been a sine qua non of economic life and has so become part of the background assumptions that national leaders have not even felt it necessary to articulate in any specifically pro-global discourse, unlike Ireland and Britain. Moreover, as we have already seen, both countries have undertaken more reforms with regard to both the old and the new social risks.

In Sweden, public attitudes toward globalization have not even been affected at moments of major reform of welfare and work. This is because such reforms did little to jeopardize the basic postwar commitment to equality and universality of access, maintaining a very high level of benefits and services despite moderate cuts and the introduction of modest user fees (Benner and Vad 2000). Thus, in their discourse, social-democratic governments consistently presented themselves as defending basic welfare state values of equality, even as they cut benefits in order to "save the welfare state" (Schmidt 2000). For the Swedish public, Europeanization has been much more in question than globalization, mainly because of fears of the negative impact of the European Monetary Union on the welfare state, as evidenced by the fact that the referenda on EMU membership have repeatedly failed.

Enlargement related to insourcing of workers, moreover, has not been much of an issue. But immigration more generally, as it relates to third country nationals, has become an issue, with anti-immigrant feeling growing with regard to immigrants' potential demands on the welfare state if they are jobless and without skills. Sweden, however, has been much less xenophobic in this regard than Denmark, which recently instituted the most draconian immigration rules in all of Europe.

The Dutch experience of reform has been much more fraught. Significant reform of the labor markets came in the early 1980s, bringing not only a return to cooperative labor management relations and wage restraint after their breakdown in the 1970s but also a veritable revolution with regard to part-time and temporary work as well as gender relations through the entry of women into the workforce (Visser and Hemerijck 1997). The transformation of the labor market was followed in the early 1990s by significant welfare reform (Hemerijck, Visser, and Unger 2000), promoted by a "crisis narrative" that the Netherlands was a "sick country," given the number of workers out on disability—one in seven (Kuiper 2004; Schmidt 2000). But while cognitive arguments about the necessity of reform enabled the government to push through major changes in the disability and pensions systems, the lack of normative legitimization led to the government's massive defeat in 1994. Only when a new government was able to argue credibly not only that it had ensured a better economy with "jobs, jobs, and more jobs" but also that it safe-guarded social equity even as it produced liberalizing efficiency, did reform gain public acceptance, as confirmed by the government's landslide electoral victory in 1998 (Levy 1999; Schmidt 2000). Since then, governments have continued broad-scale liberalization programs, such that the public has seen economic success as linked to neoliberal reform and, despite economic stagnation in recent years, continues to support it as well as to maintain a positive attitude toward globalization. Attitudes toward Europeanization have also been largely positive, at least until the negative vote in the referendum on the Constitutional Treaty, which reflected concerns about immigration as well as the inflationary impact of the euro.

To Germany—as the lead economy in Europe and for long a global competitor, given its strong export sector—global competitive pressure did not represent the kind of challenge that it did for the United Kingdom or even the Netherlands until quite late. Only in the early and mid-1990s, in conjunction with the country's unification, did globalization surface as a problem rather than an opportunity. It was not until the Social Democrats took power in the late 1990s, however, that major reform was promised (Manow and Seils 2000). But it immediately hit roadblocks in the government itself, which was unable to speak in one voice, as the pro-global, pro-welfare reform discourse of social-democratic chancellor Gerhard Schröder, was contradicted by the neo-Keynesian discourse of Social-Democratic Party leader and minister of finance Oskar Lafontaine. Lafontaine's resignation after four months did not help matters, however. Schröder's discourse was unconvincing to the public, first, as he sought to borrow from the British discourse of the "third-way" in summer 1999 and then from the French socialist discourse in the fall. He was convincing only when he came out swinging against the Mannesmann takeover by Vodafone and tried to save Holzman from bankruptcy—none of which did much for the government's reform efforts or for public attitudes toward globalization (Schmidt 2002, Ch. 6). Moreover, while economic policy reform proceeded apace, employment reforms went nowhere, the result of the split in the SPD between "traditionalists" in charge of the Labor Ministry and "modernizers" in the Economics Ministry (Zöhlnhofer 2004). Only with the Hartz IV reforms on pensions and unemployment compensation did Schröder gain in credibility, the reforms in legitimacy, and his rather thin discourse in persuasiveness. But this was mainly because he held to the reform despite battering in Länder elections, weekly Sunday protests, and a massive slide in public opinion.

For all this, however, Germany still has a long way to go with respect to reform, in particular with regard to cushioning the effects of job loss on those most vulnerable to the new social risks. This, plus continued high unemployment, has made nearshore insourcing an increasingly contentious issue, as the public worried, for example, about the replacement of 25,000 German butchers by Polish or Czech immigrants in fall 2004, or about automotive workers feeling the squeeze on wages and work conditions in exchange for industry promises to maintain employment in Germany rather than moving east (Barysch 2006). Given all of this, it may seem all the more surprising that the German public remains largely positive with regard to the effects of globalization, although it helps explain their more negative view of globalization with regard to employment (see figure 7.1).

France is the real outlier on attitudes toward globalization and Europeanization, however. With regard to Europeanization, in the 2005 Eurobarometer poll (eb 64.fr 2005), whereas two in three Europeans (73 percent) feared most the transfer of jobs to other member-states where production is cheaper came, nine in ten of the French (89 percent) did so. But even more dramatic are attitudes toward globalization. Most telling is an in-depth, 2003 Eurobarometer poll on globalization, in which a clustering of questions related to negative attitudes about globalization—as bad for the economy, bad for employment, bad for jobs, and bad for you—show the French to be off the charts compared to all other countries.

The problem for France has been that ever since the early 1980s, French policy elites have been in search of a new discourse that would serve to

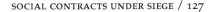
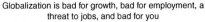
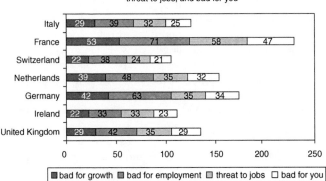

Figure 7.1 Negative Effects of Globalization
Source: Eurobarometer 2003 (Flash EB no. 151b).

legitimize the country's liberalizing economic transformation in a way that would resonate with national values of "social solidarity." In its absence, successive governments of the left and right have more often than not justified neoliberal policy change by reference to the challenges of globalization, while claiming that further Europeanization served as a shield against globalization, and that neither liberalization nor Europeanization would do anything to jeopardize "social solidarity." Governments' attempts to reform in response to the crisis of the welfare state as well as the need to meet the Maastricht criteria for the EMU were repeatedly stymied as a result of a lack of discourse that spoke to the appropriateness—rather than just the necessity—of reform (Schmidt 1996, 2002 Ch. 6). Even when the Socialists in the late 1990s finally did come up with a discourse that served to legitimate reform by balancing arguments about efficiency with normative arguments about equity—for example, by claiming "neither to soak the rich nor let them shirk their obligations" with regard to tax reforms—they did not tackle the major pension problems for fear of protests (Levy 1999; Schmidt 2000). Their discourse did, however, help set the stage for the public acceptance of a significant reform of public sector pensions by the right-wing government of Raffarin in 2004, despite Raffarin's minimal discourse (Natali and Rhodes 2004). But the attempted reform of work rules by the de Villepin government, as noted earlier, failed miserably, due not just to inadequate policies but also to inadequate discourse.

In the interim, moreover, because political elites consistently blamed the need for welfare reform on outside pressures from globalization and

Europeanization rather than admit that the problems were internal to France (Smith 2004), they encouraged the antiglobalization and anti-Europeanization feelings that came to the fore in the referendum on the Constitutional Treaty, thus contributing to its failure. This came as much from the right as from the left—the Socialists' refrain on globalization was "yes to the market economy but no to the market society," while on Europe it was to defend the "European social model" against the excesses of "Anglo-Saxon liberalism" and United States–led globalization (Schmidt 1996; Gordon and Meunier 2001). Most notable is President Chirac, who in his first televised appearance on the Constitutional Treaty, responding to concerns that the EU was "too liberal", claimed that he would protect France by fighting in the EU against "Anglo-Saxon ultra-neo-liberalism," if only the French voted "yes" on the referendum. No wonder that the French voted "no." It did not help that the services directive, which would have allowed workers from Eastern Europe to work in the West under home country rules, was floated a couple of months before the referendum, which conjured up fears of "Polish plumbers" coming to take French jobs and precipitated a "race to the bottom" in social protections.

In Italy, state paralysis and incompetence throughout the postwar period until the 1990s ensured that Europeanization was seen as the "rescue of the nation-state" (Ferrera and Gualmini 2004). Moreover, Italian industry thrived in the context of globalization, ensuring positive public attitudes toward it as well. In the 1990s, moreover, Italy was able to muster a highly successful discourse to promote major welfare reforms that had been all but impossible in the 1970s and 1980s. Center-left governments' discourse spoke to the necessity of reform in order to return to financial health and to join the European Monetary Union at the same time that they made normative appeals to national pride with regard to joining the euro and to social equity—to end unfairness and corruption as well as to give *piu ai figli, meno ai padri* (more to the sons, less to the fathers), so as to ensure intergenerational solidarity (Ferrera and Gualmini 2004; Schmidt 2000). Since 2001, under Berlusconi, however, there has been little reform of either the work or the welfare arena, the result of the failure not just of legitimating discourse capable of ensuring union cooperation but also of will, given a leader more interested in passing legislation focused on solving his own legal problems and ensuring his party's political future. In the interim, the economy slowed tremendously, leading to a discourse—both inside and outside the country—portraying Italy as the "sick man" of Europe. This makes it all the more surprising that the Italians have remained so strongly pro-global. A reversal in attitudes may be occurring, however, ever since the quotas went off China with the end of the Multifibre Agreement, and as Chinese imports together with offshoring to Asia more generally have taken a great toll on the Italian textile and shoe sectors, the backbone of the "third Italy" and largely responsible for its continued economic health since the 1980s.

Conclusion

Public attitudes in European countries to the challenges of offshoring and nearshoring, in short, are related not only to levels of economic growth or unemployment but also to the ways in which systems of work and welfare serve to cushion its effects and national discourses serve to legitimate it. For the moment, public attitudes differ across European countries, with "liberal" Anglo-Saxon and "social-democratic" Scandinavian countries generally less concerned about offshoring and nearshoring than "conservative" Continental and Mediterranean countries. However, if the number of losers of offshoring and nearshoring continues to climb, affecting more and more segments of the labor force in more and more countries, then national work and welfare systems will find it harder and harder to cushion the effects, and national leaders will be increasingly hard put to come up with sufficiently legitimating discourses across Europe.

CHAPTER EIGHT
THE EUROPEAN TRAP: JOBS ON THE RUN, DEMOCRACY AT STAKE

Hans-Peter Martin

Offshore outsourcing has dramatic political implications of which most political decision makers are far from being aware. In the European Union, it will not only continue to undermine the welfare states and significantly reduce the size of the middle class in its key member states, but it will also contribute to challenging the very foundations of democracy in the individual nation states.

And among citizens, offshore outsourcing will contribute to the lack of political acceptance of the Union—making it ever more difficult to legitimize democratically the project of the European Union as a whole. While the EU institutions based in Brussels fatefully continue to concentrate primarily on themselves, Germany as the most important EU nation state and with growing worries among its citizens plays a crucial role in the ongoing process.

To tackle the upcoming severe crisis, new democratic tools in the decision-making process and full transparency are indispensable prerequisites—and so is professional political leadership instead of traditional party politics. But in the end, a global social contract will have to be implemented to prevent globalization and offshore outsourcing from backfiring—with waves of protectionism and new wars.

The Dismantling of the Social Contract in Western Europe

"We are already in a pre-revolutionary situation," said the French social scientist and philosopher Paul Virilio at the end of the year 2005, when inhabitants of the problem-ridden Paris suburbs, the Beaulieus, took their frustration over the lack of decent jobs to the streets with unprecedented violence, and riots followed in a large number of other French cities

(Leick 2005). It is only a matter of time until similar uproars will occur in other European cities, namely in the deprived quarters of Berlin or Duisburg, one of the centers of the former coal and steel industries in the German state of North Rhine-Westphalia, where the renowned economic miracle, the *Wirtschaftswunder*, took off in the 1950s.

The reasons for this foreseeable development are manifold. Offshore outsourcing is a significant one—in quantifiable terms as well as in the subjective perception of more and more citizens. Over the past years, entire steel plants were dismantled and moved to China, part of an ongoing process of deindustrialization throughout Western Europe (Wösler 2002). Undoubtedly, offshore outsourcing can also contribute to the stabilization and success of a Western European–based company, given the present global economic prerequisites. But even in Germany, the world's leading exporter of goods, more industrial jobs were transferred to other countries during the period 2000–2005 than newly created at home (Hage 2007). This would not be troublesome if the job losses could be fully compensated for in other sectors with similarly well-paid jobs. But that is less and less the case.

There are no authoritative official statistics on the extent of offshoring, indicating once again a serious lack of available reliable data in crucial policy fields. But consultants such as Forrester Research already argued in 2004 over a "Two-speed Europe: Why one million jobs will move offshore" (Parker 2004). And the IT sector too is going to be more and more affected. The perception of looming widespread job losses is slowly reaching the mindset of more and more employees (Kirkegaard 2005). Ever since the fall of the Berlin Wall in 1989, an increasing number of jobs have been transferred to the East. Economies that had benefited from offshore outsourcing before, namely Portugal, are stagnating. After 1989, Czech, Hungarian, and Polish workforces were seen as attractive alternatives to the comparatively highly paid West European workers, despite the significantly lower productivity in these former countries of the Eastern bloc. Soon Romanian and Bulgarian workers and production sites joined the gamble for cheap labor. Now, the Ukraine is becoming an attractive destination for offshoring. But even in these countries the competitive pressures from Chinese and Vietnamese low-wage workers are increasingly being felt. "As globalization accelerates, for more and more industries offshoring and offshore outsourcing strategies are no longer merely an option," argues Kirkegaard (2005, 14), "they are already a competitive imperative for companies."

And even if jobs are not actually outsourced, the threat of offshoring has been used by factory owners in innumerable negotiations with union representatives or even individual workers.[1] Globalization and the establishment of a global labor market have brought about a dramatic shift of power between capital and work (e.g., Richard Freeman, this volume).

The result has been a major shift in the income patterns of Western European societies. "The income gap between the wages of employees and the income of companies has continued to increase," states Walter Radermacher, president of the Federal Statistical Agency of Germany. From 2000 until the end of 2006, the share of the wages in national income decreased from 72.2 to 66.2 percent in Germany, whereas the share of corporate profits and other capital income grew commensurately (Der Speigel 2007).

In this globalization process, the tax base in most nation states is seriously affected, since it is quite easy for companies to avoid paying significant taxes—due to a lack of common tax regulation and collection enforcement throughout the member states of the European Union. As a result, the differences between regions keep growing, while smaller nation states in particular try their fortune in tax races to the bottom. For example, since 1992, Austria has attracted a growing number of international companies with a very tempting tax reduction scheme for foundations. And in 2004, neighboring Slovakia introduced a flat tax of 19 percent. In early 2007, the nation state of Macedonia, a neighbor of Greece, founded only in 1991 and now an EU and NATO candidate country, presented itself in splashy ads across international business papers, such as the *Financial Times*, as the "New Business Heaven in Europe."[2] As of 2008, Macedonia offers the "lowest flat tax on profit—10 per cent," the "lowest flat tax on income—10 per cent" and "zero tax on reinvested profit," while the labor force is being described as "abundant and competitive" with an average gross monthly salary of only €370 Euro.[3]

Still, many policymakers in Western European countries believe that by strengthening the service sector the ongoing offshoring of fairly well-paid industrial jobs can mostly be compensated, but following the arguments by other authors in this book, this will become more and more difficult (e.g., Burke and Epstein, Standing). Already by now, the daily layouts for regional newspapers in western Austria or southern Germany are done in Hungary or Bulgaria; for mid-sized companies it has become commonplace to offshore their bookkeeping. In general though, the ongoing developments favor larger entities because the handling of transnational production and services requires international work and skill capacities. This adds momentum to the ongoing wave of mergers and acquisitions. Once set up, TNCs find it again easier to reduce their tax burden further—a vicious cycle.

These overall trends will also make it ever more difficult for smaller countries to find their policy niches. Even with sophisticated flexicurity models, as they have been developed in Denmark, offshore outsourcing will contribute more and more to the undermining of the social welfare states as they have been established successfully over decades throughout Western Europe. At the moment, many companies find themselves in the best of two worlds. With their headquarters and R&D facilities in the heartland of the EU, they can still benefit from pleasant surroundings, low crime rates, and a well-built infrastructure, benefiting at the same time from offshoring production and services. But this will not be sustainable, as the basis for the social contract is eroding—a sufficient number of good jobs and a balanced tax system.

Already, the general feeling of insecurity is growing throughout Western Europe. In 2006, four-fifths of all Germans identified unemployment as the most relevant and urgent problem; in France and Poland this opinion was shared by two-thirds of the population, significantly more than in earlier years (GfK Gruppe 2006). For example, in 2003, not even half of the French population named unemployment as the most pressing challenge (GfK Gruppe 2003). In 2006, 49 percent of citizens across all twenty five EU-member states saw unemployment as one of the two most important issues facing their country (European Commission 2006b).

In 2005, 36 percent of all Germans were personally afraid to "experience economic hardship," compared to just 24.7 percent in 2001 (Wort & Bild Verlag 2005). Even though more than half of all German employees considered the economic situation of their company to be "good" or "very good" in 2006, 25 percent were "afraid" or "very afraid" of losing their job (PressEecho 2006). In response to the question whether it would be easy to find an adequate new job in case of job loss, 20 percent of all West Germans (with a completed degree) answered in the affirmative in 1994; in 2004, it was only 14 percent (Statistisches Bundesamt 2006). And in a survey of all EU citizens, including the new member states, 17 percent expect their economic situation to get worse (European Commission 2006b). Even the reduced willingness to have children, the dramatic reduction of birth rates, can increasingly be attributed to this mood of doom.

Workforces can and will become ever more flexible throughout Europe—in terms of the timing of working hours and their geographic relocation. But with the loss of traditional jobs in production and services, not everyone can turn into a college graduate to still find a well-paying job. Not only are there not enough universities out there, but also not everybody is an Einstein. On the other hand, the number of hair dressers and restaurant waiters a society needs is also limited.

Taking the demographic factor into account along with the necessity for more young people to support a growing elderly population, the crisis will accelerate even more. In this process, globalization with its ongoing process of offshore outsourcing will lead to significantly lower net income derived from wages in most of Western Europe. The growing frustration over nonexistent decent job opportunities could therefore even lead to new wars, civil wars, even within the borders of the European Union—despite ongoing GDP growth.

We live in a dangerously poor-rich world.

But all these developments are not the result of fundamental economic laws, of developments comparable to a law of nature. Instead, it is mostly the political decisions that have made all this possible.

Europe at a Disadvantage

At the beginning of this new age of globalization, the European continent finds itself at a comparative disadvantage. Economic policies, tax schemes, and social security systems are all based and decided upon in nation states, most of them remarkably small. Even the leading economic powers of Europe—Germany, Great Britain, France, Italy, and Spain—lack the relevant size to matter on their own.

At first, the reunification process in Germany was mismanaged in economic matters, mainly by applying a highly overvalued currency exchange rate in former East Germany. Then, the enlargement of the EU from twelve member states until 1995 to twenty-seven at the beginning of 2007 came about too quickly. Due to the lack of political consent and harmonization, member states can now be played out against each other very easily by international investors and companies. Leading manufacturers have developed special skills in applying for significant EU subsidies in new member states and then moving on with their production lines as soon as the subsidies expire and other countries are offering new financial support.

A lack of a common European identity and language makes it very difficult for the nonelites to communicate and to develop a common spirit or a unified sense of urgency. In business terms, this also slows down the possibilities for ongoing integration. Ireland as a small but vital economic tiger is often cited as a showcase example of the success of EU integration strategies. But proximity to the Anglo-Saxon world and a common language definitely helped the country to prosper, advantages not shared by other EU member states. The fact that English is the IT language per se is more likely to enhance the future prospects of India and even China than of Eastern Europe, given their broad variety of native languages. Also, with no common European public sphere, common problems are not commonly or even concomitantly discussed in the different countries. Regional and provincial approaches to issues prevail, as does the lack of perception of the magnitude and relevance of an issue. Under these circumstances problems are often erroneously described as problems of "another country" rather than as a common problem. On the other hand, solutions found in one of the nation states might easily be at the expense of its neighbors.

At the same time the common European market has turned into a safe haven of investment, with the obligation of opening public tenders to

EU-wide competition and the possibility of challenging business practices that violate the common rules on the EU level, the so-called *aquis communitaire.*

But economic integration has not been followed by adequate political integration. Economic integration is developing in a fractured political environment. The EU, conceived by its political builders as a political entity *sui generis*, lacks the most relevant factors of a functioning democratic setting, namely sufficiently democratically legitimized institutions, a tested rule of law, and a system of adequate checks and balances.

The European legislative process is organized in a complicated triangle between the EU Commission, the Council of Ministers, and the European Parliament. Only the EU Commission has the right to propose new legislation, that is, EU directives and EU regulations. It consists of one commissioner per member state, appointed by the national government and the bulk of the EU civil servants. All legislation has to be approved by the Council of Ministers, most of the relevant issues by unanimity. A growing number of legislative acts also need the approval of a majority or qualified majority in the European Parliament, whose 785 members are directly elected by the citizens every five years. Twice a year, the European Council, consisting of the heads of the national government, meets. They frame the binding guidelines for the work of the EU institutions.

At the heart of the problem is the Council of Ministers, in reality the power house of European politics. Each of the nine councils, ranging from foreign policy to fishery, consists of the heads of the national ministries, hence members of the executive branch of government. In Brussels or Luxemburg, where they frequently meet, the ministers though turn into legislative politicians, deciding on innumerable guidelines that later in the process have to be turned into national law. The European Parliament only has co-decision rights in a limited number of fields. Therefore, the essential legislative functions in the EU lie in the hands of the executive, despite all principles of the separation of powers. Even worse, the EU decisions are taken behind closed doors.

It has become a common practice for members of the national executive from the larger countries to take regulative matters, for which they would not find the necessary majority at their national parliamentary level, to Brussels. There, they find an open willingness among EU civil servants to put forward an EU directive covering the issue. On the other hand, national governments at home blame the EU institutions for unpopular decisions even though they took part in the decision-making process. In this political nirvana, it is more and more the courts (namely the European Court of Justice) instead of democratically legitimized parliamentary bodies, that decide politically sensitive issues.

A survey by the German Federal Ministry of Justice of all legislative acts of Germany between 1998 and 2004 revealed that 84 percent had their origin in Brussels, only 16 percent in Berlin. The former German president Roman Herzog called this, in a widely publicized article at the beginning of 2007, a "substantial process of erosion," because "every EU directive that the Federal Government decides in the Council of Ministers (in Brussels) has to be implemented into German law." Herzog concludes: "Therefore the question comes up, if the Federal Republic of Germany can still be called without qualifications a parliamentary democracy" (Herzog and Gerken 2007).

What Herzog deplores about Germany applies to all EU member states. As a result, throughout Europe citizens lack overall confidence in the EU institutions. Even the European Parliament with its directly elected representatives reaches just modest levels of acceptance. Only 52 percent of all Europeans trust this institution. Within one year, trust in the EU as a whole has declined by three percentage points to 45 percent in 2006 (European Commission 2006c).

From an overall perspective, the United States is in quite a few areas comparatively better off than the EU-member states, in some aspects even better than China and India. It cannot come as surprise that the EU is now of less and less relevance in discussions about policy approaches to tackle the new challenges. Europe finds itself squeezed between the United States and India-China, with no nation state of relevant size on its soil.

This is illustrated in a striking way by the more and more popular world maps on sale in the stores of Beijing (or Sydney) these days. They portray China (or Australia) in the center and Europe as far out of reach as Alaska seems to be on traditional maps of the globe.

In that context, models of a social welfare state developed in Europe are also becoming of less interest in other parts of the world. On the contrary, Europe is being perceived as old fashioned, even as out of touch with reality.

Inside the Beltway of Brussels

Who or what is to be blamed? It is a series of factors. First, with the fall of the iron curtain, the strategic desire of the West to present a "social showcase" in Western European countries to fend off the temptation of the Communist ideology disappeared. Second, a necessity to deregulate and focus on business success, especially on shareholder value, turned into the prevailing thinking in global media. "Neoliberalism" became mainstream. Third, the United States, the only remaining superpower, pursued neoliberal policies globally, promoting the rapid development of a financial market that could function globally in real time due to the spread of information technology.

Globalization turned into an Americanization of the world. And with this mentality, offshore outsourcing was mainly seen through the eyes of prospective winners, especially companies and shareholders. The concept of a fair and sustainable society was largely pushed to the back.

But it can also be argued that history could have taken a different course if the European states that reemerged after World Ware II had followed a similarly stringent course of unification and pursued their common goals, like the emerging United States of America did 200 years earlier. In 1957, France and Germany founded the common "Coal and Steel Union." But unlike the growing economic interrelationship, the political integration did not move forward as intended. Partly, politicians in the national capitals are to be held responsible.

But the growing EU elite based in Brussels did a lot of harm to the positive image of an integrated Europe, especially to the possibility of a United States of Europe. Since it seemed to be difficult to turn Brussels into an attractive workplace for career civil servants, they were and are offered double of what they are paid in their national positions. Far away from public (media) scrutiny, an enormous amount of additional perks and privileges followed as a result of hidden negotiations between civil servants and the Council of Ministers. Consequently, Brussels has turned into a workplace hardly anybody wants to leave, and where more and more bureaucrats want to work: 36,500 civil servants are now on the payroll of the European tax payer, with enormous tax benefits and an average monthly pension of €5509 Euro—from the receptionist to the general manager of a large commission department.

The general atmosphere in Brussels can now be described as incestuous as Washington DC "inside the beltway" was perceived until the Watergate scandal broke in 1973/74. Even though there are now more accredited journalists working out of Brussels than the U.S. capital, independent NGOs are still a rare species, especially ones that would observe the decision-making process closely, such as US-Watch. And most journalists are "part of the crowd;" frequently, they or their partners are involved in some EU-financed project.

More than 3000 working groups with representatives mainly from industrial lobbies are counseling the commission in the preparation of new EU legislation; but even the names of their members are being kept secret. There is nothing comparable among the EU institutions to the Lobbying Disclosure Act of 1995, adopted by the 104th U.S. Congress, that lays out very detailed disclosure requirements for lobbyists and their activities and contacts. Therefore it is almost logical that, according to commission officials, proposals for EU directives have been taken directly from industry lobbyists. In the European Parliament, it is a widely reported practise for members to take amendments, particularly to legislative proposals, desired by industry and present them word-for-word as their own amendments.

And the EU is far from having a Freedom of Information Act as developed in the United States over the past decades, granting all interested citizens access to a broad variety of relevant documents, at least after a specified number of years.

In its deeds, the EU Commission resembles a "government." But the twenty-seven commissioners cannot be individually impeached; they can only be voted out of power collectively by the European Parliament—a predemocratic habit quite common in European nation states in the nineteenth century. Unlike the United States, there is also no major turnover in elite personnel when a new commission takes office every five years. And many European parliamentarians have found a comfortable way to stay on as party advisors in the European capital, even if they are not reelected to the Parliament. Also, each parliamentarian can earn a higher net income every month than any prime minister in Europe—by riding the gravy train of the enormous lump sum benefits and pension privileges being provided.

In reality, with no direct Europe-wide election determining the composition of the EU Commission, a grand coalition of conservatives and social democrats has run the EU affairs for decades. It is as if Republicans and Democrats had shared each U.S. presidency and session in Congress, no matter what the outcome of elections had been.

As a consequence, a detached EU elite in its "ivory tower" (as quite a few EU politicians and civil servants describe it themselves) does not deliver the desired results in democratic and economic terms. The disappointment with this state of affairs is the main reason why the peoples of France and the Netherlands turned down the proposed European Constitution in the 2005 public referenda, realizing that the new constitution would not have changed the fundamental flaws of the present EU.

Germany Pays the Bill—for How Much Longer?

To date German tax payers have footed the bill of the European Union to a considerable extent. Every year they contribute more than a fifth to the EU budget of now €112 with twenty-seven member states.[4] After World War II, the very foundation of a European union was grounded in the political desire to overcome wars between European states, mainly between Germany and France. With the ongoing *Wirtschaftswunder* it was financially possible and in the economic interest of the heavily export-oriented German companies to contribute far more to the EU budget than an even share of the burden would have warranted. The much praised generosity of the German net contributor helped to open and develop markets, namely on the Iberian Peninsula, when Spain and Portugal joined the European Community in 1986. It was also one of the conditions taken for granted, mainly by French political decision makers, for supporting the reunification process of the two Germanys in the years from 1989 to 1991.

For the average German citizen all this made sense. Over decades the growth of his/her salary reflected the ongoing boom of the German economy. Productivity gains and higher exports translated into higher wages, mainly due to a well-organized and dedicated trade union movement. Thus all sides benefited: the companies prospered, the employees enjoyed ever growing living standards, and the reputation of the Federal Republic of Germany grew worldwide.

With the fall of the iron curtain, together with the spread of new technologies, the liberalization of financial markets and the drastic reduction of tariffs and tariff barriers, the level playing field of competitive companies became global. Offshore outsourcing contributed significantly to the changes in the distribution of economic wealth. The bargaining power of trade unions has decreased dramatically, as they mostly represent a constantly decreasing share of the national labor force in a particular sector of an industry. This process is enhanced by internal structural and organizational problems of the trade union movement. Certainly, offshore outsourcing is by far not the only reason for the enormous redistribution of wealth, but the threat (or necessity) of offshoring can be used in every negotiation with almost every employee, service provider, and mid-sized company in the supply chain of a TNC.

Countries with an extensive middle class with comparatively high income levels are affected most. Therefore it is not a surprise that real wages in Germany have been declining for several years. The wage decline was attributed to domestic policy mistakes and company mismanagement as long as national economic growth lagged behind the EU average. But in 2006, the German economy grew by 2.7 percent, the highest rate since 2000, and the average wage increased by only 1.2 percent. It did not even keep up with the inflation rate of 1.7 percent (Frankfurter Allgemeine Zeitung 2007a). In contrast to expectations at the time of reunification, the new federal states of former East Germany have not caught up with the West. In more than half of the provinces of these five new German states, more than 19 percent of the population under the age of sixty-five now live off social security (Bundesagentur für Arbeit 2007).

For many years, German employees and the vast majority of middle-class citizens succumbed to the argument of the lack of national competitiveness. But the belief in a general turn around, along with a new rise of German economic strength, is being questioned more and more. A growing number of employees see their jobs threatened despite overall economic growth and skyrocketing corporate profits. The fear of unemployment is the most pressing political issue for 70 percent of all Germans (European Commission 2006c).

As a result, discontent is growing with traditional politicians and the democratic system in general. Voter turnout has reached unprecedented low levels. Only 33.6 percent of all eligible voters participated in the election for the mayor of Frankfurt in January 2007 (Frankfurter Allgemeine Zeitung 2007b). In regional elections, voter turnout regularly misses the 60 percent mark. Even at the end of the highly controversial election campaign to the Bundestag, the German national assembly, in 2005, only 77.8 percent of the voters cast their votes, compared to 90.7 per cent in 1972, for example. In innumerable elections the "party" of nonvoters is now the strongest of all. Whereas these developments might not lead to astonishment in the Anglo-Saxon world with its longstanding, well-established democratic institutions, such a decline in voter interest in Germany is an alarming figure by post—World War II standards on the European continent.

Even worse, in November 2006, a stunning survey showed that more than half of the German population now is seriously disappointed with democracy in general (Krupa 2007). Similar developments can be perceived in many other European nation states, particularly in Western Europe.

Along with the discontent with the national political establishment, the disappointment is being increasingly directed at Brussels. Until recently, it was impossible to criticize the EU in Germany without being almost automatically branded either as far left wing or a nationalist. It is only a matter of time when the taboo that still surrounds the European Union in Germany will fall.

But by now, mainstream publications of the influential, conservatively oriented publishing house Springer—with their longstanding support for "a common European House"—publish more and more articles critical of the state that the European Union is in. And they are not shy to question the overall benefit of the high net contribution of the German state.[5]

This occurs at a time when the EU institutions find it extremely difficult to agree on the minimum reforms needed to keep them operating after the high-speed EU enlargement to twenty-seven members. In Germany, always a country renowned for its organizational skills, this leads to a growing "shaking of heads."

The consequences are foreseeable. At the very same time that the democratic institutions in the home nation states are increasingly questioned, the European Union will be questioned even more. In 2009, when national elections in Germany will coincide with Europe-wide elections to the European Parliament, many voters will likely express their growing disillusion with the EU.

Given the constraints on the national budget in times of relatively decreasing tax revenues from TNCs and mid-sized companies, the question of the net payment burden of Germany in the EU will reach political center stage. This coincides with the development that a growing number of TNCs based in Germany employ the majority of their staff now in other countries, with only headquarters and strategic staff remaining in Germany. According to the 2006 edition of *Eurobarometer*, the official statistical data survey of the European Union, 70 percent of all Germans believe that EU membership now has a negative effect on their national labor market, compared to 51 percent of all EU citizens (European Commission 2006c).

This growing disappointment with the EU will have to lead to a policy shift against Brussels. The popular success of the former British prime minister Margaret Thatcher in the financial negotiations with the EU twenty-five years ago ("I want our money back") can serve as a blueprint of what is to be expected.

But with a considerable reduction of payments from Germany, the EU institutions will find it even more difficult to meet their tasks. In the past, during EU summits it was the political representatives of Germany who opened their national coffers at the last minute and made special additional financial pledges to overcome a negotiating gridlock. It last occurred during the negotiations about the new Financial Perspective 2007–2013 in December 2005 (Financial Times Deutschland 2005).

Unfortunately, most political leaders are far from realizing the political consequences of all this, most of it being the result of wrong political decisions in the first place.

But the mood is turning.

Transparency, Democracy, and a Global Social Contract

With all the experience I have collected as a journalist, author, and EU politician, my prognosis is a dire one. We are living in a world with two major nation states, the United States and China, as the key economic players in the foreseeable future—a trading system greatly shaped by their influence, a system of safe investments and profits for TNCs with financial global markets benefiting from all these developments and reinforcing the process. Under these global circumstances, offshore outsourcing will not only continue, but it will also have a severe impact mainly on Western Europe with its highly developed social welfare schemes.

As long as the primacy of politics is not reestablished, it is very hard to imagine how the comparatively high gross salaries in the Western EU can be maintained, regardless of how "flexibly" some countries might react. The large gap in wage and infrastructure costs between the EU and the emerging economies can simply not be bridged in many sectors.

As a result, in the future, the income patterns all over Europe will resemble more and more the ones in the United States or even in developing countries. Very few individuals will earn very much, but the middle class will probably be halved by today's standards. And the not so smart and well-educated will work at minimum wage levels.

A fairer, more equal landscape of incomes though would require a fundamental turnaround in the consciousness of voters and politicians alike. Only through more unbiased information and utmost transparency can this reality be understood by all stakeholders. In the end, a redistribution of wealth can only be generated by broadly accepted political institutions.

To achieve such an openly informed society in Europe will be extremely difficult. A lot will depend on the use of the worldwide net in the exchange of information and the ability to interact and network, especially among the younger generation. Mounting pressure on the EU institutions could lead to the kind of access to information that would make it possible for millions of interested citizens to track and question the spending of budget money.

Furthermore, the political elite has to redefine its role and understand the necessity to regain the confidence of the citizens. In an enlightened society with the information tools of modern technology, the times of patriarchal and nondemocratic decision-making processes are over. The everyday use of the Internet opens radically different possibilities to exercise democratic rights, including online voting on current issues.

The traditional European party system has proven to be incapable of coping with the challenges. Instead, at least as an addition, interested citizens should be enabled to run for offices without party affiliation and/or the necessity to lobby for substantial campaign money. It also has to be taken into account that neither the movement of social democratic parties, that still strongly defines itself as the representatives of the most affected groups of society, nor Christian Social Democrats, with similar goals, nor trade unions have shown the necessary understanding of the problems lying ahead. Their system of full-time functionaries, concerned mainly with their own structures, is structurally appalling to politically interested citizens.

Therefore, other forms of citizen participation can and have to be developed. The exercise to write up an entirely new, serious democratic European constitution could be one of the promising steps ahead. There is no doubt that the debate on controlled free trade will start, and the winner/loser-pattern will become ever more complicated.

The already heated debate about global warming has to lead to a re-evaluation of the terms of transporting goods. Taking the real global economic and ecological costs of transportation into account would not only foster the cause of the environment, but it would also change the cost-benefit analysis of offshore outsourcing to geographically far away destinations.

It is an opportunity and a danger to see the world becoming one. But a consequence of all these developments has to be the understanding that more and more economic problems can be tackled only on a global scale. Fair minimum wages, with consideration of local and regional purchasing power, have to be taken into account everywhere. And only open, efficiently managed welfare states can prevent mankind from going to war again.

To succeed, we need nothing short of a global social contract.

Quite a lot of this might sound illusionary. But there is no peaceful alternative to the realization of this illusion.

Notes

1. A prominent example are the negotiations of the management of Daimler Chrysler in Stuttgart about the future location of the assembly line for the production of car engines for the E class models in 2004.
2. Advertisement in the Financial Times, European edition, January 29, 2007, page 5.
3. Advertisement in the Financial Times, European edition, January 29, 2007, page 5.
4. In 2005, Germany's contribution was €20.1 billion of the overall budget of €100.8 billion (European Commission 2006d).
5. For example, regular commentaries in 2006 by Dan Hannan, a Eurosceptic Member of the European Parliament, in Die Welt, a growing number of critical articles in the mass daily Bild, or the lengthy piece of former president Roman Herzog (2007).

PART IV
OFFSHORING FOR DEVELOPMENT?

CHAPTER NINE

OFFSHORE OUTSOURCING OF SERVICES: TRENDS AND CHALLENGES FOR DEVELOPING COUNTRIES

Luis Abugattas Majluf

Introduction

The outsourcing of business functions and services by firms in developed countries to suppliers in other countries has been a source of growing academic and political debate in the developed world, especially in the United States. An increasing body of literature has sought to identify the drivers behind offshore outsourcing and to assess its benefits and disadvantages (Bartels 2005, Outsourcing Institute 2005, Hölzl, Reinstaller and Windrum 2005). Most authors have focused on the implications for the home economy (e.g., Mann 2003, Schultze 2004, Garner 2004, Jensen and Kletzer 2005, NAPA 2006, ACM 2006). And the issue has also figured prominently in recent work of international institutions because of potential systemic implications (UNCTAD 2003a, 2004, WTO 2005, Bartels 2005, ILO 2006, OECD 2005b).

While there is considerable disagreement about the costs and benefits of offshore outsourcing for developed countries, there seems to be much greater agreement on the positive impact of offshoring of services on developing countries. The growth of offshoring is thought to offer tremendous opportunities for all developing countries, creating a global marketplace in services in which they enjoy a competitive advantage (UNCTAD 2005c, Mattoo and Wunchs 2004). It might even enable developing countries to skip the industrial development stage, turning their services sectors into the main engine of economic growth and development (Radwan and Gihani 2005). Not surprisingly, service offshoring has played an important role in the negotiations on services under the General Agreements on Trade in Services (GATS) in the context of the Doha Work Program in the World

Trade Organization (WTO). Some developing countries have been particularly vocal in seeking from the major offshoring countries specific commitments on cross-border trade in services.

But such unmitigated optimism about the development benefits of service offshoring is unwarranted. There are very few studies of its impact on host countries, and the existing ones focus mainly on the experience of India, the country that has led the way among developing countries in the offshoring process (Suri in this volume, Joseph 2002, Kumar and Joseph 2005, Srinivasan 2005). In fact, much of the emerging conventional wisdom is based on an extrapolation of the Indian experience as a potential development alternative available to other developing countries.

This chapter analyses the potential contribution of services offshoring to the advancement of developing countries. First, I discuss the current trends and the main issues regarding the relocation of jobs from developed countries to offshore locations, highlighting the fact that it is a process in which developed countries are predominant both as offshoring and host countries. Therefore services offshoring is currently not predominantly a North-South issue. This fact has important implications for our understanding of the drivers of offshoring and its future evolution. I then explore the extent to which offshoring could provide a development option for developing countries. I argue that the potential benefits of services offshoring for developing countries are usually overstated, both in terms of the number of jobs that could be created and the number of developing countries that could benefit.

A number of issues arise with respect to the sustainability of the offshoring process in light of technological developments and changes in business practices, supply side constraints, the potential effects of increasing competition, and the vulnerability of the offshoring process to firms' behavior and market signals. An area that requires further analysis is the effect of offhoring on the host country. The available evidence suggests that the beneficial spillovers in the host economy might be quite limited. Finally, the chapter addresses the main challenges developing countries face in entering the offshoring business and the role that public policies could play in improving their prospects.

Offshoring of Services: Main Trends and Issues

Outsourcing takes place when one company delegates responsibility for performing a function or series of tasks to another company. This process, which has also been called "externalization," indicates an increasing division of labor linked to technological innovation and changing business practices. When the other company performing the task is located in a different country, outsourcing becomes *offshoring*. The international relocation of labor-intensive services, such as data entry and call centers, started in the 1980s and has intensified during the last decade. But the relocation of more high-value-added business processes and services has been on the rise as well.

Competitive pressures make service offshoring a key element of cost reduction in firms' global strategies. As advances and diffusion of information technology enhance systems compatibility among different firms and thus reduce transactions costs, offshoring becomes more profitable (Bartels 2005). Conventional wisdom suggests that many more developing countries can enter the offshoring market, that the improvements in technology will allow for a further increase in the number and types of activities that can be offshored, that companies might seek new suppliers in order to diversify risk, that countries can enter niche markets and that early entrants into the offshoring market may "graduate" from certain types of offshore activities as they move up the value chain (UNCTAD 2005b).

We can identify three distinct segments in the offshoring market for services: information technology-enabled back office processes (ITE-BOP), software services (SS), and online delivery of professional services (ODPS). ITE-BOP are activities that could be done inside companies, in most sectors of the economy, but which are outsourced to reap the cost reductions from specialization and economies of scale. They are primarily export-oriented activities in developing countries. The skills required to undertake these tasks range from low skills in routine clerical work, for example, data processing and order-taking services, to technical work requiring some level of job-specific training as in call centers, to higher skills in some business processes servicing, such as accounting, financial and administrative tasks.

Software services comprise custom-based solutions, systems integration, data base management, and IT consultancy. And the online delivery of professional services occurs primarily in engineering, law, health, and R&D. These are knowledge-intense activities, requiring in most cases professional training and certification in a particular area. In these services the development of the industry and its international competitiveness are mainly sustained by the domestic market. In the case of the software industry, for example, domestic developments have been the primary drivers behind the growth of the industry, with India as an important exception (Arora and Gambardella 2005). In reality, it is not always easy to draw the boundaries between the different market segments, as any particular offshoring service might combine elements of all three categories.

It is currently impossible to get an accurate measure of the value of service offshoring, due to the lack of comprehensive and internationally harmonized data. Estimates differ widely by source. Discrepancies in the data arise with respect to the size of global IT expenditures, the size of the outsourcing market, and the share of offshoring in the total outsourcing market.

A WTO survey (2005) of different estimates and data problems concluded that worldwide IT and software expenditures were in the order of $650 billion to $710 billion in 2003. Total outsourced IT services (excluding software) were around $285 billion, and offshored services were between $40 billion and $45 billion. If software services had been included, the total value of outsourced services would have been significantly higher. An OECD study (2004) estimated the value of the global service offshoring market in 2003 at anywhere between $10 billion on the low end and $50 billion on the high end, while McKinsey's (McKinsey Global Institute 2005) estimate was $37.7 billion.

The studies show that the bulk of service outsourcing still takes place in the domestic economy. The WTO study suggests that offshoring represents only 15.6 percent of the worldwide market for outsourcing services. And a study by the research firm NelsonHall, cited in Suri (2005), estimated that offshoring accounted for only 2 percent of the total contract value of outsourced business processes in 2003, and that its participation was expected to rise to 6 percent by 2008. At this stage, it is impossible to estimate the size of the three different segments of the offshoring market. Available information indicates that the bulk of offshoring takes place in software services. ITE-BOP still represent a smaller share of the total business, though their share is expected to increase considerably (UNCTAD 2004). And ODPS remain comparatively small, around 10 percent of the total market of offshore services (Suri 2005).

The debate on the impact of offshoring has focused on the effects of "exporting jobs" from industrialized to low-cost developing countries. Contrary to common perceptions, the data show that service offshoring is primarily a North-North and not a North-South phenomenon (Amiti and Wei 2005). In the case of the Unites States, the main offshoring economy, 85 percent of this trade is with other OECD countries. Another important feature is the predominance of captive offshoring, that is, trade with subsidiary companies. It is estimated that up to 70 percent of offshoring involves captive units in the foreign country. As a result, offshoring mostly takes the form of intrafirm trade, and trade flows are closely associated with flows of foreign direct investment.

Offshoring is concentrated in a relatively small number of countries. The main offshoring countries are the United States and the United Kingdom, with the former accounting for more than 70 percent of all worldwide offshoring, and the latter representing two thirds of all European offshoring activity. On the receiving end, five countries account for almost 84 percent of the worldwide offshoring industry. India is the main provider with 32 percent of the total market, followed by Ireland with 23 percent, Canada with 10 percent, Israel with 9.5 percent, and China with 9 percent

(McKinsey Global Institute 2005). Country concentration has increased further in recent years. India accounts for over 80 percent of all offshoring activity in developing countries. And 82 percent of its exports of software and IT-enabled services go to the United States and the United Kingdom (UNCTAD 2004). Therefore, the geographical spread of offshoring from developed to developing countries has been quite limited to date. Nevertheless, a pattern of specialization is slowly emerging, with new entrants beginning to provide different offshoring services.[1]

Offshoring for Development?

Many authors view the emerging new international division of labor as an opportunity for developing countries to redefine their integration into the world economy, with respect to employment, exports, growth, and overall welfare (Primo Braga 1996, UNCTAD 2005c, NelsonHall 2004, cited in Suri 2005). In this section, I challenge the unequivocally positive assessment of the implications of offshore outsourcing for developing countries by exploring four questions: (1) how big are the potential employment gains? (2) who is more likely to benefit? (3) how sustainable is the process? and (4) what are the knowledge spillovers in the host economies?

Employment Generation: How Big Are the Gains?

The current optimism in developing countries and the concerns in industrialized countries derive from broad estimates of the potential long-term employment effects of offshoring. There are large variations among the estimates though. An early study by the World Bank (1995) suggested that 1–5 percent of total employment in the G-7 countries could be affected by offshoring. More recent OECD estimates (2006, 2005b) claim that close to 20 percent of total employment in OECD countries is susceptible to relocation; other studies, economy-wide and sector-specific ones, also predict significant potential long-term job effects (Bardhan and Kroll 2003, Deloitte Research 2003). According to McKinsey (McKinsey Global Institute 2005), 160 million jobs, or about 11 percent of the projected 1.46 billion service jobs worldwide in 2008, could in theory be carried out remotely, and 9 percent of all service jobs in the United States could be offshored. Nevertheless, the report stresses that not all the offshoring potential will actually materialize due to regulatory restrictions, company policies, supply constraints, and specific concerns about language and culture. In fact, the McKinsey report predicts that only 2.6 percent of all offshorable service jobs will have moved abroad by 2008.

Estimates of the actual loss of jobs in developed countries due to service offshoring vary considerably. Forrester Research calculates that by 2003, 315,000 jobs had been offshored in the Unites States, and predicts a cumulative job loss of 3.4 million jobs by 2015 (McCarthy 2004). Jaffee (2004) estimates a possible cumulative loss of 3.7 million jobs over 15 years. Estimates of the total jobs actually relocated to developing countries are even harder to find. In a study of eight sectors in 2003, McKinsey (Quarterly 2005) estimates that 565,000 jobs were performed in low-wage countries for companies or consumers in developed countries, and it expected the number to increase to 1.2 million by 2008. McKinsey estimates that up to 2003, only 37.6 percent of all jobs relocated as a result of offshoring went to low-cost developing countries and that by 2008 only 29.3 percent of all offshored jobs will have gone to these countries. In 2003–2004, 813,000 people were employed in the ITE-BOPs and SS sectors in India, the leading recipient of offshoring services among developing countries. Around 500,000 of them were primarily in export-oriented activities (260,000 in SS and 245,000 in ITE-BOPs). If these data were compatible with the McKinsey estimates, it would suggest that the employment effects from service offshoring to developing countries have been concentrated primarily in India.

In summary, the available data suggest that to date the employment impact of service offshoring on host developing countries has been positive, though by no means impressive, particularly in light of the high share of job relocation to other developed countries, and the high concentration of offshore-related job creation in services in one developing country, India. Even the highest forecasts for the medium term suggest that the overall employment effect in developing countries could be quite limited and rather insignificant considering the pressing employment needs of these countries.

Distribution of Development Gains:
Country Concentration

We have seen already that India is the dominant supplier of offshore services among developing countries. Even though a few other countries have been able to enter the business, for example, China, it seems unlikely that offshoring of services will spread widely in the developing world in the foreseeable future. Many developing countries will probably remain marginalized from the process of service offshoring.

Developed countries will continue to play an important role as suppliers of offshored services. The extent to which developing countries can make inroads into offshoring services currently supplied by developed economies will largely determine the growth and diffusion of offshoring in the developing world. Additional opportunities may arise from further specialization in the industry, as developed countries retain the technology-intensive end of the offshoring business while some of the more labor-intensive and low-technology activities are relocated to developing countries.

It is likely that the same developing countries that supply offshore services today will also attract the bulk of offshoring activity in the future. Different indices measuring countries' attractiveness as offshore locations coincide in ranking the same countries as the top destinations for future offshoring activity. Surveys about the future offshoring plans of firms in developed countries indicate that most offshoring will still be concentrated in the same locations (Kearney 2004, McKinsey Global Institute 2005). With respect to software services, it may be difficult for developing countries to reproduce the experience of today's successful countries, as it took an extraordinary confluence of events for export-oriented software industries to develop in India, Ireland, and Israel (Arora 2005).

On the other hand, there are some documented cases where offshoring has spread to new developing countries. One driver behind the shift of offshoring activity to other developing countries is the internationalization of firms from the first comers in the offshoring market. Firms in India, for example, are relocating some of their offshoring activity to other developing countries in order to maintain competitiveness, as domestic wages are increasing. This relocation is taking place mainly to neighboring countries with an untapped supply of adequate personnel and lower labor costs and the minimum context requirements for offshoring. Some firms from successful developing countries have also tapped offshoring opportunities in other countries in order to preempt the emergence of competitors.

Developing countries might be able to break into niche markets in the offshoring business, if they have the right location-specific assets or advantages from language and cultural affinities. If a country is located in the same or similar time zone and can be reached in a short flight from the outsourcer's site, nearshoring may be a promising possibility permitting the entry of new players into the market (Meyer 2006, Abbot and Jones 2002). Detailed research is needed to assess the niche market potential that can be developed by countries currently excluded from offshoring.

The Sustainability of Offshoring Growth

Most of the forecasts of services offshoring are based on the assumption that the impressive growth rates of the past can be sustained in the medium and long-term. There are indications, however, that offshoring growth might already be leveling off. In addition, there are forces at work that could significantly limit host countries' benefits from offshoring.

The Impact of Technology and Business Practices
While certain technological developments have made offshoring possible, others might prevent developing countries from reaping all the benefits from the process. Labor-displacing technology is not a new phenomena, it has been with us since the industrial revolution. But today we are witnessing an impressive shortening of the time frame during which the impact of new technological developments and business methods are felt in the labor market.

The growing sophistication of voice recognition and voice-to-data technology, for example, is already mechanizing many jobs in the ITE-BOP segment of the offshoring market. Some argue that these developments could render a significant share of the industry obsolete within a few years. Nearly 60 percent of work done offshore is customer management services, 85 percent of which is voice-based (NelsonHall 2004 cited in Suri 2005). Not all these jobs can be mechanized, of course, but a significant share of these is vulnerable to new technological developments. Yet this is the market segment that provides the highest benefits to developing countries in terms of jobs and incomes.[2]

Innovative business practices, seeking more efficiency and better responses to market demands, are also having an impact. There is growing customer involvement in the provision of many services which tends to eliminate some of the back-office processes that are being offshored by firms in developed countries, for example, an increasing reliance on electronic ticketing in the airline industry and self-service in the banking industry. This reduction in the need to outsource data encoding, for example, has already affected some Caribbean countries that developed the data entry industry to serve companies in the airline and banking sectors. The call center industry may also be transformed by the rising reliance of firms on "virtual call centers," where the service is provided from the homes of the employees. A number of companies in the United States are already shifting from conventional call centers to virtual ones.

New concerns about data and network security, privacy, risks for national capabilities and sovereignty, and application of domestic regulations in cross-border transactions are likely to have an impact on business offshoring practices (ACM 2006). An important challenge for developing countries is how to keep pace with overall technological developments so that they can position themselves for entering the high-tech, high value-added end of the offshoring market. This is particularly difficult in light of the enormous and increasing amounts of R&D subsidies to firms in developed countries, estimated at $250 billion annually (Abugattas 2005).

Increasing Competition and Vulnerability
With respect to the promotion of labor-intensive manufactured exports from developing countries, a number of authors have warned against the

viability of such a strategy, if too many countries pursue it at the same time. If many, in particular large, developing countries try to increase their labor-intensive exports considerably, they may face the risk of rising protectionist sentiments in importing countries, and a decline in the terms of trade to such an extent that the benefits of an increased volume of exports is more than offset by the loss due to lower prices (Mayer 2003). Increased international competition coupled with productivity improvements in exporting countries may thus lead to "immiserizing growth" (Kaplinsky 2000).

Such a "fallacy of composition" argument may well carry over to the case of labor-intensive services (Jaffee 2004). There are already some indications that increased competition among developing countries to participate in the main markets for offshore services is generating a strong downward pressure on prices and firms' profitability; and a protectionist backlash in major importing countries is evident. As more developing countries try to enter the market, even if they are not successful in the long-term, they would be exerting additional competitive pressure on prices and therefore on domestic wages in the industry, limiting the anticipated income effects of employment. Depending on the price effects, some offshoring locations with higher wages and overall costs and more rigid labor markets might be priced out of the market.

Anecdotal evidence suggests that the offshoring industry in developing countries might be highly vulnerable to offshoring firms' behavior and to market signals. Captive offshoring entails few sunken costs and therefore has a tendency of being "foot-loose." As a result, companies can relocate fairly rapidly in response to changes in risk and profitability. The industry is also particularly sensitive to market signals. This has been shown in the call center segment, where in response to adverse customer reactions, firms in France and the United Kingdom, for example, have relocated call centers back to the home country or to other locations.

Supply-Side Constraints
Most of the analysis of offshoring assumes an almost unlimited supply of adequately qualified labor in the insourcing location. Therefore, a country could benefit from increasing volumes of exports for a significant period of time, while expanding domestic employment with higher salaries than those paid in traditional economic activities. The case of India, a country with a large educated population and a significant number of new skilled workers entering the market each year, gives some indication that the assumption of an unlimited supply of labor does not hold. Wages in the offshoring industry in India have been rising significantly in recent years suggesting an increasing shortage of the right type of labor for the industry. Some estimates indicate that wages have been rising at 30 percent annually in some segments of the industry. Most estimates by private consulting

firms put the cost savings for offshoring firms at 10 to 30 percent of what it would cost to undertake the task in-house or outsource it in the domestic market. Therefore, the margin for internalizing higher labor costs is limited.

Spillover Effects in the Host Country

A central issue in assessing the potential development gains of offshoring is the extent of positive spillovers generated in the host economy. Unfortunately, there are very few studies analyzing this issue. Most of the conventional wisdom derives from an extrapolation of conclusions based on studies of the impact of foreign direct investment in general on host countries, or from studies of this issue in India, with an emphasis on software services. The potential spillover effects will depend, inter alia, on the segment of the business (ITE-BOP, SS, or ODPS) and on the business model through which the activity is undertaken (captive offshoring or outsourcing to a third party abroad).

Technology and Knowledge Spillovers

Technology and knowledge spillovers from service offshoring are the most important potential benefits for the developing host countries. The realization of such spillovers presupposes a foreign presence, that is, captive offshoring, and they might happen at the intraindustry level benefiting domestic companies, or throughout the economy enhancing overall systemic efficiency. The higher technology segments of the market are more likely to generate this positive outcome. In the case of ITE-BOP, the potential for spillovers is necessarily more limited, as they are not very technology intensive. Some studies suggest that the software services segment in India has generated few knowledge spillovers to the domestic economy. Most export-oriented activities operate as "export-enclaves" with limited linkages with the domestic economy (D'Costa 2003, Kumar and Joseph 2005, UNCTAD 2004).

There is also evidence that the scope for linkages between foreign affiliates and local firms is especially limited in the area of software development (Kumar 2001). Most of the software developed is highly customized with little application elsewhere. The high export concentration of the industry in India might also have limited the diffusion of ICT technology in the domestic economy. Knowledge spillovers can also happen through the movement of skilled personnel from high-technology export firms to domestic companies. Evidence from the Indian case suggests, however, that the opposite might be occurring, with export firms luring skilled personnel from domestic companies in different sectors of the economy.

Knowledge spillovers can also take place in a more diffused manner, through frequent interactions between domestic and foreign firms, and the demonstration effect of foreign firms in the domestic economy. But it is difficult to measure the existence of such spillovers. A lot of in-depth analysis of a wider set of countries and market segments is needed to gain a better understanding of the extent to which offshoring generates positive technology and knowledge spillovers in the host country.

Upgrading of Human Capital
Another possible positive impact of offshoring on development is the enhancement of human capital. The higher the skill level required by the activity, the higher the drive for enhancing human capital. Upgrading of skills takes place when firms engaged in offshoring undertake substantial in-house training, or if the workplace encourages learning-by-doing, as has been the case, for example, in Singapore and the Philippines (ILO 2003). Even in the ITE-BOP segment, there is potential for skill upgrading. Many jobs in the low-skill segment of the industry constitute the market entry for new people, and these jobs stimulate updating of skills (Richardson 1999). Many governments in developing countries provide fiscal incentives for investment in training to promote in-house training in the offshoring business.

Offshoring can also have a wider systemic impact on the development of human capital in the host economy, if it serves as a driver for improvements of the national education system. This effect can emerge from the demand side by increasing the returns to education, motivating individuals to seek better qualifications and putting pressure on educational institutions. From the supply side, this effect could happen if the business sector demands from the government and the education institutions that programs are upgraded and adjusted to their needs. These effects will materialize only to the extent that public education policies are implemented adequately, thus requiring a certain critical mass of offshoring interests to be able to influence policy decisions. The successful offshoring cases highlight the fact that there were significant investments in education and coordination with the industry to adjust the supply of skills and education to the particular demands of the firms, thus making it possible to sustain the activity and increase productivity.

Limiting "Brain Drain"
By providing adequately remunerated domestic job opportunities to highly educated individuals, offshoring may contribute to skill retention in the host country. There are no empirical studies documenting the extent to which this is actually happening in developing countries currently engaged in offshoring. However, studies on migration show that

income opportunities are only one of the variables explaining the decision to migrate. It is interesting to note though that offshoring has enticed some expatriates to return to their home country to set up business. This has been the case in India (Kumar 2001) as well as in Ireland (Sands 2005). Large diaspora populations have facilitated connections between the export firms and their product markets, creating a natural inflow of expertise when expatriates return from working with companies abroad (Kapur and McHale 2005, Arora et al. 2001). Offshoring makes "brain circulation" possible between the offshoring and the insourcing countries, allowing workers to upgrade skills abroad and then use them in their home country.

Challenges and Policy Issues for New Entrants

A number of factors need to be taken into consideration when assessing the potential for offshoring spreading to a large number of developing countries, and some of the challenges confronting new entrants in the offshoring business. Particularly important factors are agglomeration economies, incumbent advantages, availability of human resources, and the role of public policies.

Constraining Factors

Agglomeration economies explain the increasing concentration of economic activity in certain locations, at the global and national levels. Leamer and Storper (2001) argue that there are significant agglomeration tendencies even for intellectual and innovative activities. Agglomeration is driven by the availability of infrastructure, skill base, and other resources, and by the synergies produced by the close proximity of firms. At the same time, a critical mass of activity is needed to promote the enhancement of the required infrastructure and skill base to sustain firm activities. Agglomeration economies are operating already in some of the main offshoring locations in developing countries, increasing the attractiveness for new ventures to select such locations. The pattern of concentration in the software development industry in India attests to the drive for agglomeration at the national level. For many new entrants it will be difficult, if possible at all, to achieve the required critical mass of activity to foster economies of agglomeration.

Countries that are already providing offshore services also enjoy "incumbent advantages." Offshored services have certain characteristics that enhance incumbent advantages. Most of the services are customized, and in many high-value services, price is not necessarily the determining factor in the choice of location. They imply a high level of expertise and credence value, and clients often find it difficult to assess ex-ante competing offerings and sometimes feel unqualified to fully assess the information they obtain. A supplier's previous relationship with a client and experience in networks significantly reduce information-gathering transaction costs incurred by the client in issuing new contracts. Intangibles such as brand awareness or reputation and perceived leverage also provide significant incumbency advantages.

The competitiveness of the offshoring industry rests in its "connectivity," the development of associated telecommunications services and other infrastructure, and the extent of diffusion of ICT in the economy. Most developing countries have embarked on the liberalization of the telecommunications sector. But in many cases, liberalization has not led to a competitive environment able to sustain the modernization needed to diffuse these services throughout the economy. In many countries, the size of the domestic market and international traffic flows are too small to attract the requisite investments in telecommunications infrastructure. The location of countries with respect to the availability of optical lines is another factor that may marginalize some countries from entering the offshoring business. In Africa, for example, the francophone West Coast, which lies on the route of the high-quality fibre optic link between Europe and Latin America, is emerging as a preferred destination for some French companies' offshoring services, taking advantage as well of the language and the available infrastructure (Gray 2004).

A supply of skilled labor is needed to engage in offshoring. McKinsey (McKinsey Global Institute 2005) highlights the wide gap between the overall supply of skills and the employability of human resources in the offshoring industry. The upgrading of educational systems is a long-term process, which provides incumbents with the opportunity to further capture new opportunities arising in the offshoring of services. The skill levels needed to undertake ITE-BOP offshoring is, however, less demanding. In this segment of the market, new entrants among developing countries may have a greater opportunity to attract offshoring business in the short-term, if they have the requisite degree of connectivity and competitive costs.

Public Policy Options for Supporting New Entrants

Available evidence strongly suggests that public policies have played a significant role in the countries that have been successful in exporting services, in particular through offshoring, and that public policies are equally necessary to ensure that service exports contribute to the achievement of national policy objectives (ACM 2006).

Many developing countries are adopting active policies to promote the development of these activities in their territories, including extensive government support programs. The basic pillars of the strategies are measures to develop telecommunications infrastructure, increase utilization rates, strengthen capacities in ICT-based services, and promote services exports (UNCTAD 2003b). Development of telecommunications and enhancement of the economy's connectivity are crucial. There are a number of interesting examples of state intervention that aim at closing the "digital divide," supporting the use of IT services by firms (in particular SMEs) and creating a favorable environment where offshoring can flourish. In Korea, government support was instrumental in developing broadband services. In Singapore, the government uses grants to support the development of the communications networks and R&D in advanced telecommunications and to encourage the development of enhanced capacities in innovative services. The Multi-media Corridor Project in Malaysia and the Nusantara-21 Project in Indonesia are other interesting examples.

Based on infant industry considerations, support is provided for the development of more dynamic high-tech activities, including services, among them R&D services, information technology services, and software services. Government support to strengthen domestic capacities in the services sector varies across countries, but the observed tendency is to implement comprehensive packages that address human resource development, infrastructure development, telecommunication capabilities, and the development of the software industry. Some countries have established technology parks, offering certain benefits to attract firms to them. Other measures include direct grants, tax holidays, investment incentives, duty-free imports, allowances for human resources development, R&D subsidies, access to telecommunications under preferential rates, and access to credit at subsidized interest rates. Government support of exports is also rapidly spreading across the regions of the world, as countries implement different measures to enhance the competitiveness of their domestic firms to allow them to compete in both the domestic and the international market. Many developing countries include services under the provisions of Export Free Zones, hoping to promote the export of services, in particular through offshoring.

Incentives to attract FDI are highly popular in developing countries (UNCTAD 2004) and may affect the geographical distribution of offshoring, since most offshoring is to captive units. Agarwal (1986) has found a strong relation between incentives and capital investment in certain industries, including banking and high-technology services. Evidence suggests that export-oriented investments are more responsive to host country incentive packages and that in the developing country context incentives can matter (Chalk 2001). However, FDI incentives need to be viewed with a lot of skepticism. To the extent that foreign investors receive more favorable treatment than domestic companies that provide similar competitive services, which is already the case in some developing countries, incentives would promote captive offshoring more than the development of indigenous capacities. Also, these policies may provoke a race to the bottom, unleashing "bidding wars" and limiting the fiscal contribution of offshoring to the host country.

The potential for developing countries to enter the offshoring business might depend to a large extent on the appropriateness and efficacy of the supporting measures they implement. In this regard the institutional capabilities of different countries to put in place "industrial policies" might be a determining factor of success.

Conclusion

Emerging conventional wisdom is overstating the potential development gains of service offshoring for developing countries. Offshoring offers opportunities to these countries, but those may be limited in terms of their overall dimension as well as in the number of possible beneficiaries. Incumbents will enjoy significant advantages and may well receive the bulk of development gains. New entrants may be able to exploit market niches. There are a number of questions concerning the sustainability of gains, questions that require further analysis. Establishing a business-friendly environment is not sufficient to be a successful participant in the offshoring market. Public policies have played and will continue to play a crucial role in fostering the competitiveness of domestic firms and in assuring development gains for developing countries.

Notes

1. The Philippines, China, Thailand, Singapore, Hong Kong, Brazil, Mexico, and South Africa are identified as emerging players. Also, some transition economies in Eastern Europe have started to cater to the European market.
2. This is happening in the medical transcription industry in India, for example, which has experienced a nine percent revenue loss per annum in recent years (Suri 2005).

CHAPTER TEN

OFFSHORE OUTSOURCING OF SERVICES AS A CATALYST OF ECONOMIC DEVELOPMENT: THE CASE OF INDIA

Navdeep Suri*

Introduction

Rapid advances in Information and Communications Technology over the last decade have introduced an element of tradability into a wide range of services that were hitherto tied to the geographical location of the consumer. As a result, a growing number of organizations are choosing to concentrate on their core activities by outsourcing an array of ancillary services to other organizations that can deliver them more efficiently and at a lower cost. Others are taking advantage of falling international telecom rates to set up units in developing countries, which offer lower labor costs or larger pools of skilled workers, leading to the phenomenon of offshored services. Typically, offshored services include customer contact centers, data entry operations, telemarketing, and basic technical support at the lower end of the spectrum; processing of financial transactions such as credit card billing, insurance claims, and debt collection in the middle of the spectrum; and professional services such as design and engineering, R&D, investment analysis, medical diagnostics at the higher end. The fact that these services include discrete business processes and rely heavily on information technology has given rise to the sometimes overlapping terminology of IT-enabled services (ITES) and Business Process Outsourcing (BPO). There is a growing body of evidence to support the view that despite the hardship faced by individuals who become unemployed when their work is outsourced, at the macroeconomic level, offshore outsourcing remains a win-win proposition for host as well as client countries. One study demonstrates that every dollar of outsourcing from the United States to India creates $1.45 of value, of which the U.S. economy captures $1.12 while India receives 33 cents (McKinsey Global Institute 2003).

This offshoring of services has emerged as one of the fastest growing sectors of international trade. Being a labor-intensive activity, it offers a natural comparative advantage to countries with an educated and skilled workforce and lower labor costs. India has clearly emerged as the leader of the pack in the outsourcing field and its burgeoning ITES/BPO industry has made it the model that several other countries aspire to emulate. It has grown from a modest $565 million in FY 2000–2001to $6.2 billion in FY 2006–2007and is expected to rise to $8.5 billion by FY 2007–2008 (NASSCOM 2006). Most experts expect this trend line of 35–40 percent year-on-year growth of ITES/BPO exports to continue for the next several years. McKinsey estimates that when robust growth in exports of pure IT services such as applications development and maintenance is also taken into account, total IT and ITES export revenues could reach $60 billion by 2010, with the prospect of a further $15–20 billion in export revenues over the next 5 to 10 years through deep and enduring innovation by industry participants. The study is based on the calculation that the potential market for global offshoring of services exceeds $300 billion, of which hardly 10 percent or so has been realized so far. This leaves considerable scope for additional growth as the industry matures, as more industries begin to outsource an increasingly wider range of processes, and as companies that have been late to recognize the benefits of outsourcing start coming to the table. The projections, however, are based on the assumption that governments at the federal and state levels, software industry body NASSCOM (National Association of Software and Service Companies) and key industry players will take the steps necessary to maintain India's leadership position in the sector by overcoming the challenges that clearly loom large on the horizon.

This chapter looks at the evolution of the IT-ITES industry in India, the different streams in which the ITES-BPO sector has evolved, the benefits that it has brought to the Indian economy, and the steps taken proactively to ensure the continued growth of this industry. The benefits include the contribution of offshored IT/ITES to the generation of direct and indirect employment, greater participation of women in the workforce, development of smaller towns and cities, balance of payments stability, building of Brand India equity and its consequent impact on India's export of manufactured goods. There is also a tangible impact on the development and modernization of a range of other sectors including telecommunications, real estate, retail, banking, insurance, entertainment, customer services, and others. Recognition of the very substantial

benefits of the offshore outsourcing industry to India's economic development has prompted the Government of India and industry bodies such as
NASSCOM to take specific steps focusing on education and training, quality awareness, and security issues. India's success in this sector has inspired a
number of other developing countries to try and emulate the Indian story,
though they face significant obstacles in the process.

The Indian IT Story

Starting around the 1960s and 1970s, a number of graduates from the pres-
tigious Indian Institutes of Technology (IITs) migrated to the United States
in search of better economic opportunities. Many made it to the top eche-
lons of major IT companies such as Intel, AMD, Motorola, IBM, Texas
Instruments, and HP. During the late 1980s and early 1990s, these members of the Indian diaspora (nonresident Indians or NRIs, as they are
commonly known) are believed to have played a key role in encouraging
their companies to set up Research and Development operations in India.
A few others returned to India to establish start-ups that would later
become industry leaders. The success of these initial ventures and the exposure of senior company executives to the abundant mathematical talent and
programming skills available in places such as Bangalore, Chennai, and
Hyderabad led them to hire Indian companies to tackle the Y2K or the
millennium bug problem of the late 1990s.

The Y2K scare proved to be a bonanza for Indian IT companies such as
TCS, Infosys, Wipro, and Satyam. It gave them an opportunity to deploy
large numbers of programmers at onshore locations in the United States
and other countries and at offshore locations in India itself to fix the software bug that was expected to wreak havoc in the developed countries.
Sending IT managers and programmers overseas and successfully resolving
the Y2K issues enabled Indian companies to establish their credentials with
the CIOs and heads of the IT divisions of major companies. It also coin-
cided with the downturn in the U.S. economic cycle. Outsourcing of business processes to India emerged as a logical choice for managers trying to
trim operating costs. The fact that engineers working in a large IT facility in
Bangalore could fix the problem for a company in San Francisco or
Houston also established the technical viability of the decision to offshore
other processes.

In the initial stages, companies such as GE established large, captive
facilities in India to provide credit card processing and an array of other
services for their parent companies. The GE operation soon grew to a point
where it was providing similar services to other clients. Some companies
such as Citibank and Bank of America sent senior NRI executives to head

their operations in India, leveraging their knowledge of the Indian market and their understanding of the parent company's culture. These executives initially played an important role in persuading their companies to offshore a growing range of services to India. Later, some left their parent companies to set up highly successful BPO companies of their own. Former Citibank India head Jaitirath Rao became president of Mphasis and even the chairman of the software industry body NASSCOM, while Vikram Talwar became CEO of EXL. Raman Roy of GE's BPO facility similarly parted company to first found Spectramind and later start another venture after selling his stake to IT major Wipro. The three companies figure among India's twenty largest BPO companies, and each of them has established its own commercial presence in several countries to service existing clients and to secure additional business. They have also moved to acquiring companies in the United States and elsewhere to obtain access to major clients and niche markets. Taken together, they offer a remarkable example of the kind of cross-pollination of ideas and technologies that has sparked the growth of India's ITES industry.

NASSCOM has emerged as a key player in driving the growth of the ITES/BPO industry by virtue of its position as a premier trade body and chamber of commerce of the IT software and services industry in India. NASSCOM also projects itself as a global trade body with over 1050 members, of which over 150 are global companies from the United States, the United Kingdom, the European Union, Japan, and China. NASSCOM member companies are in the business of software development, software services, software products, and IT-enabled/BPO services. The body has taken key initiatives in partnership with industry and government to look at emerging trends in this sector and to put in place systems aimed at sustaining India's leadership.

Development Benefits from ITES/BPO Sector

The rapid growth of the ITES/BPO sector since the turn of the century has had a visible impact on India's economic development. Some of these development benefits—the direct and indirect employment in the industry, the foreign exchange earnings, the rise of hightech BPO facilities cropping up in metropolitan areas across the country, the changing face of some of the smaller cities attracting BPO companies—are fairly visible. Other benefits, however, are less tangible and these include the impact on areas such as telecommunications, real estate, banking, insurance, retail, entertainment, and air travel as well as the significant transformation of India's brand equity.

Employment and Income Effects

The share of the IT-ITES industry in India's GDP has more than doubled in a five-year span: from 1.9 percent in FY 1999–2000 to 4.8 percent in FY 2005–2006 (Indian Institute of Foreign Trade 2006). NASSCOM estimates that direct employment in the IT-ITES sector has grown from a mere 284,000 in FY 2000–2001 to 1.3 million in FY 2006–2007. The NASSCOM-McKinsey report 2005 projects this figure to rise to at least 2.5 million by FY 2010–2011. Employment in the burgeoning ITES space has been rising much faster than in IT services. Over 100,000 new jobs were created in the ITES/BPO sector in FY 2006–2007 taking the total to 415,000. The NASSCOM-McKinsey report estimates this figure to rise to 1.4 million by 2010.

A look at the indirect and induced employment generated by these IT-ITES jobs, however, provides a truer picture of the cumulative impact. NASSCOM estimates that in FY 2006–2007, the 1.3 million strong work-force in this sector created over 3 million additional jobs (NASSCOM-Hewitt 2005) through expenditures on vendors providing construction, transportation, catering, telecom, security, janitorial, and other services. The induced employment generated by this sector is harder to quantify but is no less significant when the impact of employees' expenditure on food, clothing, housing, utilities, recreation, health, banking, and other areas is taken into account. An employment survey by Ma Foi management con-sultants predicts the creation of some 60,000 new jobs each month in the Information Technology and related sectors—the highest amongst the eighteen sectors involved in its survey of employment growth in India. While these numbers are clearly having an impact in terms of employment opportunities in metropolises and in a few smaller cities, their impact in a country of over 1 billion people, 70 percent of whom live in rural areas, should not be overstated.

The ITES/BPO sector also has a significant impact on income growth and consumption. To attract high-quality staff and to compensate for the odd working hours, most BPOs companies pay wages that are signifi-cantly above those paid to employees with similar qualifications working in the domestic sector. Most locally recruited employees continue to live with their families even after getting employment. In the case of rela-tively low-income families, the salary of the son or daughter working in a BPO company usually becomes a very substantial contribution to the family's income stream and soon produces a discernible improvement in its standard of living—a phenomenon that is especially visible in some of the smaller cities and townships that have attracted large BPO facilities.

For employees coming from more affluent families, the salary earned while working in a BPO means an immediate increase in disposable income and a capacity to spend on mobile phones, branded clothes, films, and other consumer goods. The mushrooming growth of shopping malls, restaurants, cafes, and cinema multiplexes in the vicinity of several BPO clusters is testimony to the vigor of marketing men targeting the disposable incomes and high spending propensity of these young men and women.

Empowering Impact on Women

For educated young women, in particular, the clean, air-conditioned, and sanitized environment offered by most BPO facilities have proven to be a strong magnet. Estimates indicate that women account for anywhere from 40 to 60 percent of BPO staff. For many, it is their first job after graduation and an opportunity to strive for economic independence at a crucial stage of their lives. In many developing societies, family pressure tends to push women into marriage at a relatively early age, often denying them the opportunity for an economically productive career. A BPO job is increasingly sought by young women to keep parental pressure at bay and stake out a possible career.

BPO companies are also beginning to make a conscious effort to recruit more women at middle and senior management levels. IBM Daksh is one company that is deliberately focusing on a "diversity program" aimed at putting more women in senior positions and offering placement agencies 1percent over and above their standard rate for women candidates. Genpact, India's largest BPO company, similarly offers Rs. 6,000 for successful referrals of senior women candidates as compared to the normal incentive of Rs. 5,000.

Learning and Spillovers

The sector also has come to be recognized as a useful starting point in the career progression of young graduates. Most BPO facilities tend to be state of the art in terms of technology since they depend upon using the latest developments in Information and Communications Technology for their efficient functioning. They often provide local staff with their first experience of the kind of office environment, work ethics, and business practices that prevails in companies in the developed countries.

With the maturing of the BPO industry, skills acquired in the offshore sector are progressively transferred to domestic operations as well. Organizations in the telecommunications, banking and insurance sectors, for instance, have been able to get rid of antiquated customer service systems and move quickly to modern call centres that can respond much more efficiently to customer requests. The transition has taken place within the space of a couple of years and has been possible largely on account of experience gained by local companies in serving offshore clients. The process has been facilitated by the availability of a pool of workers trained at offshore call centers but who are keen to trade the rigors of a night-time job serving offshore clients in the United States or the United Kingdom for a day-time job with a local company, even if it means a 20 percent pay cut.

India has also benefited from the fact that modern, competitively priced telecommunications facilities are a prerequisite for a viable BPO sector, spurring the government to introduce competition in the telecom sector through private domestic and foreign operators. An emphasis on satellite-based communications, greater use of fiber optics and wireless networks, introduction of VoIP-based telecommunications, and availability of greater bandwidth at a lower cost are some of the other benefits that India has derived on account of the crucial role of efficient telecommunications in developing their BPO sector.

Boost for Air Travel

Air travel is an unlikely area to benefit from offshored services, but in cities such as Hyderabad and Bangalore, the IT-ITES industry has emerged as a key driver for the boom in international air travel, compelling them to embark on the construction of huge international airports to overcome the growing bottlenecks at the existing facilities. Although offshore outsourcing would normally see the bulk of work being done within locations in India, the nature of work requires frequent travel to client sites in the host country for a variety of purposes including market development, scoping of projects, precontract negotiations, knowledge transfer and transitioning of projects, testing and implementation at site, sales and marketing, trouble shooting and maintenance support, onsite operations for meeting needs such as disaster recovery and management, emergency response services, and professional services in key areas that cannot be outsourced for offshore development. One study estimates that by 2010, the IT-ITES industry will account for 1 million international airline trips annually, constituting perhaps 20 percent of all airline trips undertaken by Indians at that time.

Promotion of Decentralized Growth

With traditional IT destinations such as Bangalore, Delhi, Mumbai, and Hyderabad approaching a saturation point in terms of the available talent pool and physical infrastructure, many of the major IT companies have started to move to the hitherto neglected Tier II and Tier III cities and townships. Cities hosting major universities and technical institutions and offering significantly lower real estate prices than the IT metros enjoy a clear preference, and in some cases the positive intervention by state governments to attract MNC and local IT giants provides an additional incentive. This is particularly true in the case of states such as Tamil Nadu, Andhra Pradesh, Gujarat, Maharashtra, Kerala, and West Bengal where the chief ministers have taken it upon themselves to become the IT ambassadors by putting in place a liberalized regulatory framework, offering generous incentives and positioning their regions as the IT destination of choice. Pune has already set up two IT parks with state-of-the-art facilities, while Visakhapatnam is in the process of establishing its own exclusive IT-zone spread over 300 acres.

Some of these efforts are clearly beginning to show results. Infosys COO M.D. Pai describes Jaipur, Kolkata, Mangalore, Bhubaneshwar, Vishakhapatnam, and Pune as the IT-ITES destinations of the future, even as his company makes significant investments in infrastructure and training facilities in Mysore and Chennai. Genpact, the formerly GE-owned BPO, has moved into Jaipur with a second major facility, while Wipro is expanding into cities such as Trichy and Coimbatore. TCS, similarly, has made a major foray into Kolkata and is now looking at setting up a software research and development facility in Gujarat.

The trend toward a move away from the IT metros is providing significant development benefits to the successful Tier II and III cities, typically reflected in more decentralized growth, creation of sophisticated ICT infrastructure, and a rapid improvement in employment opportunities for educated youth. The trend will gain further momentum if the central government accepts the recommendations of a NASSCOM-McKinsey report that makes a strong case for at least 10 to 12 new integrated townships with international airports and other infrastructure.

Foreign Exchange Contribution

Exports from the IT-ITES sector grew from $13.3 billion in FY 2003–2004 to $18.2 billion in FY 2004–2005 to an estimated $23.9 billion in FY 2005–2006 (Indian Institute of Foreign Trade 2006).The healthy foreign exchange earnings of around $22.5 billion from IT-ITES exports in FY 2006–2007 have helped India sustain the steady growth in its foreign exchange reserves despite the high crude oil prices that have had an adverse impact on the trade balance. Unlike the severe shock to the economy during the oil price hikes of 1973, 1980, and 1990, export earnings from the IT sector have cushioned the impact and protected the value of the Indian rupee despite a merchandise trade deficit of nearly $45 billion. This, in turn, has helped in improving the country's international risk profile.

Moving Up the Value Chain

Until fairly recently, India was widely perceived as an exotic but impoverished country that manufactured some textiles and other low-end products. As a manufacturer and exporter, it was seen in the low-price, low-quality quadrant of the matrix. However, the rise of India as an IT powerhouse has brought about a substantial change in perceptions. As IT, by definition, is seen as a high-technology area, Indians are increasingly regarded as educated, smart, and skilled. This perception is strengthened by the increasingly sophisticated services that are being outsourced to India in sectors such as healthcare, finance, accounting, engineering, design and R&D. Global corporate leaders have frequently spoken about the manner in which India has moved from a cost-arbitrage proposition for outsourced services to one that provides higher quality, innovation, and greater efficiency in business processes, even describing the BPO business as a "Trojan Horse" that creates new openings for Indian IT companies and enables them to progressively move up the value chain. While the cost savings are substantial, the strength of India's ITES model lies in the manner in which successful ITES companies have been able to move up the value chain into a wide range of BPO activities including purchasing and order functionality procurement, accounting, insurance management, human resource and benefits management, and a vast array of internal corporate control functions. More recently, the same companies are moving into medical, legal, and actuarial functions. Engineering services outsourcing is another new area, and NASSCOM estimates that over 150 MNCs have already set up captive R&D facilities in India.

The testimonials of international consultancy firms, financial services companies, and global engineering leaders about the quality of their operations in India have had a significant impact on India's brand equity, moving the country toward the good quality–high value quadrant of the matrix. As the "Made in India" brand acquires international credibility, it is beginning to have a positive spin-off on India's manufacturing exports in sectors ranging from automobiles and steel to pharmaceuticals and high-fashion apparel.

The Emergence of Indian IT Multinationals

The rapid growth of offshore outsourcing to India has also seen the emergence of the first real Indian multinationals that have begun to make an impact around the globe. Start-ups such as Infosys and Wipro have reached a turnover of over $2 billion in less than a generation, catching up with more mature players such as TCS. Growing consistently at rates of over 30 percent per year, they now operate in multiple geographies and are positioning to compete directly with global leaders such as IBM, Accenture, and EDS. TCS, for instance, now boasts of a substantial presence in every continent, with regional offices spread from Beijing to London, from Asuncion to Budapest, and from San Francisco to Johannesburg. Equally significant is the pace of mergers and acquisitions set by some of the larger Indian IT companies in their quest for "inorganic growth" as they scan the markets for small to mid-sized companies that possess niche technologies or bring healthy client lists to the table. Infosys and Wipro have been particularly aggressive in their drive to acquire relevant companies in Europe and the United States, showing the path to others such as HCL, ICICI Onesource, Patni, EXL to follow their example.

A second indicator of the emergence of Indian IT multinationals is their ability and willingness to recruit employees from across the globe. Infosys, for instance, has become a sought-after destination for internship programs of several reputed American universities, while TCS has set itself the target of having 10 percent of its global workforce comprised of non-Indians. One example is Technovate eSolutions, a Delhi-based ITES company, that could be heralding a new facet of India's strengths in this sector. It serves clients from eleven countries in nine different languages, and at least 10 percent of its 900 employees are from Europe (Pandey 2004).

The success of India's IT industry and the reputation enjoyed by some of the industry leaders has enabled them to wield an influence that extends far beyond their own industry. Infosys founder N.R. Narayanmurthy, for instance, has become a respected voice on issues ranging from accountability and good governance to corporate social responsibility and academic freedom. His successor Nandan Nilekeni advises the city of Bangalore on infrastructure development issues. Shareholder value created by companies such as Infosys, TCS, and Satyam have spawned thousands of millionaires and ignited the imagination of millions more.

At a different level, the success of the IT leaders in establishing themselves as global players in their own right has raised the benchmark for a number of other companies that were hitherto content to operate within India's sheltered domestic market. While Tata Steel's recent bid to acquire Corus attracted international headlines, it is only the latest in a series of high-profile acquisitions by Indian companies. Even without counting the Corus deal, 2006 would go down in India's contemporary economic history as the year when inbound FDI was dwarfed by outward FDI on account of a whole slew of foreign acquisitions by Indian corporations. Companies ranging from Mahindras (automobiles, tractors), Suzlon (wind energy equipment),

Reliance (refining, petrochemicals), Bharat Forge and Sundaram Fastners (automotive components), to Ranbaxy, Cipla, Dr. Reddy's (pharmaceuticals) now believe that they have the requisite blend of entrepreneurship, technology, and managerial competence to target global markets and compete with established leaders in their respective domains.

Sustaining India's leadership

As India's ITES/ BPO sector gathers steam and the development benefits start streaming into secondary and tertiary sectors and into smaller cities and towns, governments at the federal and state levels have worked closely with NASSCOM to develop an ambitious program that focuses on education and training, quality assurance systems, and security parameters and aims at maintaining India's leadership position in this sector. There is also a recognition that continued growth of offshored services faces significant policy barriers in the form of protectionist legislation in the United States and Europe and through visa restrictions that impede mobility of technical personnel. India, therefore, has emerged as a key advocate of liberalized trade in services under Mode 1 and of unrestricted movement of specialized personnel under Mode 4 of Article 1 of the General Agreement in Trade in Services (GATS) (Mattoo and Wunsch 2004).

Education and Training

As a labor-intensive industry, the ITES/ BPO sector depends heavily on the availability of skilled labor at a relatively low cost. Countries that seek to take advantage of the opportunities available in this sector must develop a cogent set of policies to ensure that they can produce a sufficient number of persons with the skill-sets relevant to this sector. Even in a country such as India, which possesses a large pool of skilled workers, there is a growing recognition that a shortage of workers in several specific areas could inhibit future growth. The shortage will stem not from the lack of available seats at educational institutions, but rather from the nature of skills and training imparted at these institutions. The NASSCOM-McKinsey 2005 report in fact projects a shortage of 500,000 professionals in different market segments by 2010 unless corrective action is taken.

This issue was also studied in some detail by the Task Force on Meeting the Human Resources Challenge for IT and IT enabled services, coordinated by the Ministry of Communications and Information Technology, Government of India. It recommends that India must adopt a comprehensive strategy aimed at meeting the human resource requirements of the ITES/BPO sector by making sure that the educational system provides the right skill-sets, by establishing a standard to certify the quality of skills provided and by encouraging people to get certified and employed in this sector.

NASSCOM has taken the lead in implementing the recommendations of the Task Force and taking the necessary steps to ensure the continued availability of trained manpower for the rapidly growing IT-ITES industry. Some of its key initiatives include the IT Workforce Development Initiative, the Nasscom Assessment of Competence Program, and the National Skills Registry for IT professionals.

The *IT Workforce Development* (ITWD) initiative is aimed at fostering a closer interaction between industry and academia so that academic institutions recognize the changing skill sets needed in today's students to find employment in the IT industry. Toward this end, NASSCOM has entered into an institutional arrangement with the University Grants Commission (UGC) and the All India Council for Technical Education to strengthen professional education in line with the IT industry's requirement for skilled professionals and to keep academia abreast of the rapid changes in technology and corresponding change in skill-set requirements. These efforts are being bolstered by the in-house training programs instituted by industry majors, and the collaborative initiatives of a number of other companies with counterpart educational institutions.

While TCS, WIPRO, Satyam, and virtually every major IT company has set up a sizeable in-house training facility to meet its huge appetite for new workers, the case of Infosys stands out for the sheer scale of its operations. The company is adding a new 9,000 seat training centre to its existing 4,500 seat training facility in Mysore. The expansion would make it the largest training facility of its kind in the world, operating in three shifts and providing training to 40,000 employees annually.

The trend of close collaboration between industry and academic organizations is also gathering momentum. While NASSCOM has organized a series of IT-ITES industry-academia meetings in Tier II cities such as Jaipur, Lucknow, Vishakapatnam, Coimbatore, and Dharwad, private companies such as Zensar, Xansa, Pixtel, and others have initiated mentorship programs with technical colleges as part of the NASSCOM-UGC memorandum. Other companies such as Satyam, Mind Tree, Patni, Accenture, and Microsoft have started faculty training programs in key colleges and universities.

The partnership between Zensar Technologies and Vishwakarma Institute of Technology (VIT) perhaps offers a glimpse of the shape of things to come. Zensar is setting up a virtual global delivery platform that will enable VIT to function as a virtual training and development extension of Sensor's own software development campus. This will allow VIT students to work on live Zensar projects and expose them to mature software engineering processes and practices, creating "business-ready" professionals once they graduate from the college.

The *NASSCOM Assessment of Competence* (NAC) program aims to meet the possible talent shortage in the ITES-BPO sector by putting in place a standard assessment and certification process that can help in assessing candidates on key skills and create a uniform platform for recruitment and training purposes. Hewitt Associates, a leading HR consultancy, has been engaged as program manager for NAC and is responsible for designing and rolling out the NAC program.

The NAC program seeks to test the aptitude of potential recruits for ITES-BPO companies on seven separate sets of skills including listening, typing, verbal ability, spoken English, comprehension and writing ability, office software usage, numerical and analytical skills, and concentration and accuracy. NASSCOM formally launched the pilot testing phase of NAC in August 2005 and during the ensuing year, 6000 candidates, 22 ITES-BPO companies, and several state governments and educational institutions participated in it. Following successful completion of the pilot phase, the national rollout of NAC started in November 2006.

The *National Skills Registry for IT Professionals* (NSR-ITP) is another NASSCOM initiative to create, operate, and maintain a national database of employees working in the ITES/BPO industry in India. NSR is a voluntary effort that encourages employees and employers to join hands in preventing misuse of employee identity and misrepresentation by employees in their resumes. By providing third-party-verified personal, qualification, and career information of IT professionals, NSR is expected to allow prospective employers the opportunity to view the verified resumes of professionals in a nationwide database, provided access to the information is authorised by the professional. NSR was launched in January 2006 and with 22 leading IT companies already signed on to the initiative, Nasscom hopes to rapidly cover the 25 top IT companies that account for 70 percent of the industry workforce.

Quality Awareness

Quality has emerged as a key issue in the success of an ITES/ BPO operation, helping service providers differentiate themselves and claim an edge over competitors in major global contracts. Quality certifications serve as a road map for a sustained improvement in processes, adding value and strengthening relationships between vendors and clients. They also provide parameters for appraising the performance of service providers in a consistent and comparable manner, allowing clients to separate the high-performance vendors from those with a more ordinary record.

Analysts consider the conscious drive undertaken by India's IT industry toward internationally recognized certification as an important factor in raising the comfort level of new clients, moving up the value chain and sustaining the industry on a high-growth trajectory. The industry has moved through three distinct phases in its quest for high-level certification. In the first phase, the emphasis was on the creation of basic processes to handle all activities related to order fulfilment. The European ISO 9000 standard served as a useful benchmark for this purpose.

In the second phase, the focus shifted to more sophisticated software engineering and IT companies to align their Quality Management Systems with the Capability Maturity Model (CMM)[1] developed by the Software Engineering Institute at Carnegie Mellon University, submitting their systems to one or more assessments at increasing levels of maturity. The success of this drive is seen in the fact that India today has more SEI CMM Level 5 companies than any other country, including the United States.

In the third phase, the focus has shifted to instituting processes, metrics, and a framework for improvement in all areas of activity ranging from billing and collection and sales to HRD and after-sales support. Companies have attempted to achieve this by aligning their internal practices with the People CMM framework and by using the Six Sigma methodology[2] to reduce quality variations and by putting in place systems that ensure end-to-end quality in all company operations.

Somewhat more recent is the race by ITES/BPO operators to acquire COPC (Customer Operations Performance Centre) certification. Developed by a team of leading consumers of ITES such as American Express, Motorola, and Microsoft, the COPC certificate has become the de facto standard to which customer contact centers aspire. It assures clients that their call centre has a strong quality record and requires the call centre operator to comply with a set of 32 parameters in order to get COPC certification, including client satisfaction; end-user satisfaction; timeliness, quality and accuracy of responses; efficiency, speed, and productivity; telecommunications and computer infrastructure; HRD policies related to recruitment, training, and compensation; and other areas.

eSCM (e Services Capability Model), also developed at Carnegie Mellon University, is a system specifically designed to assess the capabilities of service providers to clients in the ITES/BPO sector even as it guides the service providers by specifying practices to be implemented and institutionalized. A growing number of Indian BPO companies are also working to acquire eSCM certification.

The apparent obsession with attaining progressively higher and more stringent quality certifications played an important role in changing perceptions of Brand India in IT from low cost/ good value to high quality/

high value. To give a further boost to the process, the Ministry of Information Technology has entered into licensing arrangements with Carnegie Mellon University so that the Standardization, Testing and Quality Certification (STQC) Directorate in the ministry can undertake the task of certification, testing and training of trainers and assessors in India. The directorate also publishes a list of certificate issuing authorities for SEI CMM Level 2 and above, while the Ministry of Commerce provides specific recognition to key certifying organizations under its EXIM policy (NASSCOM 2004).

Security

In an environment marked by periodic attacks on data by computer viruses, hackers, and even terrorist groups and the ever-present fear of data loss through unscrupulous individuals or data destruction on account of natural disasters, the issue of information security and data privacy is becoming increasingly important among large corporations and global organizations. These concerns have gained particular importance with the offshoring of services, as sensitive information related to financial, medical, insurance, or personal aspects gets handled and processed by service providers in remote locations.

International customers therefore require service providers to put increasingly stringent information security measures in place as a precondition to signing a contract, as a breach in information security could have serious financial and legal implications for the client. NASSCOM and leading Indian companies have taken the lead in accepting stringent security requirements as a prerequisite and worked toward putting in place robust systems that not only reassure their clients but also counter some of the backlash against offshoring that centers its arguments on data privacy issues.

At the federal level, the government has also played an important role by putting in place forward-looking legislation that deals with information security and copyright issues. This comes in the form of the IT Act of 2000, which covers data security and cyber crimes, and the Indian Copyright Act, which provides protection to intellectual property and computer programs. In addition, the STQC Directorate has launched an independent, third-party certification scheme for Information Security Management Systems, and the Indian Computer Emergency Response Team (CERT) has been set up to deal with virus and other information security threats.

Conclusion

India has clearly emerged as a winner from the offshore outsourcing of services. Developing countries such as India tend to benefit on account of low wage costs that accompany the skill set that they offer. Wage costs in India's IT sector, however, are rising at around 15 percent annually, and it is inevitable that some of the lower-end work will gradually migrate to cheaper destinations even as Indian companies progressively move up the value chain. But as various reputed studies have shown, the developed countries, too, are winners as they reap the benefits of higher productivity, corporate savings, and repatriated profits. At the same time, they do face the challenge of upgrading the skill levels of workers and putting in place systems that provide retraining and soften the impact of job loss on workers whose jobs are offshored.

India's success in creating a strong ITES/BPO sector has encouraged several other developing countries with low wage costs and a reasonable pool of skilled manpower to try and emulate India's example. Some have enjoyed limited success. But a number of others have been unable to make significant gains because of poor telecommunications and power infrastructure, absence of an adequate domestic legal environment and of supporting services in fields such as banking, insurance, accountancy, and due to a continued perception in developed countries that quality would suffer or that vital data would be at risk.

For India, the ITES-BPO boom has opened unexpected avenues for growth and there is sometimes a temptation to see it as some kind of panacea and to gloss over many of the serious development issues that confront the country. Offshoring of services to India is *not* going to solve the problems of poor infrastructure, inadequate primary and secondary education, severe rural unemployment and underemployment, dismal access to healthcare facilities for the underprivileged, and other similarly daunting problems. Each of these issues requires a separate and specific solution.

Nevertheless, the robust performance of the IT-ITES sector has clearly contributed to India's accelerated economic growth and to the palpable sense of optimism that presently pervades several sectors of the economy. GDP has grown at 8 percent per year in the last four years, and most analysts expect a further acceleration of 9–10 percent in the coming years. In purchasing-power-parity terms, India overtook Germany in 2005 to become the world's fourth largest economy behind the United States, China, and Japan. Poverty is declining in relative as well as absolute terms, and the sense of confidence and optimism that permeates a significant section of the urban Indian landscape today has created a growth momentum that will have a profound impact on international geopolitics in the years to come.

A nation that accounts for over one-sixth of the world's population is coming out of two centuries of slumber induced by colonial rule to reclaim a status that it had enjoyed in the global economy for over two thousand years. And when economic historians record this reemergence of India, they may well be tempted to look at the country's success in the IT-ITES sector during the last decade as one of the key elements in the process.

Notes

* The views expressed in this chapter are personal and do not represent the position of the Government of India.

1. The Software Engineering Institute (SEI) was established in 1984 at the Carnegie Mellon University with funding from the U.S. government. The Capability Maturity Model for Software (CMM) of SEI is a framework that describes the key elements of an effective software process, tracking the progression from an ad hoc, immature process to a mature, disciplined process covering practices pertaining to planning, engineering and managing software development and maintenance. It reflects five maturity levels, with each level providing a layer in the foundation for continuous process improvement. Achieving each level of the maturity model institutionalizes a different component in the process, resulting in an overall increase in the process capability of the organization.
2. Six Sigma is both a management practice and a capability measure and offers a relatively faster route to maturity in a nascent industry like the ITES/BPO sector. It provides companies with a robust metrics system for measuring, tracking and managing the business and progressively reducing the level of its faults tolerance.

CHAPTER ELEVEN

OFFSHORE OUTSOURCING AND INDUSTRIAL RESTRUCTURING: NEW EUROPE'S SUCCESS

*Bartlomiej Kaminski**

Introduction

The reintegration of former centrally planned economies into global markets and their accession to the European Union (EU) offer a unique vantage point to study the impact of North-South deep integration on industrial restructuring. The accession process meant that Central Europe (hereafter CEEC-10 or New Europe) became like an EU member in terms of policies and integration, and that it had unfettered access to the EU single market for industrial products.[1] In that context, transnational corporations (TNCs) were eager to incorporate CEEC-10's industrial production into their global value chains, a process that revamped these countries' industrial landscape and turned them into internationally competitive economies. As a result, the CEEC-10's share in world trade rose from 1.9 percent in 1994 to 3.2 percent in 2003.

In this chapter, I assess the scope and impact of offshore outsourcing on industrial restructuring of the economies of the CEEC-10 as revealed in their trade performance. The analysis is based on an eclectic approach using firm surveys and a production and distribution network analysis of foreign trade data (developed in Kaminski and Ng 2001 and 2005). The major findings can be summarized as follows: First, the type of offshore outsourcing to CEEC-10 has evolved significantly over time, shifting from subcontracting and "nonequity"-based networks to offshore outsourcing driven by "equity-based" production networks. Countries that attracted significant FDI (foreign direct investment) inflows earlier moved faster toward integration into global markets based on participation in "equity-based" production networks. Second, the analysis shows that offshore outsourcing to

New Europe has contributed significantly to industrial restructuring and the emergence of internationally competitive industries. Many capital- and technology-intensive industries would have been condemned to extinction or stagnation, had it not been for FDI. In contrast to many developing countries, offshore outsourcing did not create enclaves in the CEEC-10. Rather, it fostered the development of backward linkages, technology transfer, and competitiveness. Last but not least, the analysis underscores the importance of the quality of governance and unrestrained access to larger markets for maximizing FDI inflows and positive spillovers to the host economy. The EU accession process has been a critical force behind the shift from market-seeking, horizontal investments to efficiency-seeking investments incorporating the CEEC-10 into global production networks. Cost advantages rather than access to protected domestic markets have become the major motivation for foreign investors.

From Outsourcing to Offshore Outsourcing: Participation in Global Production and Distribution Networks

Using foreign trade data to determine the scope of offshore outsourcing suffers from two major shortcomings: information is limited to foreign trade activities and it is difficult, if not impossible, to link trade data to particular firms.[2] Kaminski and Ng (2001 and 2005) have developed a taxonomy that allows us to identify at least some goods flows that can be attributed to global production and distribution networks. Outsourcing and offshoring drives trade within these networks, which can usefully be linked to Gereffi's (1999) dichotomy of buyer-driven and producer-driven commodity chains or networks.

Both types of networks represent a different mode of participation in the global division of labor, in terms of factor content and intensity of external links. TNCs in producer-driven chains often belong to global oligopolies, where there are only a handful of competitors, while buyer-driven commodity chains are characterized by highly competitive, locally owned, and globally dispersed production systems (Gereffi, 1999, 43). Buyer-driven networks tend to exist in industries in which large retailers, branded marketers, and branded manufacturers play the key role in setting up decentralized production networks worldwide. Such networks are prevalent in labor-intensive, consumer goods sectors, such as apparel, footwear, and furniture. Their products are finished goods made to the specifications of a foreign buyer. Buyer-driven networks involve largely nonequity links, that is, subcontracting and alliances, with profits coming from a combination of high-value research, design, sales, marketing, and financial services, and not from scale, volume, and technological advantage, as in producer-driven networks.

Producer-driven networks refer to vertically integrated arrangements, that is, ownership of successive stages of production by one corporate entity, thus necessitating FDI inflows. In producer-driven supply networks, the production process tends to be highly fragmented and increasingly spread across borders. Such networks, coordinated by large multinational corporations, are mainly present in capital- and skilled labor–intensive industries such as automobiles, computers, semiconductors, and heavy machinery. The link between FDI and network trade seems to be ever-present for producer-driven networks. The weight of the two networks in CEEC-10 exports has shifted from buyer-driven to producer-driven networks in the course of the last decade.

While the networks identified below for trade analysis clearly do not cover all outsourcing and offshore arrangements, their exports account for a significant and growing share of manufactured exports. Exports of both networks grew at an average annual rate of 18 percent during 1995–2004, with their aggregate share in exports of manufactures (excluding chemicals) rising from 32 percent in 1995 to 46 percent in 2004. Hence, conclusions from the trade analysis provide important insights into industrial restructuring and its driving forces in New Europe after the collapse of central planning.

'Buyer-Driven' Networks: Move to Higher-Value-Added Products

Clothing and furniture, representative of the buyer-driven network, tend to be owned by local producers who operate, in a global value chain supplying products according to specifications provided by large multinational retailers.[3] But while the apparel value chain often involves only the use of local unskilled labor and simple cut-make-trim operations for fabrics supplied by buyers, the furniture network is more diversified and complex requiring a larger local input of skills and investment in capital assets.

During the initial stages of the transition clothing was the most important driver behind the growth of industrial products. But this did not last long. Except for Bulgaria until 2001 and Lithuania and Romania until 1999, clothing exports lost their growth momentum in the other CEEC-10 before 1995 (see table 11.1). As wages were rising, many of the offshoring operations in the clothing sector shifted to economies less advanced in the transformation process in order to take advantage of lower labor costs.

In contrast to the apparel value chain, the furniture network is less sensitive to a rise in labor costs and creates more opportunities for knowledge

Table 11.1 Developments in Buyer-Driven Network Exports: Clothing and Furniture, 1995–2003

		Clothing network			Furniture network			Parts in furniture network exports	
	Peak year	Share in peak year	Share in 2003	Average growth in 1995–2003	Share in 1995	Share in 2003	Average growth in 1995–2003	1995	2003
Bulgaria	2001	37.7	31.2	5.1	1.7	3.1	18.0	14	23
Czech R.	1993	7.4	2.0	−11.1	2.6	3.1	13.3	37	69
Estonia	1993	27.5	7.0	−10.5	6.7	8.1	17.8	23	46
Hungary	1992	20.8	3.1	−15.8	3.3	2.4	15.2	41	77
Latvia	1994	22.7	14.6	−1.5	7.0	8.9	13.4	38	38
Lithuania	1999	34.8	19.3	−4.0	3.9	9.2	24.8	10	28
Poland	1993	21.4	4.3	−15.4	9.2	9.7	11.4	11	32
Romania	1999	37.1	29.5	0.7	9.7	5.8	4.5	3	17
Slovak R.	1994	8.9	3.3	−8.7	3.3	4.8	17.3	13	25
Slovenia	1992	15.6	3.7	−12.2	6.9	9.0	7.6	46	68

Note: Respective shares of network exports in total exports of manufactured goods excluding chemicals. For SITC items included in both networks, see Kaminski and Ng (2005).

Source: Computations based on world import data from UN COMTRADE Statistics.

transfer and productivity spillovers, with multinationals often providing assistance in technology development, production management, and personnel training (Javorcik 2004). Because of the greater complexity of the tasks involved, the relationship between a supplier and the multinational retailer tends to be based on a more long-term mutual commitment. In addition, skills acquired in this way can be used to specialize in activities beyond simple assembly operations; for instance, in the production of specialized parts or higher-value-added furniture. Indeed, the emergence of parts as the main driver of this industry's growth indicates significant progress in industrial restructuring and the ability of producers to enter higher levels of the furniture value chain (see the last columns in table 11.1).[4]

Dynamics of Trade in Producer-Driven Networks

Over the last two decades, the increasing fragmentation of production has resulted in the disappearance or dramatic restructuring of global and vertically integrated firms and in the emergence of vertically integrated firms connected through complex and borderless supply chains. The automotive and electrical industries have developed the most elaborate global production and distribution networks (Szanyi 2004). Here I focus on the participation of the CEEC-10 in two producer-driven networks: the automotive network and the IT network. The components and parts identified in the networks belong only to the first tier of a supply chain. If lower tiers could be identified and included as well, the total reach of network trade would undoubtedly be much larger.

CEEC-10 exports from producer-driven networks have been sizeable and growing, and since 1997 they have been much larger than exports from buyer-driven networks. Exports from producer-driven networks grew at an average rate of 27 percent, and imports increased at 14 percent per year in 1995–2003. Their share in total manufactured exports increased from 14 percent in 1995 to 33 percent in 2003.

Three features of producer-driven network trade in the CEEC-10 stand out. First, New Europe moved from a position of net importer to that of net exporter indicating gradual change in their export specialization. Total networks' exports in terms of their imports increased from 56 percent in 1995 to 79 percent in 1999 and 99 percent in 2002. But in 2003 exports rose to $56 billion, 37 percent above the value of imports.

Second, in line with world trends, trade related to the IT network expanded faster than that linked to the automotive network. The share of IT exports in producer-driven networks increased from 24 percent in 1995 to 38 percent in 2003, and its share in imports from 47 percent to 63 percent, respectively. Third, the dynamics of this trade were spectacular by world standards. The share of the CEEC-10 in world exports of IT products and parts increased from 0.3 percent in 1995 to 2.4 percent in 2003, and in imports from 1 percent to 2.1 percent. Their share in world automotive exports grew from 1.2 percent to 3.9 percent, and in imports from 1.9 percent to 3.4 percent.

Links between Producer-Driven Networks and Offshore Outsourcing

Empirical evidence points to a powerful link between the stock of FDI in manufacturing and exports from producer-driven networks, as demonstrated by trade and FDI in the CEEC-10. Countries with larger FDI stocks in manufacturing tend to specialize and export more producer-driven network products than countries with a lower FDI stock in manufacturing. In 2003, the correlation coefficient between the FDI stock in manufacturing and network-linked exports (both per capita) was 88 percent. Hungary, followed by the Czech Republic, had both the largest FDI stock per capita and the largest network-linked exports per capita (accounting for more than half of the network-linked exports of the CEEC-10), while Bulgaria and Latvia scored the lowest on both counts (see table 11.2). In 1995, the share of network products in manufactured exports exceeded 25 percent only for Estonia. But eight years later, this share was larger than 25 percent for four other countries—the Czech Republic (34.4 percent), Hungary (53.8 percent), Poland (26.2 percent), and Slovakia (40.5 percent).

Over the last ten to fifteen years, the variation across CEEC-10 economies has been falling, both in terms of the share of exports from producer-driven network exports and FDI inflows. The CEEC-10 economies have been moving in a geese-like pattern, following the earliest leader—Hungary (Damijan and Rojec 2004). Between 1995 and 2003, the simple average of the shares of exports from producer-driven networks in total exports increased from 20 percent to 24 percent, with the coefficient of variation falling from 73 percent to 66 percent. The growing export specialization in producer-driven network products and parts has been accompanied by a growing alignment between CEEC-10 shares in FDI inflows and their respective shares in regional GDP.[5]

Country- and industry-specific studies provide ample evidence of the role of offshore outsourcing in setting up producer-driven networks in New Europe. Developments in the automotive sector show that without TNCs' involvement local firms would have been doomed to failure. The companies taken over by TNCs not only survived but prospered, with the Czech

Table 11.2 FDI Stock in Manufacturing and Exports from Producer-Driven Networks, 2003

	FDI per capita in manufacturing (US$)	Network exports per capita (US$)	Percentage of network exports in manufactured exports (excluding chemicals)			Value of total network exports	
						Index 1999	Index 2003
	2003	2003	1995	1999	2003	1995 = 100	1999 = 100
Bulgaria	428	22	7.6	4.9	3.9	61	183
Czech R.	1,338	1,391	15.5	24.3	34.4	217	267
Estonia	548	844	25.1	27.8	29.9	197	224
Hungary	1,694	1,847	18.1	52.2	53.8	814	180
Latvia	230	32	10.9	3.3	4.9	39	261
Lithuania	314	220	18.5	13.8	19.1	104	337
Poland	547	275	11.9	19.5	26.2	219	278
Romania	262	59	4.1	5.7	9.7	164	372
Slovakia	624	1,339	11.2	30.5	40.5	362	305
Slovenia	824	1,094	19.7	21.5	22.0	112	147

Source: Trade figures—UN COMTRADE Statistics. FDI figures—cumulative net FDI inflows 1990–2003 calculated based on data from IMF International Financial Statistics combined with information on the shares of FDI in the manufacturing sector taken from various national sources.

Republic, Hungary, Poland, and Slovakia emerging as regional powerhouses (Meyer 2000; Richet 2004). Similarly, firms such as Nokia, Thomson, Siemens, Philips, IBM, General Electric, and their suppliers are present in all countries that attracted sizable FDI inflows and were successful in developing the IT sector.

The major motivation for offshore outsourcing by TNCs in these producer-driven networks has been the search for lower costs (efficiency-seeking FDI). In the aftermath of the collapse of central planning, market-seeking was the dominant motive for FDI in the industrial sectors.[6] But subsequently, efficiency-seeking FDI became more important. In contrast to market-seeking FDI, efficiency-seeking FDI does not substitute for trade but stimulates it, as corroborated by the trade performance of those CEEC-10 countries that have been most involved in producer-driven network trade. Beginning with the "Big Privatization" of 1995 in Hungary, market-seeking investments focused mainly on services in the second half of the 1990s, whereas investments in manufacturing were increasingly efficiency-seeking. That is true for the other CEEC-10 economies as well, due to the progressive opening of their economies and their integration into EU-designed structures.

Concluding Observation

Offshore outsourcing, mainly by TNCs located in the EU, has had a dramatic impact on the trade patterns of the CEEC-10 and their mode of integrating into global markets. Thanks first to offshoring in buyer-driven networks and then in producer-driven networks, New Europe has moved from interindustry trade, characteristic of the central planning era, to intraindustry and intraproduct trade. Offshoring has been instrumental in incorporating several New European economies into a new global division of labor based on production fragmentation (Kierzkowski 2001). Countries with a larger stock of FDI in manufacturing have also been more involved in producer-driven network trade, which has contributed to expanding exports.

Offshore Outsourcing: Impact on the CEEC-10

A review of the extensive literature on FDI in the CEEC-10 economies during the transition years is beyond the scope of this chapter. It is important to note though that—contrary to initial concerns—firms with FDI triggered only a temporary worsening of the balance of trade and subsequently contributed to expanding exports. And after the initial shedding of labor, firms with FDI increased output, productivity and employment, as shown by panel data of Hungarian firms (Kaminski and Riboud 2000). Some studies found no positive horizontal spillovers from FDI, but they did not find evidence of negative horizontal spillover either.[7] Horizontal effects may be unlikely to develop simply because firms with FDI do not benefit from transferring knowledge to their competitors. And knowledge spillovers within an industry from demonstration effect may be counterbalanced by the competition effect, as domestic firms experience lower productivity with the fall in production volumes exacerbating their fixed costs.[8] Much more likely and important are vertical effects, or backward linkages.

But as Saggi (2002, 353) has pointed out, "the notion of vertical technology transfer has not received adequate attention from economists."[9] There is at least one exception discussing the experience of a transition economy. Using firm-level panel data, Javorcik (2004) shows that the productivity of Lithuanian firms is positively correlated with the extent of contacts with multinational customers.

Scope of Backward Linkages: Evidence from Trade Data

As argued earlier, insourcing through FDI has been instrumental in incorporating the CEEC-10 economies into the new global division of labor based on production fragmentation. Since the trade data indicate that countries that received the most FDI inflows also experienced the largest vertical integration into global production and distribution networks, it is important to analyze whether these FDI inflows generated backward linkages.

Import intensity, defined here as the share of imports of network-related parts in total network-related exports is one rough measure of the degree to which final goods producers create backward linkages. Together with information on the total exports of a network and its net external position, it allows us to assess the extent to which domestic inputs have replaced imports over time.

The indicators summarized in table 11.3 suggest significant expansion in the scope of backward linkages. Note that with the expansion of network exports, the dependence on imported parts appears to be falling. Import intensities of networks tend to decline suggesting an even stronger expansion in domestic sourcing; albeit not necessarily from locally owned firms. The available data suggest that the apparent shift toward local sourcing can be attributed to both the development of backward linkages with locally owned firms and to the phenomenon of "sequential investments," that is, major investors being followed by their suppliers.

Scope of Backward Linkages: Evidence from Surveys

International experience, confirmed by firm-level studies in Central Europe, suggests that foreign affiliates increase local sourcing over time,

Table 11.3 Trade Indicators of the Automotive Network and the Information Technology Network, 1995, 1999, and 2004

	Total exports (US$ million)			Exports as a percentage of imports	Import intensity		
	1995	1999	2003	2003	1995	1999	2003
3. A. Automotive Network							
Bulgaria	0	68	62	6	43	151	284
Czech Republic	1,966	4,631	9,049	164	44	35	36
Estonia	119	100	319	40	40	70	53
Hungary	737	4,979	7,928	123	56	53	47
Latvia	50	12	29	6	27	506	370
Lithuania	102	96	447	45	24	97	38
Poland	1,325	2,660	8,213	99	30	120	42
Romania	203	206	753	54	35	93	66
Slovak Republic	546	2,031	6,365	164	74	51	44
Slovenia	1,161	1,329	1,899	101	35	50	42
3. B. Information Technology Network							
Bulgaria	0	27	112	18	124	315	194
Czech Republic	485	691	5,144	85	150	123	56
Estonia	138	409	820	89	117	66	54
Hungary	540	5,414	10,760	125	82	59	50
Latvia	23	16	45	14	136	378	191
Lithuania	115	129	313	60	45	59	49
Poland	405	1,126	2,306	45	168	110	90
Romania	14	148	567	34	2124	225	121
Slovak Republic	108	333	840	58	191	104	85
Slovenia	139	129	250	38	108	118	91

Source: Calculated from UN COMTRADE data base.

although they purchase locally a lower share of their inputs than domestic firms (UNCTAD 2000, 134). In Hungary, the share of domestically owned firms in supplies of material inputs to foreign-owned firms rose from 16 percent in 1997 to 21 percent in 1998. In Poland, a survey of some 30 foreign affiliates in 1997 found that three quarters of their inputs were sourced from local firms, compared to 65 percent at the time of their establishment in the early 1990s. In the Czech Republic, Volkswagen-Skoda was sourcing roughly three-quarters of its inputs from domestic suppliers in the mid-1990s. Of Skoda's 279 registered suppliers, 174 (62 percent) were Czech-owned, 19 were Slovak-owned, and 86 were foreign affiliates and joint ventures with firms from the United States, the United Kingdom,

Germany, Italy, and France. Volkswagen Slovakia has been successful at increasing its sourcing from firms operating in the country, though not all of them are locally owned. While Volkswagen Slovakia had only 4 direct and 9 indirect domestic suppliers in 1997, the numbers increased to 30 and 35, respectively, in 2000, with the value of inputs sourced locally rising 36 times during this period (Javorcik and Kaminski 2004).

A 2003 World Bank study of 119 majority-owned foreign subsidiaries across manufacturing sectors in the Czech Republic sheds additional light on the sourcing patterns and decision-making processes of multinationals. The results suggest that TNCs are actively engaged in local sourcing in the Czech Republic. Ninety percent of respondents reported purchasing inputs from at least one Czech company.[10] The median multinational in the sample had a sourcing relationship with ten Czech suppliers, while a TNC in the top quartile of TNCs sourced from at least thirty local suppliers. Czech companies were the most important supplier group followed by other European suppliers (located in the EU-15 or Central Europe) and then by other TNCs operating in the Czech Republic (Javorcik and Kaminski 2006b). Responding to a question about the current share of inputs purchased from each type of supplier (in terms of value), TNCs indicated sourcing on average 48.3 percent of inputs from Czech enterprises, as compared to 33.3 and 12.6 percent from firms in the European Union/Eastern Europe and multinationals located in the Czech Republic, respectively.

"Sequential Investments" and Backward Linkages

Efficiency-seeking foreign investors in the CEEC-10 have not only increasingly incorporated domestic firms into their supply chains, but have also induced "sequential investments," as developments in the automotive sector illustrate. The entry of large automotive producers has acted as a magnet prompting supplying firms to either relocate or establish production facilities locally without closing down respective capacities in their countries of origin. The most compelling example is the case of the automotive sector in the Czech Republic and Slovakia. Volkswagen Slovakia has attracted many foreign investors stimulating domestic production of electrical equipment, machinery, metallurgical products, and industrial chemicals. SAS Automotive, a fully owned subsidiary of SAS Autosystemtechnik GmbH (a joint-venture of Siemens Automotive and Sommer Allibert Industrie AG), established production facilities in Bratislava in 2000. It is closely integrated with Volkswagen supplying the German manufacturer with completely assembled cockpits consisting of dashboards, electronic components, air-conditioning, airbags, steering rods, and pedals (Javorcik and Kaminski 2004). The $2.6 billion VW investment in Skoda Auto in the

Czech Republic, following the 1991 privatization, has attracted both other global car producers (PSA Peugeot and Toyota) and large international firms specializing in automotive parts and components. They established in-country production through the purchase and modernization of local firms or through greenfield investments. More than half of the top 100 world suppliers of automotive parts and components are currently producing in the Czech Republic and Slovakia.[11]

Geographic proximity to Germany, Hungary, and Slovakia meant that auto-part producers operating in the Czech Republic became suppliers to auto manufacturers in many European countries. The proximity and links to the German car industry also explain the dominance of German-based firms in the sector. Brand name companies in automotive components, such as Robert Bosch and Siemens, continue to expand their activities not only in the Czech Republic and Slovakia but also in Poland and Romania. Firms from other EU countries have been following suit, especially from Italy and France, as well as from other countries, including the United States, Canada, the Republic of Korea and, more recently, Japan.

FDI and the Factor Content of Exports

In New Europe, firms with FDI not only outperformed locally owned firms but also displayed a much stronger export orientation. Hungary, which experienced the strongest growth in producer-driven exports among the CEEC-10 during the 1990s, is a good example. Based on a survey of 125 studies of privatization, Djankov and Murrell (2000) concluded that privatizations to foreign investors have produced the best managed and most internationally competitive firms. In contrast, mass privatization schemes led to the worst results in terms of restructuring previously state-owned firms. Hungary, a country with the largest share of producer-driven network trade, relied on privatization to outsiders, mainly foreign investors. Foreign-owned firms already accounted for more than 50 percent of total exports in 1994 (Kaminski and Riboud 2000).

Javorcik and Kaminski (2006a) show that countries that had a larger FDI stock per capita in manufacturing also had a higher share of skilled labor and capital-intensive products in total exports. The correlation coefficient between the two variables was 84 percent. Ultimately, the driving force behind the decision to insource, embedded in FDI, was to take better advantage of resources available locally. This resource has been relatively cheap skilled labor (Marin 2004), and the outcome has been the gain of a competitive advantage in products using skilled labor in combination with TNCs' capital and technology.

Concluding Observation

Foreign-owned firms have increasingly shaped New Europe's trade patterns. They tend to be export-oriented, have increasingly employed skilled labor, and have engaged in capital-intensive activities in most CEEC-10 countries. These are critical factors in being able to move up the technology level and catch up with the more developed countries of the EU (Welfens and Borbly 2006).

The Importance of the EU Factor for FDI in the CEEC-10

There is widespread agreement in the literature that North-North FDI flows generate welfare effects. But some of these benefits may fail to materialize in North-South FDI flows, that is, in developing countries. Two sets of factors are usually responsible for such failure. First, ill-founded policies to attract foreign investment may wipe out the positive effect of FDI on real income. Excessive indirect subsidies (protection) or direct subsidies (tax holidays, project-specific investment in infrastructure) to foreign firms may raise the domestic price well above the international price. Second, indirect benefits (vertical and horizontal spillovers) may be weak or nonexistent, if domestic firms are unable to take advantage of new opportunities. Lall (1992) links significant positive spillovers to the availability of local skills and technological prowess to adapt techniques used elsewhere.

The EU factor, which denotes institutional and policy constraints imposed by the EU accession process, combined with the Pan-European Agreement on Cumulation of Rules of Origin, first reduced and subsequently eliminated the discretion of CEEC-10 governments to resort to excessive indirect and direct subsidies.[12] The EU factor has produced the best effects of a North-South type of regional integration. It has provided the template for domestic and external liberalization. And it has created a huge market for industrial products, linking the CEEC-10 not only with the EU-15, but also among themselves and with other European countries. In consequence, access to any national market was tantamount to access to 29 national markets. Duty-free access to the future EU-25 and several other European economies combined with the policy framework allowing unfettered distribution of production capacities in the territory of each signatory of the Pan-European Agreement has created a very attractive environment for TNCs, since multinationals do not have to worry about meeting usually very cumbersome rules of origin requirements.

Furthermore, CEEC-10 endowments in skilled labor and the quality of their infrastructure were well above the levels implied by the countries' relatively low levels of GDP per capita.[13] This has resulted in a much greater capacity to absorb imported technologies, especially considering the large pool of relatively highly educated labor. Lall's condition for the development of backward linkages, that is, the availability of local skills and technological prowess to adapt sophisticated techniques, was met in the CEEC-10.

New Europe was uniquely positioned to emerge as a clear winner from offshore outsourcing. In addition to its endowment in highly skilled and disciplined labor and proximity to the EU, the CEEC-10 benefited greatly from the EU factor. The EU accession process has created a business-friendly environment for foreign and domestic investors alike. The emergence of a pan-European free-trade area for industrial products in the second half of the 1990s has had a positive impact on the scope and quality of offshore outsourcing by TNCs, as they were searching for cost reductions.

Conclusion

Offshore outsourcing driven by FDI has been responsible for the integration of firms located in the CEEC-10 into global networks with growing intensity in skilled labor, capital, and R&D. FDI has helped to close the gap that had emerged during the initial transition period between endowments in high-skilled labor and the large share of unskilled labor-intensive products in exports. Earlier recipients of FDI witnessed the disappearance of this dissonance faster than slow reformers. The factor content of CEEC-10 exports has been moving toward skilled labor and capital-intensive products.

New Europe's success did not come at the expense of their major source of offshore outsourcing, the EU-15. On the contrary, offshore outsourcing has been a positive-sum game. In 2002, the year before the first wave of the EU's enlargement to the east, the EU-15 imported $147 billion from the CEEC-10 (67 percent of those countries' exports) and exported around $149 billion to them. Since the collapse of central planning, CEEC-10 trade has risen at double digit rates. The empirical research based on disaggregated data also suggests that relocation of manufacturing and service activities from the EU-15 to New Europe has been limited and has not contributed to unemployment in the EU-15 (Hunya and Sass 2005, Marin 2004, Stefanova 2006).

Offshore outsourcing has not created enclaves within the CEEC-10 economies. On the contrary, backward linkages have grown substantially. So has the presence of input-supplying TNCs. Last but not least, the EU-factor has been largely responsible for changes in the domestic business climate and for the favorable conditions of access to New Europe's most important markets. Taken together, these factors have boosted offshore outsourcing and their positive welfare effects. Over time, the motives behind foreign investment inflows have shifted from market-seeking and privatization-driven FDI to efficiency-seeking FDI, including its higher stage of more complex net-work-type integrated investments. The pace of moving to more complex forms of integration has depended on the scope of reforms, attitudes to foreign capital, and the chosen mode of privatization.

Notes

* The author is grateful to Eva Paus for constructive comments on an earlier version of this paper. The usual caveats apply.

1. They include new members of the EU—Czech Republic, Estonia, Hungary, Latvia, Lithuania, Poland, Slovak Republic, Slovenia—as well as Bulgaria and Romania which acceded to the EU on January 1, 2007.
2. Statistics are directly available, but only for a very specific form of subcontracting-outward processing referred to in the U.S. as "production sharing" and in the UK as "jobbing contract."
3. Although participation in furniture or clothing global chains does not necessarily require foreign investment, it is often associated with FDI. A good example is Romania's clothing sector, which is characterized by much higher foreign penetration than in other CEEC-10 (Hunya 2002, 391). A large number of small Italian firms appear to dominate both clothing and leather industries in Romania (Kaminski and Ng 2004).
4. There were only three exceptions to this trend: Hungarian and Romanian exports of furniture network products and parts lagged behind the growth of other manufactures; and the share of parts in network exports of Latvia did not change between 1995 and 2003.
5. The CEEC-10 laggards have been catching up with radical reformers (Hungary), and, as a result, there has been a growing convergence in terms of quality of governance and the progress in establishing competition-supporting institutions (Javorcik and Kaminski 2006b).
6. See Lankes and Venables (1996) and Lankes and Stern (1998).
7. See for instance Djankov and Murrell (2000) on the Czech Republic, Zukowska-Gagelmann (2000) on Poland, and Konings (2001) on Bulgaria, Romania, and Poland.
8. Indeed, according to the 2003 World Bank surveys designed to identify effects of horizontal spillovers, 48 percent of Czech respondents and 30 percent of Latvian firms pointed to increased competition in their sectors due to the presence of foreign-owned companies, with 29 percent in both countries complaining about the loss of market share. On the other hand, 24 percent of Czech firms and 15 percent of Latvian firms pointed to exposure to information about new technologies—an indication of a demonstration effect (see Javorcik and Kaminski 2006b).
9. Spillovers either take place through backward linkages, that is, contacts between domestic suppliers of intermediate inputs and their multinational clients, or through forward linkages arising from FDI output used as an input in other kinds of local production. For a theoretical discussion of spillovers through backward linkages, see Rodriguez-Clare (1996) and Markusen and Venables (1999); for case studies, see Moran (2001).

10. Note that the question specifically asked respondents not to include suppliers of services, such as catering or cleaning. For the review of the survey results see Javorcik and Kaminski (2006b).
11. For more details, see *The Auto Parts Market*, US & Foreign Commercial Service and U.S. Department of State, Washington, DC, 2002.
12. The so-called pan-European cumulation program—adopted by the EU Council in July 1996—linked 29 countries including the CEEC-10, Turkey and the European Economic Area (EU and EFTA) through a system of diagonal cumulation, which allows imports from these countries to be treated as local inputs. The Agreement, which went into effect on January 1, 1997, set the stage for the formation of a single European trading bloc as of January 1, 2002.
13. The share of the economically active population with secondary education was 66 percent in the CEEC-10, well above the average level of 47 percent in the "old" EU (EUROSTAT and World Development Indicators 2004).

CHAPTER TWELVE

THE IMPACT OF FOREIGN INVESTMENT ON CHINA'S INDUSTRIAL INNOVATION

*Gary H. Jefferson**

Introduction

Over the last two decades, China has received large inflows of foreign direct investment, and since 2000 (FDI), the country has emerged as the leading recipient of FDI. While FDI per capita in China is not substantially higher than for all of Southeast Asia, the sheer size of China's population has enabled the country to stand out as the world's leading FDI recipient.

If India is the developing country that has benefited most from offshore outsourcing of services, China is the country that has attracted large amounts of FDI linked to offshoring in the manufacturing sector. One consequence of the extensive FDI in China and the fact that its indigenous industrial technologies are relatively backward compared with overseas technologies is that foreign firms now account for over half of China's total exports and more than four-fifths of the country's high-tech exports (NBS 2005, 626, 642).

The large flows of FDI to China have provided well-established benefits to China's economy, including contributions to investment, employment, and exports. In addition, by serving as a conduit for foreign technology, FDI may generate technological spillovers and competition for domestic firms that motivate them to engage more aggressively in research and development leading both to imitation and innovation. As a result, an important consequence of outsourcing manufacturing through FDI may extend to stimulating R&D operations in China. That is, in addition to creating a stream of manufacturing exports back to the countries of FDI origin, FDI may also be leading to the outsourcing of research and development from the OECD countries to China. This chapter focuses on the extent to which FDI has advanced industrial innovation in China.

Much of the literature on China's science and technology system (S&T system) is divided over the issue of the respective roles of the domestic and foreign sectors in driving China's technological advance. George Gilboy (2004), for example, takes a decidedly skeptical view of the capabilities of China's domestic S&T system, characterizing China's domestically owned firms as hampered by.

> an "industrial strategic culture" that encourages them to seek short-term profits . . . (and) forego investment in long-term technology development and diffusion . . . . Most Chinese industrial firms . . . have not increased their commitment to developing new technologies . . . . R&D expenditure as a percentage of value added at China's industrial firms is only about one percent, seven times less than the average in countries of the OECD. (43).

Contrary to this proposition, I argue that while foreign-funded firms have substantially expanded the scope of R&D efforts in China, they have not been the key drivers of China's R&D intensity, at least not through their *direct* contribution. China's domestic industrial enterprises account for the large majority of R&D spending and patenting activity. In 2005, China's enterprise sector accounted for 62.3 percent of the nation's total R&D financing and 68.3 percent of total performed R&D. Among China's large and medium-sized industrial enterprises domestically owned enterprises accounted for nearly 75 percent of all R&D (NBS-MOST 2006, 7).

Nonetheless, technological and competitive spillovers from the foreign sector have played an important *indirect* role in the advancement of industrial innovation. They have motivated and facilitated domestic firms' ability to increase their R&D intensity and to patent their innovations. In addition, purchases of imported technology have contributed significantly to raising domestic firms' returns to R&D and hence to their demand for R&D resources.

FDI has also contributed greatly to the production of patentable technologies within the domestic enterprise sector. In 2005, 476,264 patent applications were filed with China's State Patenting Office. Among these, 127,397 applications were filed by the industrial enterprise sector.[1] From this perspective, FDI in China has gone beyond creating the enclave effect associated with the original special economic zones and has instead motivated domestic firms to deepen their R&D effort and technology performance, by expanding the supply of technological opportunity and competition. These FDI spillovers are contributing to innovative capabilities and to the prospect for dynamic technology development in China's domestic industrial enterprises.

Most of the research in this chapter is based on a panel of data that spans China's approximately 25,000 large and medium-sized enterprises and includes measures of foreign investment, R&D spending, patent activity, and other measures of technology activity that can be used to investigate the impact of FDI on China's innovative performance. In the following section, I review the role of FDI in China. Section 1 documents China's rising FDI and R&D intensity. Sections 2 and 3 investigate the impact of FDI on China's innovative performance, with section 2 focusing on FDI's direct contributions and section 3 on its indirect contributions. The important role of technology imports as complements to in-house R&D is examined in section 4. Section 5 describes the recent emergence of MNE research centers. Section 6 reviews the key conclusions of the chapter and examines the policy implications, both in China and in the United States, for FDI in the emerging pattern of R&D outsourcing that we observe in China.

*　*　*

China's Rising FDI and Innovation Intensity

FDI in China has grown dramatically over the past 25 years. Annual flows have remained above $40 billion since 1996, rising to $64 billion in 2004.[2] After having risen to more than 6 percent of GDP in 1994, FDI now accounts for approximately 4 percent of China's GDP. FDI has played a growing role in financing the investment in China's fixed assets (see table 12.1). The rise in the FDI share from only 3.6 percent in 1985 to 5.3 percent in 2004 disguises the nearly 24 percent annual growth of FDI over this period, nearly three times that of the economy as a whole.

Table 12.1　Foreign Direct Investment

Year	Total (billions of US $)	Percentage of total investment in fixed assets
1981	2.23	3.8
1985	3.16	3.6
1990	6.06	6.3
1995	27.66	11.2
2000	20.44	5.1
2002	25.12	4.6
2004	39.59	5.3

Note: Exchange rates (yuan: dollar): 1981 = 1.6, 1985 = 2.9, 1990 = 4.7, and 1995–2004 = 8.3.

Source: NBS (2005), p. 186.

FDI has played a critical role in the Chinese economy. In 2004, the 242,284 registered foreign-funded enterprises (FFEs)[3] accounted for 27.8 percent of total industrial value added, 57 percent of China's total exports (NBS 2005, pp. 626, 642), and about 85 percent of China's high-tech exports (Naughton 2007, Ch. 17). These data offer an unambiguous connection between the phenomena of FDI in China and the offshore out-sourcing of production by MNEs that are the source of the foreign invest-ment. Among the firms formally designated as "above size" (*guimo yishang*), that is firms with annual sales of more than 5 million Rmb (i.e., about $650,000), FFEs accounted for 24.6 percent of total industrial assets (NBS 2005, 493, 505).

To gauge China's growing R&D intensity, we compare its R&D trajec-tory with that of the large OECD economies. Among the seven large OECD economies with populations of over 40 million, the United States, Japan, the United Kingdom, Germany, France, Italy, and South Korea, all but Italy cur-rently have R&D ratios in the range of 2–3 percent (see figure 12.1). Singapore and Taiwan have recently made the transition from a low-intensity R&D country (R&D as a share of GDP is less than 1 percent) to a high-intensity R&D country, where the R&D ratio is greater than 2 percent. Each of these countries went through an "S&T takeoff," when their R&D ratios first rose to 1 percent and continued to climb until they leveled off in the 2–3 percent range. On average, the six OECD economies needed ten years for such an R&D transition.

China's R&D trajectory surpassed the 1 percent threshold in 2000; by 2005, its R&D intensity had risen to 1.4 percent.[4] But just because China's

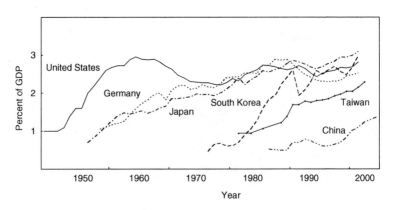

Figure 12.1   S&T Takeoff in Comparative and Historical Perspective
Source: Gao and Jefferson (forthcoming).

R&D intensity has risen well above 1 percent and continues to rise, we cannot infer that China is necessarily in the midst of an S&T takeoff that will soon elevate its level of R&D intensity to that of the large OECD economies. Nonetheless, Gao and Jefferson (forthcoming) argue that many of the conditions that are associated with S&T takeoff seem to have taken root in China's economy. These include the transition from the consumption of final goods that are low in technology content to those high in technology content, the accumulation of complements to R&D, such as education and IT investments that drive up the returns to R&D, access to the world's knowledge base, a lag in the wages of R&D workers behind their rising productivity, and market size.

Table 12.2 shows the change in R&D intensity among China's large and medium-sized industrial enterprises (LMEs) between 1999 and 2004. For

Table 12.2 R&D Intensity and Patent Applications by Ownership Type

	No. of firms		R&D/VA ratio		No. of patent applications	
	1999	2004	1999	2004	1999	2004
State-owned						
Population	11,184	4,537	3.68	5.39	3,099	4,672
Balanced sample	2,305	1,907	3.47	8.15	1,307	2,364
Collectively owned						
Population	3,408	1,320	1.74	1.64	1,776	1,288
Balanced sample	307	155	2.49	1.97	444	102
HMT (Hong Kong, Macao, and Taiwan)						
Population	1,567	4,202	4.59	1.67	469	4,929
Balanced sample	228	212	2.09	4.54	130	480
FOR (foreign)						
Population	1,966	4,697	3.03	2.49	465	9,091
Balanced sample	292	351	2.23	3.11	208	714
Shareholding						
Population	3,478	8,297	5.89	4.27	1,650	16,044
Balanced sample	425	1,080	3.39	6.43	374	5,242
Private						
Population	316	4,509	1.41	1.95	117	6,264
Balanced sample	12	164	0.23	3.85	0	324
Other domestic						
Population	149	47	3.82	3.07	26	15
Balanced sample	20	7	13.25	7.19	12	0
Total						
Population	22,068	27,609	3.7	3.25	7,602	42,303
Balanced sample	3,589	3,876	3.24	6.58	2,475	9,226

Source: National Bureau of Statistics, Large and medium-size industrial enterprise data set, 1999–2004.

the total population of LMEs, the ratio of R&D expenditure to value added declined during this period. By contrast, the balanced sample shows a doubling of R&D intensity. The balanced sample includes only those firms that reported in both 1999 and 2004, that is, those that survived for the duration of the period, though they may have changed ownership category. The difference is due to the fact that within the full population of LMEs, we see large numbers of new entrants whose R&D operations are small or nonexistent.[5] Nonetheless, in 2004, at 3.25 percent, the R&D intensity of the roughly 27,000 industrial enterprises was two to three times larger than China's overall R&D/GDP ratio of 1.3 percent in that year.

R&D spending and rising R&D intensity are, strictly speaking, but inputs to the innovation process. They do not guarantee that China-based firms will be successful innovators. To get a sense of the ability of China's industry to innovate, we examine patent applications filed with China's State Patent Office. China has witnessed a dramatic increase in patent applications over the last decade, from about 69,000 in 1995 to nearly 280,000 in 2004 (see figure 12.2). Over the same period, total patents granted also showed a significant increase, from under 42,000 to more than 150,000. In the next section, I investigate the respective roles of the domestic and foreign sectors in the growth of R&D and patent applications in China.

* * *

The Impact of FDI on Innovation Intensity: The Direct Contribution

Foreign direct investment may motivate industrial innovation through direct and indirect channels. First, foreign-funded firms may establish R&D operations that facilitate the application of established product lines, both to exploit China's supply of relatively abundant labor and to fit the tastes of China's emerging middle class. Through this channel, foreign-funded firms contribute directly to the total R&D effort.

To investigate the proposition that firms with FDI participation dominate R&D operations in China, we turn to our data set for China's industrial LMEs. Table 12.2 shows the contribution of different ownership types to innovative activity in China. The data compares R&D intensity and patent applications for 1999 and 2004 for each of seven different ownership types. FDI data are distributed across two types of firms. The first, listed as HMT refers to investment from Hong Kong, Macao, and Taiwan; the second category FOR refers to all other foreign investment, which principally originates from the OECD economies and South East Asia. The number of firms in both categories has increased considerably between 1999 and 2004.

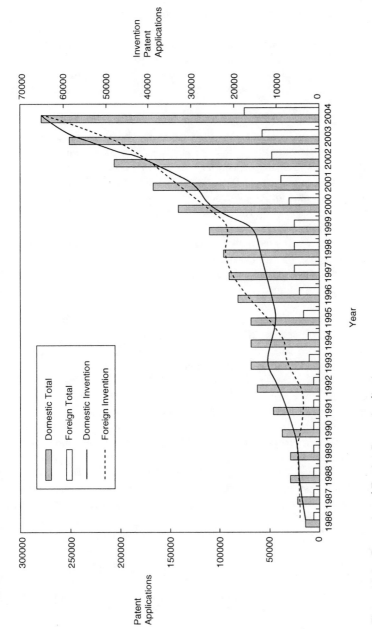

Figure 12.2 Domestic and Foreign Patent Applications

Source: Hu and Jefferson (2006).

As a result of the aggressive conversion programs of the late 1990s and early part of the present decade, the number of state-owned and collectively owned firms declined significantly. But the number of firms classified as "shareholding enterprises" (*gufenzhi chiye*), which may be either privately held or publicly traded firms, and "private enterprises" (*siying chiye*) has skyrocketed, reflecting in part the conversion of SOEs and COEs to new ownership types and in part the entry of new firms or graduation of small-sized firms to LME status.

The population of SOEs registered an increase in R&D intensity during the period under consideration. Given that the SOE restructuring program tended to liquidate or convert the smaller state-owned enterprises to non-SOE ownership status, it is not surprising that the declining number of SOEs tended to be larger in size and increase their R&D intensity. The only other ownership group for which the population exhibits an increase in its R&D intensity is private firms. This increase most likely reflects the exceptionally low R&D intensity of comparatively few firms that reported "private" status in 1999. During the following five years, the number of private firms exploded. While these new entries raised the overall R&D intensity of this ownership category, in 2004, the R&D intensity of private firms remained among the lowest of the LME population.

Both categories of foreign firms show a declining R&D intensity for the whole population of firms. Since both the FOR and HMT ownership categories experienced an increase in their populations of roughly 60 percent over this period, the decline in R&D intensity is most likely the result of the entry of newer and smaller FFEs. In 2004, the R&D intensities for both the FOR and the HMT firms are substantially less than those for the total LME population, which includes both types of these FDI firms.

We conclude from this examination of the performance of China's LMEs that although the FOR and HMT firms account for a substantial share of R&D, they have not led the way in the intensification of R&D spending in China. At the end of 2004, the highest R&D intensities were reported in the populations of SOEs (5.39 percent) and shareholding firms (4.27 percent). Both exhibited higher R&D intensities than the population of foreign-funded firms (2.49 percent).

FDI can also make substantial contributions to patenting activity. While patent applications arise from R&D activity for China's foreign and domestic firms alike, the FFEs may have a higher propensity to patent due to their familiarity with patenting procedures and their determination to secure intellectual property in the face of domestic competitors who wish to copy their innovations. Moreover, as shown in recent research, U.S. and European innovators have engaged in strategic competitive behavior whereby they seek patent protection for strategic reasons to create legal challenges for competitors with intellectual property that competes in similar product space (Jaffe and Lerner 2004). The presence of FFEs may also create spillovers that indirectly motivate patent activity among Chinese firms. Concentrations of FDI may enable domestic firms to generate innovations worthy of patenting, and moreover, like their foreign counterparts, domestic firms may seek to secure portfolios of patents for strategic competitive purposes. Thus, as with the impact of FFEs on R&D intensity, FFEs can also motivate greater patenting activity through both direct and indirect channels.

We find that the surge in total patents is more pronounced for domestic than for foreign applicants (see figure 12.2). However, China produces three patent types: invention, utility model, and design patents. Compared to utility model and design patents, invention patents must meet a somewhat higher standard of novelty and therefore receive protection for a longer duration than the other two types of patents, that is, fifteen years versus ten years. We saw earlier that domestic firms enjoy a substantial advantage in total patent applications. But with respect to invention patent applications, foreign and domestic firms have followed a similar trajectory, with roughly the same number of filings in 2004.

There was an increase in patenting applications by China's large and medium-size industrial enterprises across the board from 1999 to 2004 (see table 12.2). For the population of LMEs, patent applications rose nearly sixfold, while the balanced sample shows a 3.7-fold increase. Among the enterprises in each category in 2004, the patent applications per enterprise were 1.53 for the full population and 2.38 for the balanced sample. The highest ratio was 4.85 for the balanced sample of shareholding firms followed by the balanced samples for the HMT (2.26) and the FOR (2.03) firms. The large number of patent applications by shareholding firms most likely reflects the fact that this ownership category includes many of China's largest high-technology firms, such as Huawei, Bird of Ningbo, and TCL that file hundreds of patent applications every year.

In conclusion, foreign firms accounted for about 21.4 percent of total patent filings in 2004 and for about one-half of the higher-quality invention patent applications. In that same year, among China's subset of large and medium-size enterprises only, foreign-funded firms accounted for just under one-third of total LME patent applications. That the proportion of patents accounted for by the FFEs is larger in the LME data set is unsurprising, since the vast majority of FFEs qualify as large or medium-size

enterprises, whereas the small-scale enterprises that round out the population of China's industrial enterprises are nearly all domestically owned firms.

* * *

The Impact of FDI on Innovation Intensity:
The Indirect Impact

Foreign direct investment may elevate R&D intensity through two channels: either directly through the spending of FFEs on R&D or indirectly, by
inducing domestic firms to spend more extensively on R&D activity than
they would otherwise. As suggested earlier, such indirect inducements may
arise from the expanded technology opportunity and/or competition associated with high concentrations of FDI.

To test the hypothesis that FDI concentration in industries motivates
greater R&D intensity by China's domestic firms, we use the LME data to
estimate the impact of the growth of FDI concentration across 4-digit
industries on the growth of individual firm-level R&D intensity within
each of these industries. Our estimation results show that a 1 percentage
point increase in the share of FDI in the total assets of a 4-digit industry on
average motivates an increase of 0.06 percent in the R&D intensity of the
domestic firms residing within that industry. These results confirm our
intuition that new inflows of FDI into individual Chinese industries motivate domestic firms to intensify their R&D effort.

Gong and Jefferson (2007) corroborate these findings. Using a broader set
of data spanning China's 240,000 "above size" enterprises, they find that concentrations of foreign FDI at the 3-digit industry level are robustly associated
with both a higher probability of performing R&D intensity and with an
increase in R&D intensity. Breaking out their results by ownership type, they
find that China's state-owned and private firms both tend to intensify their
R&D effort in response to concentrations of industry investment from the foreign sector. By comparison, concentrations of HMT investment appear only
to motivate greater R&D intensity among collective firms.

A further result of the Gong-Jefferson study is that concentrations of both
types of industry-level FDI—FOR and HMT—tend to depress R&D intensity in foreign-funded firms and in firms with funds from Hong Kong, Macao,
or Taiwan. One possible explanation is that industries with high concentration
of FDI are industries in which technologies are relatively advanced or brand
recognition is important, for example, in the computer notebook industry. For
these products, typically consumer goods whose production is offshored, FFEs
concentrate their R&D work back in their home countries. When R&D is
employed by the FFEs in China, it is largely used to adapt the outsourced
products to local tastes or to more labor-intensive production methods.

In any case, available research strongly suggests that a key explanation for the higher R&D intensities of domestic SOEs and shareholding firms shown in table 12.2 are the spillover effects of high concentrations of FDI. In this sense, foreign investment may partially explain the increase in R&D intensity in China. Its avenue of impact, however, is not dominance of R&D spending by foreign-financed firms. Rather China's rising R&D intensification appears to arise significantly from concentrations of FDI that motivate domestic firms to increase their R&D effort.

Hu and Jefferson (2006) have conducted research on the causes of the surge in patent applications and grants in China since the late 1990s. They find that domestic firms and FFEs are comparably efficient in using their R&D resources to generate patent applications. Furthermore, concentrations of industry FDI substantially affect the propensity to patent. However, these spillovers to the propensity to patent are notably greater in the domestic sector than in the foreign sector. A 1 percent increase in the concentration of industry FDI induces an increase in the incidence of patent applications by 1.6 percent in the domestic sector while leading to a negligible increase in the foreign sector. This result indicates that the patenting behavior of domestic firms in China is highly responsive to concentrations of FDI in their technology neighborhood.

One interesting implication of the Hu-Jefferson finding is that a substantial portion of the patenting conducted by FFEs is associated neither with R&D spending nor with industry FDI spillovers. This high incidence of autonomous patenting may reflect an effort by FFEs to extend patent rights within China on innovations that had already been patented in other countries, particularly when it became clear that China intended to join the WTO and enacted legislation to strengthen its patent system in 1999. Such patents can be secured independent of further R&D expenditures or spillover effects associated with concentrations of FDI.

In conclusion, available research yields substantial evidence that China's domestic firms are highly responsive to concentrations of industry FDI. Both state-owned enterprises and private firms exhibit tendencies to increase their R&D effort when they operate within the context of high industry concentrations of FDI. FFEs do not exhibit similar tendencies. In the realm of patent applications, industry FDI seems to be a powerful motivator for domestic firms—and to a far lesser extent for FFEs—to initiate patent applications.

* * *

Role of Imported Technology Markets

The research reviewed in the previous section underscores the role of FDI in motivating China's domestic industrial firms to establish and intensify their

R&D operations. Another potential source of foreign technology in China is through imported technology. While we might expect that firms that take advantage of technological opportunities created by FDI would also find ways of exploiting the existence of markets in technology inputs, Gilboy (2004, 38) argues that "Chinese firms are taking few effective steps to absorb the technology they import and diffuse it throughout the local economy, making it unlikely they will rapidly emerge as global industrial competitors." To put these claims in perspective, table 12.3 shows the importance of technology purchases in relation to in-house innovation spending within China's industrial LME sector. Purchases of imported technology in 2000 amounted to 30 percent of total internal S&T expenditure, a measure of innovative activity that is somewhat broader than R&D but closely tracks R&D expenditure. While the proportion of purchased to in-house expenditures declined to 27.6 percent in 2003, purchases of imported technology still grew at an annual rate of 18 percent during 2000 to 2003.[6]

Hu and Jefferson (2006) document important complementarities between internal R&D and technology purchases, both imported and domestic. In particular, in-house R&D shares strong complementarities with technology imports, which enable domestic firms to capture higher returns on their own R&D spending.[7] Fisher-Vanden and Jefferson also find that domestic firms that combine in-house R&D with imported technology are more likely to be active exporters. Compared with imported technology, the purchase of domestic technology played a much smaller role at just 3.7 percent of total internal S&T expenditure in 2003.

How are technology purchases distributed over domestic and foreign firms? In 2001, 1,460 LMEs recorded purchases of imported technology, over 80 percent of them were domestically owned. Furthermore, the FFEs purchased almost nothing in China's domestic technology markets. Thus, in contrast to Gilboy's claim, domestic firms are far more active participants in both the imported and domestic technology markets than their foreign

Table 12.3 LMEs' Spending in Technology Markets (billion yuan)

	2000	2003	Annual growth percentage
Internal S&T expenditure	82.4	146.8	21.2
Purchase of imported technology	24.5 (29.7%)	40.5 (27.6%)	18.2
Purchase of domestic technology	2.6 (3.2%)	5.4 (3.7%)	27.6

Note: Figure in parentheses is proportion of total internal S&T expenditures.

Source: NBS-MOST (2004), pp. 142, 149; NBS-MOST (2001).

counterparts. While the FFEs in our sample may transfer technology from their parent companies, they are substantially less connected with technology markets than their domestic counterparts. By creating incentives for domestic firms to perform R&D while also enhancing the impact of R&D by combining it with foreign technology transfer, China's fast growing foreign sector is supporting the growing capabilities of China's domestic companies to compete on world markets.

* * *

The MNE Research Centers

China's Ministry of Commerce recently reported that as of September 2005 foreign companies had established approximately 750 R&D centers in China. MNEs that have established separate R&D centers include Dupont, Ford, G.E., General Motors, IBM, Intel, Lucent Technologies, Microsoft, and Motorola. These generally were outside the industrial R&D survey data. They were also outside the annual survey of domestic research institutes administered by the Ministry of Science and Technology.

MNE-established R&D centers generally reflect one or a combination of motivations. These are the desire to enhance appeal to local markets, to gain access to skilled talent, and to ensure technology control.

Enhance Appeal to Local Market

Much of foreign R&D conducted in China is focused on adapting established products to the local Chinese market. Localized innovations include design innovations that are intended to appeal to Chinese consumers. Examples of R&D focused on localization include IBM's China Research Lab, established in 1995, with its work largely analyzing and responding to the needs of the Chinese market. Matsushita Electric Industrial Co. has two R&D centers in China, both of which are focused on applied R&D. According to Iwazaki Morio, general manager of the two centers, "Infrastructure research institutions are mainly set in mainland Japan. For Panasonic and many other transnational corporations, the core significance of establishing applied R&D institutions is to enable products to further meet [local] market demands" (Cai 2006).

Gain Access to Skilled Talent

Bell Lab under Lucent Technologies is the largest MNE research institution in China. It has more than 500 scientific researchers in Shanghai and

Beijing, 96 percent of whom possess doctoral or master's degrees (Cai 2006). Given the relatively high productivity-wage margin for the Chinese R&D personnel, we would anticipate that MNEs would skip a venue such as Seoul to take advantage of the relative value of Chinese R&D labor. Even though the returns to an R&D worker in Shanghai were but two-thirds of that of a Korean R&D worker in 2000, the salary of the Chinese worker was little more than one quarter of that of the Korean counterpart (Jefferson and Kaifeng 2004).

Strategic Motives to Ensure Technology Control

In order to establish itself as a first mover or leading player in a Chinese market, an MNE may invest in a free-standing R&D center. This positioning may be intended to establish branding advantages in the Chinese market as well as to influence Chinese policy toward the MNE in question. Proximity to the market and local technology development may also give advantage to sponsoring MNEs in their efforts to control key technologies. According to China's Ministry of Commerce, 46 percent of transnational corporations set up foreign-owned R&D centers mainly for technology control. According to the ministry's report, the MNEs use research centers to control the diffusion of critical technologies by acquiring competing R&D operations thus blocking the diffusion of competing technologies. Out of security concerns, China's government has set up a series of policy barriers for MNEs seeking to merge with related domestic R&D institutes. But, in fact, the more significant spillovers are likely to flow in the other direction—from foreign institutes to domestic R&D operations.

These research centers are unlikely to be producing leading innovations that would otherwise be made in the United States or other advance scientific centers in the OECD countries. The lead R&D manager from Sun Microsystems reported in May 2005 that China's research centers have yet to achieve the scale or quality needed to deploy the leading Sun scientists to a Chinese research setting. Among IBM's patent applications filed in China, more than 90 percent originated from its R&D Center based in the United States while that from China Research Lab accounted for less than 1 percent. These examples illustrate the tendency of major MNEs with R&D facilities in China to retain research on their core competencies at their home base and for the most part to offshore to China research relating to particular characteristics of the Chinese market or production needs.

However, the presence of these centers is likely to be conveying more advanced technologies than those currently available in China's domestic industrial firms while at the same time demonstrating to Chinese counterparts how to organize successful R&D labs with a high-end commercial orientation. Again, as with FDI in China's industrial sector, investment in foreign-funded R&D centers is likely to generate spillovers to establish and strengthen China's domestic R&D establishment.

Conclusions and Policy Implications

What role has public policy played in facilitating the accumulation of FDI in China and its contribution to China's indigenous technology development? Linkages between FDI and foreign-funded R&D investments in China and domestic Chinese R&D capabilities carry policy implications for both China and the OECD countries, including the United States.

The vast majority of FDI in China is located in its special zones that provide preferential treatment for investors. Beginning in 1979, China established its first four Special Economic Zones (SEZs) that were designed to capture foreign investment from Chinese living overseas along China's southeast coast, including Hong Kong, Taiwan, and Macao. In 1984, 14 new Open Cities were designated along the coast; they all set up Economic and Technology Development Zones (ETDZs). As a result of the lobbying of provinces and cities throughout China, there were over 100 investment zones by 2003, including High Technology Development Zones recognized by the central government, with at least one in each of China's 31 provinces.[8]

While the central government sets minimum tax requirements and abatement guidelines for foreign investment, the highly decentralized nature of the FDI approval process often results in deeper concessions to foreign investors than those formally allowed by the central government.[9] The decentralized decision-making process is sometimes referred to as the "10 plus 1" policy. Under this arrangement, foreign investors often find themselves receiving a list of concessions from one province or city that is anxious to capture their investment (say 10 concessions). The next interested province or city will then offer one more concession to add to the list thereby bringing the number to 10 + 1 and so on. Recently, China's government has given serious consideration to phasing out tax concessions to foreign companies and establishing a uniform tax code that would apply equally to domestic and foreign firms.

The large annual flows of FDI to China have been motivated by an abundant supply of relatively well-educated, low-wage labor, a vast emerging market, and a highly decentralized administrative structure that enables local jurisdictions to compete energetically for foreign investment. Against these economic conditions and administrative backdrop, arguably the major contribution of the central government has been to create a relatively stable macroeconomic environment that has encouraged confidence for foreign investors, including attention to the enforcement of intellectual property rights.

Given that FDI is likely to continue to flow to China, as will the establishment and growth of foreign-funded R&D centers, an important question is how China can maximize the extent and benefits of the spillover effects. The government has already begun to substantially expand its investment in both undergraduate and graduate training for scientists and engineers. In 2004, the number of students entering masters' and doctoral programs in science and engineering was 161,817, more than twice the number of graduates in these programs, that is, 73,614 (NBS 2005, 694).

While the sheer supply and the rate of growth of scientists and engineers are probably larger in China than any other country, there are serious issues regarding the ability of China's universities and their faculty to train world-class scientists and engineers. Among other policies, China's system of higher education needs to recognize that it operates within an international market for research talent and that requires it to compensate instructors and researchers according to international standards. Competitive salaries are needed to attract younger, talented graduates from abroad back to China's understaffed universities. While more competitive compensation schemes have been established in a few fields and in a few universities, extending the compensation incentives can yield significant further benefits.

On the OECD and U.S. side, it is unlikely—and perhaps undesirable—that the developed economies will attempt to stem the offshoring of R&D operations. There is ample research within the innovation literature to suggest that proximity of R&D to production and sales, that is, learning by doing and learning by using, are critical inputs to the R&D process. This literature suggests that outsourcing manufacturing to a country such as China in which the scale of production and sales are immense necessitates the establishment of complementary R&D operations. As we have seen in the analysis above, the establishment of such foreign-funded manufacturing and R&D operations yields substantial spillovers that help drive the intensification and upgrading of domestic R&D operations.

While China is rapidly expanding its supply of highly trained scientists and engineers who can staff R&D operations, both in China and abroad, the United States retains a critical role in the development of successful R&D operations. In spanning many countries and multiple fields, such successful R&D operations will entail a range of tasks that include design, financing, management, strategic planning, and the deployment of R&D outcomes across countries and industries. As with offshoring in the manufacturing sector, these tasks will draw on comparative advantages enjoyed by the United States, including well-developed banking and venture capital industries, highly trained and experienced managers, and top scientists and engineers who can formulate and manage the strategic design of large-scale R&D programs. In fact, in the realm of R&D, a quality hierarchy exists as in manufacturing. The comparatively low R&D intensity of FFEs in China hides the fact that their China-based R&D operations are embedded within a network of R&D activities in the United States and other OECD and developing economies. Indeed, just as the phenomenon of FDI and R&D offshoring leads to spillovers that induce Chinese firms to establish rudimentary R&D operations, the same pattern of offshoring is also motivating the United States and other OECD MNEs to upgrade and diversify their R&D operations in order to maintain control over the development and deployment of critical technologies. From this perspective, the intensification of R&D in Chinese firms and the globalization of R&D operations in MNE are opposite sides of the same coin—the result of FDI and the offshoring of foreign-funded R&D operations.

Notes

* The author appreciates the research assistance of Guan Xiaojing and Wu Bin of China's National Bureau of Statistics. We acknowledge the support provided by the U.S. National Science Foundation (award no. SES-0519902) and the U.S. Department of Energy's Biological and Environmental Research Program (contract #DE-FG02-00ER63030) that helped support the data acquisition and research assistance provided for this project.

1. NBS-MOST (2006), 291. The balance of the patent applications originated from small-scale enterprises, research institutes, universities, government agencies, and individual residents.
2. Naughton (2007), Ch. 17. The figures cited are for actually utilized incoming FDI, including "other" investment, which is part of export processing contracts or compensation trade.
3. China's National Bureau of Statistics designates firms with foreign investment as "foreign-funded enterprises and enterprises with funds from Hong Kong, Macao, and Taiwan (waishang gangaotai touzi chiye)." In this paper we condense the reference simply to foreign-funded enterprises (FFEs).
4. As a result of the upward revision of China's GDP resulting from the 2004 census, the National Bureau of Statistics revised its estimate of the R&D/GDP ratio for 2004 from 1.44 percent to 1.27 percent.
5. The large difference in the number of firms in the balanced sample versus that in the full sample is explained by the large number of firms in the full sample that exit after 1995 or enter before 2004. A substantial portion of the exit-entry activity is associated with firms for whom their ownership designation, address, industry classification, or formal size classification changes thus entailing the reassignment of their firm identification numbers.
6. With purchases having doubled over the period 2000–2003, however, the growth of LME activity in the domestic technology market is outpacing the growth of internal S&T spending and imported technology purchases.

7. Hu, Jefferson, and Jinchang (2005) show this result within the context of a production function. Fisher-Vanden and Jefferson (2005) find this result using a cost function approach.
8. See Naughton 2007, Ch. 17 for a more complete account of the creation of these zones.
9. For example, while the statutory enterprise income tax rate is 33%, enterprises in SEZs and ETDZs are to be taxed at 15%. Zones established by provinces and coastal cities may set the rate at 24%. Enterprises designated as "high technology" may be taxed at lower rates although, in principle, not below 10%. (Naughton 2007, Ch. 17).

CHAPTER THIRTEEN

CAPTURING THE BENEFITS FROM OFFSHORE OUTSOURCING IN DEVELOPING COUNTRIES: THE CASE FOR ACTIVE POLICIES

Eva Paus and Helen Shapiro

Introduction

The increasing organization of production chains across national borders offers new opportunities for economic advancement to developing countries, as they will have a chance to attract foreign direct investment (FDI) in parts production, specific services, as well as final products. But under which circumstances will developing host countries actually be able to use participation in the global production networks of transnational corporations (TNCs) as part of a strategy for industrial upgrading and leapfrogging?

We evaluate the impact of offshore outsourcing on developing countries in terms of the contribution that foreign investment can make to the advancement of the host country's knowledge-based assets. The development of technological, production, design, and marketing capabilities is at the heart of the development process, as it allows national producers to move up the value chain and provide higher-value-added goods and services, the basis for increased productivity growth and rising real wages. While FDI may promote growth by increasing investment, employment, foreign exchange, and tax revenue, its greatest benefit for the developing country lies in its potential contribution to the development of knowledge-based assets. Such contribution can come about through different kinds of spillovers, backward linkages, or human capital effects (on-the-job training and subsequent labor mobility).

During the 1980s and 1990s, many developing countries abandoned the strategy of import-substituting industrialization (ISI) and embraced market liberalization. The new paradigm of the Washington Consensus asserted that unfettered markets would eliminate inefficiencies fostered by ISI and promote growth based on comparative advantages determined by relative prices in international markets. Thus the earlier skeptical stance toward potential development benefits from FDI gave way to a welcoming open-arms approach toward TNCs. Even more, governments started to compete fiercely for FDI in the expectation that—together with trade—it would engender renewed growth and development.

Indeed, FDI flows increased significantly over this period. Contrary to expectations, however, it has become increasingly clear over the last two decades that spillovers do not happen automatically. The large and growing body of empirical studies on FDI and spillovers shows very mixed results. Recent survey articles by Lipsey and Sjöholm (2005) and Görg and Greenaway (2004) demonstrate that, in developing countries, FDI-generated spillovers tend to be the exception rather than the rule.

We argue that the disjuncture between reality and Washington Consensus–based expectations can be explained by the notion that not all FDI is created equal and that not all developing countries have the same capabilities to capture potential spillovers. The FDI-spillover nexus is rooted in the interaction between the dynamics of transnational corporations' global value chains on the one hand and the development of host countries' absorptive capacity for spillovers on the other. The type of FDI and the global strategies of transnational corporations (TNCs) determine the *potential* for spillovers. The *realization* of that potential depends upon the ability of host country producers to compete in related products; it depends on what we call the absorptive capacity of the host economy. If there are no spillovers from FDI in a developing country, then either spillover potential was lacking or national absorptive capacity was insufficient.

Washington Consensus polices have not provided a major impetus for the expansion of indigenous knowledge-based assets. Where governments failed to address coordination failures and imperfect and missing markets, they failed to support domestic producers—directly and proactively—in competing effectively with foreign investors and they failed to develop the national capabilities necessary to benefit from positive spillover effects. In many cases, a drastic reduction of the role of the state in the economy reduced the very administrative capacity that is needed for the conceptualization and implementation of effective proactive capability-promoting policies.

Therefore, to increase the likelihood that FDI will lead to spillovers and thus contribute to the advancement of knowledge-based assets and the development of dynamic comparative advantages, governments in developing countries need to adopt more active policies. Active policies are needed to target the more "spillover-prone" FDI, in recognition of the fact that different types of FDI hold out different potential for spillovers and that TNCs are bound to have only imperfect information about all the relevant location-specific assets of a developing country. Active policies are also needed to advance national absorptive capacity, when market failures are the main reason for insufficient absorptive capability. Policies to advance absorptive capabilities are not just policies with an eye toward enabling spillovers, but rather policies that focus on advancing technological capabilities in general. In other words, policies to attract FDI and to enhance spillovers must be understood as only one part of the larger set of policies for bringing about structural change and increasing the knowledge-based assets of the country.

In the age of trade in IT-enabled services, developing countries may attract FDI in the manufacturing as well as the service sector. Even though our discussion in this chapter focuses primarily on FDI in manufacturing, the arguments about market failures and active policies hold equally for fostering spillovers from FDI in the IT-based service sector.

Because FDI and spillover policies have to be understood within this larger context of industrial advancement, we situate the current debate on offshoring and development within a broader theoretical discussion on industrial policy. We then lay out a framework to assess whether these benefits can be realized, a framework that incorporates both the nature of the FDI in question and the conditions in the host country. We conclude with a discussion of the constraints on proactive policies and suggest that while multi- and bilateral agreements circumscribe policy space, certain interventions—particularly those related to R&D—are still feasible. Moreover, whether a country will implement industrial policy depends as much on domestic political economy issues as on externally imposed limitations. With global competition for FDI increasing in the face of rapid technological change, resolving these issues takes on added urgency for those countries that are already lagging not to fall behind even further.

Theoretical Insights and Historical Lessons

In the debate on general industrial policy, a kind of schizophrenia has emerged between the worlds of theory and practice.[1] While market-driven approaches have dominated the policy realm since the 1980s, the assumption of widespread market failure, which motivated industrial policies of the 1960s, has made a comeback in development theory. In addition, new approaches to technical change and innovation, some originating in the literature on firm competitiveness, have challenged previous assumptions about firm behavior. Together, they have generated a huge literature documenting how market forces will not produce optimal results and that some kind of state intervention is necessary to promote industrialization.

Although repackaged in formalized models, the arguments behind coordinating investment or a "Big Push" have changed little since first proposed by Rosenstein-Rodan, Nurkse, and Scitovsky more than fifty years ago. In the presence of increasing returns, industrialization in one sector raises demand for other sectors and makes large-scale production in these sectors more profitable. The presence of these pecuniary externalities makes different firms' and industries' profits interdependent and thereby provides a rationale for a government-coordinated investment strategy.

The notion that countries can be stuck in a low-level equilibrium trap has also made a comeback, as it has been shown that multiple equilibria can exist in the face of pecuniary externalities driven by increasing returns. Under these conditions, making the transition from so-called cottage production equilibrium to industrialization equilibrium (Murphy, Shleifer and Vishy 1989), which entails specializing in different types of manufacturing, is the challenge countries face. This echoes a point made long ago by Gerschenkron, among others, about backwardness and inertia—that more than a market signal is required to displace the previous equilibrium in order to make nontraditional investment projects attractive (Shapiro and Taylor 1990).

What this work suggests, in contrast to traditional models of comparative advantage, is that a country's specialization pattern determines its rate of growth. As Ros (2000, 2001) explains, specializing in sectors with increasing returns allows for a higher return on capital and subsequently, a higher investment rate. This literature also offers new explanations for the success of East Asia and the relative failure of Latin America that focus not on prices and exports, but on investment. As suggested by Murphy, Schleifer, and Vishy (1989, 1025), "countries such as South Korea that have implemented a coordinated investment program can achieve industrialization of each sector at a lower explicit cost in terms of temporary tariffs and subsidies than a country that industrializes piecemeal. The reason is that potentially large implicit subsidies flow across sectors under a program of simultaneous industrialization."

Taking a slightly different tack, a number of economists have argued that some specialization patterns are more conducive to industrial advancement than others, because learning externalities and spillovers are greater in manufacturing than in primary production, and greater in some manufacturing activities than in others (e.g., Rodrik 2006a, Lall 2001). Spillover potential varies with the technology intensity of the production process. Low-technology products embody stable and well-established technologies; medium-technology products use more complex technologies and moderate levels of R&D and need higher skills and longer learning periods; and in high-technology products, technologies change fast, high R&D-investment is required and product design is of utmost importance (Lall 2001). Due to the R&D intensive nature of high-tech products, their production is likely to contain a greater element of knowledge production and involve a broader and more sophisticated set of skills. Industrial development is about producers' ability to move up the value chain and into the manufacturing of more sophisticated products. The key point is that coordination and information failures make it impossible for producers to move into the desired direction based only on market signals. And positive externalities will not be internalized without policy interventions.

The acknowledgement that sectors are not all equal in a world of differential returns to labor and capital and differential learning and spillover potentials reflects the insights from the literature on firm strategy and competitiveness. In contrast to the passive price-taking firms of comparative statics, this literature portrays successful firms as those that create and maintain barriers to entry and the rents associated with them. By exploiting "competitive" advantages based on innovation, firms are then not dependent on unsustainable cost advantages such as low wages or exchange rates. According to this logic, a firm's strategy must be to avoid price-competitive sectors, vulnerable to forces beyond its control (Porter 1990).

By extension, a "competitive" nation does not specialize in these sectors, either. In explicit contrast to theories of comparative advantage, a country's competitive advantage is determined by innovation rather than factor endowments, by the ability to diversify up the value chain and not get stuck at a particular static comparative advantage. For Porter (1990) this means that national policies should help create an environment of demanding consumers, domestic competition, strong supplier linkages, and good infrastructure.

Amsden, focusing on late-developers, also puts firms and their technological capacity at the heart of development. Their ability to shift away from primary resources to knowledge-based assets—a set of managerial and technological skills that allows them to either produce a product "at above prevailing market prices (or below market costs)"—determines a country's long-term growth (Amsden 2001, 3). In contrast to the standard emphasis on getting the macro right, the starting point for Amdsen and others is the firm (Paus 2005, Best 2001, Lall 2001, Nelson and Winter 1982, and Katz 1996).

The treatment of technology also distinguishes this work from both current and early development economists. Rather than a missing factor akin to capital or labor, knowledge or technology is portrayed as a learning process. As Lall (2003, 15) puts it, "industrial success in developing countries depends essentially on how enterprises manage the process of mastering, adapting and improving upon existing technologies. The process is difficult and prone to widespread and diffuse market failure." In this world of imperfect information and technology rents, the firm is not a competitive, price-taker implicit in most macro approaches. Moreover, public support is crucial to help build their technological capabilities, to help provide the inputs (broadly speaking) that enable producers to produce new and more sophisticated products (Rodrik 2006a).

Interestingly, the theoretical literature cited above on the need to coordinate investment or to protect firms until they reach the technological frontier or generate adequate returns fails to mention ownership, implicitly assuming that the firms are independent and nationally owned. Much of the literature on competitiveness makes similar assumptions and does not consider the ramifications of transnational firms' global strategies on national industrial development.[2]

FDI, Offshoring and Industrial Advancement

In practice, the governments of many developing countries have not considered these ramifications either. With the embrace of free-market policies in the 1980s and 1990s, governments no longer looked to promote national producers but rather expected that foreign investment and trade would bring spillovers to generate renewed economic growth. If anything, many governments have shown a distinct preference for foreign producers over national producers, as they are competing for FDI with financial incentives, outright grants, preferential tax rates, and the promise of stable rules. Governments' eagerness to attract and enshrine unencumbered foreign investment flows into and out of the country is reflected in the unprecedented number of formal investment treaties. At the end of 2005, governments worldwide had signed 2,495 bilateral investment agreements and 2,758 bilateral taxation treaties (UNCTAD 2006, xix).

A growing number of developing country governments have also established specific institutions charged with advertising the country's location-specific assets to TNCs, sometimes across all sectors in search of any type of FDI and sometimes in specific sectors. There are two main reasons behind the establishment of investment-promotion agencies. The first reason, especially important for small countries, is to counter the imperfect information that TNCs have about how the potential host country's locational advantages fit with TNCs' strategic interests. The second reason, in some countries, is the desire to overcome coordination failures among different foreign investments; in other words, the desire to draw a critical mass of foreign investors into cluster formations in the host economies so as to generate spillovers and agglomeration economies.

The rationale behind preferential treatment for foreign investors is also based on spillovers. Though rarely termed "market failure," the potential for positive externalities or spillovers for the host economy is used to justify government intervention, in that the returns to the country exceed the private returns to the foreign investor. Traditionally, the emphasis has been on technological externalities, by which other firms increase productivity through better practices or new technologies. Like the industrial policy literature more generally, the acknowledgment of imperfect competition and increasing returns has broadened the argument for intervention. As Görg and Strobl (2005, 138) explain, "Only recently has the theoretical literature pointed out that in the presence of imperfect competition and increasing returns to scale, linkages between MNCs and indigenous firms can also lead to pecuniary externalities benefiting firms in the host country . . . In a nutshell, increases in output by multinationals lead to an expansion of demand for intermediate products supplied by indigenous suppliers." Rodriguez-Clare (1996) offers one such model.

The policy discourse around FDI is distinct from the industrial policy debate in general. In contrast to their predecessors, the default policy recommendation of many contemporary theorists of market failure is still the market (Nolan and Pack 2003, World Bank 2002). However, the policy recommendations with respect to FDI and spillovers have been largely limited to attracting investment. The market imperfections that do warrant positive interventions are restricted to those related to information and FDI, so that investment promotion and subsidies to foreign firms are recommended (Moran, Graham, and Blomström 2005, 378).

There is ample empirical evidence, however, that the hoped-for spillovers from FDI do not materialize automatically.[3] The extent of spillovers depends upon the interaction between the dynamics of TNCs' global value chains, on the one hand, and the development of host countries' absorptive capacity for spillovers, on the other. The type of FDI and the global strategies of TNCs determine the *potential* for spillovers. The *realization* of that potential hinges on the ability of host country producers to compete in related products; it depends on what we call the absorptive capacity of the host economy.

The Potential for Spillovers

A generic approach to FDI does not pay sufficient attention to the fact that not all FDI is created equal with respect to its ability to generate spillovers. This point is analogous to the arguments presented above that demonstrate how the types of products a country specializes in have different ramifications for growth and industrialization. Foreign investment in resource extraction generally provides very little potential for spillovers, as it tends to be very capital intensive and have few linkages to the host economy. In contrast, FDI in the manufacturing sector has higher spillover potential. The extent varies though with the technology intensity of the production process. As a result, the spillover potential from FDI in the production of high-tech goods is particularly promising.

But regardless of technology intensity, the production of any good spans a gamut of different processes, some of which are very routine and standardized, and others that add much greater value. To the extent that late developers can draw in high-tech FDI, they are likely to attract FDI in the production of parts and processes that are more standardized. The key question and challenge is whether FDI will remain at that level, or whether—over time—TNC affiliates move up the value chain and into the production of parts or final goods with greater learning externalities and spillovers more generally.

Since supply chain development is an important channel for positive spillovers, a TNC's global sourcing strategy is a key determinant of the spillover potential of FDI. More than ever before, TNCs are developing and managing global networks where key business functions are allocated around the globe, and reallocated when required by the competitive dynamics within the industry. Different parts of the value chain may be produced by TNC affiliates themselves (internalized production) or they may be produced by unaffiliated companies through arms-lengths contracts (externalized production). The extent of internalized versus externalized production varies from TNC to TNC, depending on which activities a TNC considers to be part of its core capabilities.

Generally speaking, R&D, product design, and marketing under the company's brand name are core competencies of TNCs. Yet, over the last few years, we have witnessed a growing trend toward subcontracting of not just standardized parts, but also of aspects of design, marketing, and overall coordination (Sturgeon and Lester 2003; Yusuf 2003, UNCTAD 2002, Dicken 1998). In 2002, foreign affiliates in developing countries accounted for 18 percent of total business R&D by all foreign affiliates, an increase from 2 percent in 1996 (UNCTAD 2005a, xxvi).

In addition to the type of FDI, TNCs' interests in sourcing in the host country is another important determinant of FDI spillover potential. That interest depends on the degree of internalized production, use of global sourcing, and technological requirements. If production is highly internalized, the TNC affiliate will have little interest in sourcing beyond nontradable services and very standardized inputs such as packing materials. Or if the production of inputs requires a high degree of technological sophistication, a TNC may opt for inputs from suppliers with whom it has developed a long-standing relationship and who have a track record of high-quality production.

The Realization of Spillovers

The existence of FDI spillover potential is clearly a necessary condition for the realization of spillovers. But contrary to much of the model-theoretic literature which assumes that the existence of FDI in a host economy will lead to increased demand for inputs from domestic suppliers and thus pecuniary externalities, the existence of FDI spillover potential is not a sufficient condition for the realization of spillovers, pecuniary or otherwise. The other—equally important—factor is the host country's ability to absorb spillovers. Economy size, the learning infrastructure, and firm-level capabilities are the main determining factors of a country's absorptive capabilities.

There is relatively little policy discussion among promoters of free-market strategies about how to increase a country's absorptive capacity. This is the case, even though empirical studies indicate that the capabilities of local firms affect whether they will be suppliers to TNCs, and a number of studies suggest that the larger the productivity gap between local firms and foreign investors, the less likely it is that these positive externalities will be realized (e.g., de Mello 1997 and Best 2001). As Lall (2003, 12) characterizes much of this literature, "Access to new technology becomes equivalent to its effective use."

To the extent that there is any concern expressed about spillovers not being realized, the focus has been on removing constraints on the foreign investor and providing a hospitable business climate in general. As stated by Moran, Graham, and Blomström (2005:377), "the kinds of measures resurrected by some developing countries (i.e. domestic content requirements, joint venture mandates, and technology sharing regulations) are precisely the kinds of host policies most likely to interrupt the 'intrafirm trade' and 'parental supervision' shown in this volume to be so potent for host development. These restrictive measures lead to outdated technology, inefficient production processes, and wasteful use of host country resources."

The implicit assumption about the automaticity of supplier response ignores the uncertainties and risks associated with the learning process discussed above. It downplays how the development of a systemic learning infrastructure shapes firms' absorptive capacity. The average schooling and skill level of the workforce, the interaction between institutions of higher learning and the private sector, the existence and embeddedness of technological research institutes all have an impact.

The size of the host economy imposes obvious limitations on the number of fields in which a country can have absorption capabilities. By definition, limited human and physical resources in a small country demand a larger degree of specialization, particularly in fields where economies of scale do not play a significant role. But size is not necessarily the defining factor. For example, Mexico and Costa Rica, two countries with a similar

GDP per capita, but vastly different markets, have been able to attract significant inflows of high-tech FDI. Yet, in both countries spillovers have been limited (Paus and Gallagher 2006).

This noninterventionist approach also ignores the lessons provided by those countries that have been successful in capturing technological spillovers. There is no historical precedent for FDI single-handedly advancing a country's knowledge-based assets. Rather, what is at issue is a developing country's general strategy of promoting knowledge-based assets and how the role of FDI is defined within that context. Historical evidence suggests that countries that developed strong national capabilities and reduced the productivity gap that helps determine whether spillovers will in fact be realized have often done so through selective interventions that supported domestic firms and pressured foreign companies to invest in local R&D and to maximize spillovers.[4] Korea, for example, rewarded firms that spent certain amounts on R&D and penalized those that failed to do so. Taiwan did so as well and established R&D institutes and science parks, in which selected firms participated.

Lall (2003, 21–22) contrasts Hong Kong, which had relatively free trade and few restrictions on FDI, with Singapore, which also had relatively free trade but imposed R&D and other performance requirements on foreign firms. As a result, Hong Kong did not deepen its capabilities and has had slower growth than the other "tigers" and China. Singapore, in contrast, deepened its manufacturing production and has the third highest ratio of enterprise financed R&D to GDP in the developing world.

The experience of these countries also suggests that timing matters. As Lall (2003, 5) puts it, "industrial capabilities develop slowly, in a cumulative and path-dependent manner subject to agglomeration economies." In her survey of late developing countries, Amsden (2001) concludes that countries that opened relatively late and had supported domestic firms were more likely to retain medium- and high-tech industries. In the recent phase of mergers and acquisitions that has taken place in all of the late developing countries to enhance scale economies, in Taiwan, China, Korea, and India were more likely to have national firms strong enough to survive and/or to be viable as joint venture partners. Latin America, which did not support local innovation to the same extent, saw many of its national firms and supplier industries collapse as production has become more concentrated by TNCs, and there has been a vertical de-integration of industrial activity as imports have replaced domestically produced intermediate products. As a result of these factors, Ocampo (2004, 296) concludes that "the multiplier effects and the technological externalities generated by the high-growth activities associated with exports and FDI have been weak."

Therefore, the assumption that countries will benefit from regimes that allow TNCs to integrate local production into global sourcing networks with no restrictions ignores the degree to which this may depend on a country's capabilities at the time of liberalization. Indeed, many successful firms may have gotten their start under an import-substitution regime, even if the products they produce are no longer the same. As managerial and technological capabilities at the firm level are key to development, acknowledging this continuity of major firms is critical.[5]

To a certain extent, FDI spillover potential and domestic absorption capability interact. Where domestic capabilities exist, TNCs will be more likely to outsource some of the production. And where domestic production capabilities keep growing, the likelihood increases that the nature of FDI in the country will become more technology intensive, generating a virtuous cycle behind the advancement of domestic technological capabilities. At present the ability of developing countries to benefit from the growing offshoring/internationalization of R&D differs dramatically, in accordance with their level of development. Countries need to already have a certain level of innovation capabilities to attract the requisite FDI and benefit from it. UNCTAD (2005a) defined and calculated a proxy for such capabilities: the Innovation Capability Index.[6] The results show that different developing areas have vastly different capabilities (see table 13.1). The new EU members have much greater potential for innovation and the absorption of spillovers than South-East and East Asia. The index for Latin America and the Caribbean is roughly half that of New Europe, and Sub-Saharan Africa has by far the lowest capabilities.

Table 13.1 Innovation Capability Index (regional unweighted averages)

Region	1995	2001
Developed countries (excl. the new EU members)	0.876	0.869
The new EU members	0.665	0.707
South-East Europe and CIS	0.602	0.584
South-East and East Asia	0.492	0.518
West Asia and North Africa	0.348	0.361
Latin America and the Caribbean	0.375	0.360
South Asia	0.223	0.215
Sub-Saharan Africa	0.157	0.160

Source: UNCTAD 2005, 115.

Conclusions: Policies and Policy Space to Promote the FDI-Development Nexus

We have argued in this chapter that market failures and learning externalities necessitate policy interventions aimed at advancing knowledge-based assets in general and national absorptive capacity for FDI spillovers in particular. Historical evidence shows that the most successful latecomers in the development process were the ones that actively countered market failures. So if developing countries want to capture the benefits from offshore outsourcing, their governments have to intervene to overcome coordination, information, and other market failures.

The exact types of policies will need to vary with the level of development of a country and its specific path dependent assets—real or potential. Nonetheless, we can say a few things in general about the type of active policies needed and the urgency for adopting them.

First, multilateral, regional, and bilateral trade and investment agreements have narrowed the space for industrial policies dramatically. Policies used successfully in the past, for example, domestic content requirements for foreign investors, are no longer an option under the TRIMS Agreement of the WTO. But while performance requirements for TNCs are out, certain interventionist policies to advance domestic absorptive capabilities are still possible, for example, R&D support, provision of information and active consultation, match-making, and cluster formation (Abugattas and Paus 2006; UNCTAD 2006). In recent years, a growing number of developing countries have set up institutions that are charged with match-making functions so as to enhance the linkages and spillovers between domestic input suppliers and foreign producers in the economy. Egypt's National Supplier Development Programme, for example, provides financial support and technical assistance for national companies that it has identified as potential suppliers to transnational corporations (UNCTAD 2006, 48). Costa Rica Provee is in the same business for Costa Rica, and Enterprise Ireland has served that role since its founding in 1994. It remains to be seen whether policies aimed at advancing absorptive capacity will be as effective as the policy set in the past that included stipulations regarding TNC performance.

Second, the identification of market failures and bottlenecks and their prioritization across sectors and policy areas is not something that can be left to the government alone. Rather, as a number of economists, political scientists, and sociologists have pointed out, those choices need to be made in close consultation and cooperation among the relevant government institutions and domestic producers (e.g., Hausmann and Rodrik 2006, Evans 1995).

Third, while some policies will have to target sectors identified as strategic or most likely to succeed, other policies will be applicable to all producers, that is, horizontal policies. These noninterventionist policies are especially important in the area of upgrading and expanding the human capital base and infrastructure. While most of our discussion in this chapter has focused on the manufacturing sector, implicitly or explicitly, the discussion in other chapters of this book (e.g., Abugattas, Suri) highlights the importance of a well-functioning telecommunications sector as a necessary condition to attract IT-based FDI.

Fourth, we believe that at this juncture, the main challenge to the implementation of an industrial policy agenda in many developing countries does not lie in the policy restrictions of international agreements, formidable as they are. Rather, they frequently lie in the arena of politics and political economy. For example, after two decades of neoliberal policies and deindustrialization in Latin America, one has to wonder where the political constituency is that would exert the pressure to use the windfall from the high export prices of primary products to develop the national knowledge-based assets and linkage capability.

Finally, as global competition keeps increasing, with China, India, and Eastern Europe aggressively vying for more sophisticated FDI, proactive policies are becoming ever more urgent: from targeting specific TNCs to supporting cluster formation, to expanding technical education, to improving access to telecommunications, to aggressive support policies to develop indigenous linkage capability and integrate national firms into emerging clusters. At the same time, increased competition among countries has allowed TNCs to raise the barriers of entry for integration into their value chains; for example, a successful input supplier increasingly is the one who can supply several functions within the value chain. Concomitantly, faster technological change and greater mobility of productive capital have reduced the time period during which spillovers can actually be realized.

To reap the benefits from offshore outsourcing in this global context is a huge challenge. And it is not clear that the least developed countries in Africa or the middling developing countries in Latin America are in a position to meet the challenge. But it is clear that in the absence of active industrial policies, there is no chance that the potential promise of FDI-linked economic upgrading and development can be realized.

Notes

1. Parts of this section are based on Shapiro (forthcoming).
2. Porter's *The Competitive Advantage of Nations*, based primarily on firms in advanced, industrialized countries, deals almost exclusively with national firms. For a discussion of related works on developing countries, see Shapiro (2003).
3. Given the weak empirical evidence of actual spillovers, many voice skepticism about whether subsidies are warranted to attract FDI (e.g. Hanson 2005).

4. For details on these programs, see Lall (2003), Amsden (2001), Wade (1990), and Rodrik (1995).
5. Amsden (2001, 173) elaborates on this point.
6. The Innovation Capability Index is based on a technological activity index (composed of R&D personnel per million population, U.S. patents granted per million population, scientific publications per million population), and a human capital index (composed of the literacy rate as a share of population, secondary school enrolment as a share of the respective age group, and tertiary enrolment as a share of the respective age group). UNCTAD (2005a, 113).

REFERENCES

Abbott, Pamela, and Matthew Jones. 2002. *The Importance of Being Nearest: Nearshore Software Outsourcing and Globalization Discourse*, paper presented at Proceedings of the IFIP TC8/WG8.2 Working Conference on Global and Organizational Discourse about Information Technology.

Abugattas, Luis. 2005. *State Support Measures for Services: An Exploratory Assessment with Scanty Data*, mimeo.

Abugattas, Luis, and Eva Paus. 2006. *Policy Space for a Capability-Centered Development Strategy for Latin America*, paper presented at the Conference on "Responding to Globalization in the Americas: The Political Economy of Hemispheric Integration," Institute for the Study of the Americas, London School of Economics, June 2–4.

ACM (Association for Computing Machinery). 2006. *Globalization and Offshoring of Software*. New York: Association for Computing Machinery, a report of the ACM Job Migration Task Force, http://www.acm.org/globalizationreport/.

Aeppel, Timothy. 2005. "Rising Stock Buybacks Align with Repatriated Profits." *Wall Street Journal*, October 24.

Agarwal, J.P. 1986. *Home Country Incentives and FDI in ASEAN Economies*. Kiel, Germany, Kiel Institute for the World Economy. Working Paper No. 258.

Altshuler, Rosanne, and Harry Grubert. 2005. *The Three Parties in the Race to the Bottom: Host Governments, Home Governments and Multinational Companies*. Munich: CESifo Group, CESifo Working Paper Series No. 1613.

Amiti, Mary, and Shang-Jin Wei. 2005. "Fear of Services Outsourcing: Is It Justified?" *Economic Policy* 20 (42): 308–347.

Amsden, Alice H. 2001. *The Rise of the Rest: Challenges to the West from Late-Industrializing Economies*. New York and Oxford: Oxford University Press.

Arendt, Hannah. 1957. *The Human Condition*. Chicago, IL: University of Chicago Press.

Ark, Bart van, Robert Inklaar, and Robert McGuckin. 2003. "Changing Gear: Productivity, ICT and Service Industries: Europe and the United States." In *The Industrial Dynamics of the New Digital Economy*, ed. Jens Froslev Christensen and Peter Maskell. Cheltenham, UK and Northampton, MA: Edward Elgar Publishing, Inc.

Arndt, Sven W., and Henryk Kierzkowski, eds. 2001. *Fragmentation: New Production Patterns in the World Economy*. New York and Oxford: Oxford University Press.

Arora, Ashish. 2005. *The Emerging Offshore Software Industries and the United States Economy*, mimeo.

Arora, Ashish, and Alfonso Gambardella. 2005. "The Globalization of the Software Industry: Perspectives and Opportunities for Developed and Developing Countries." In *Innovation Policy and the Economy (Volume 5)*, ed. Adam Jaffe, Josh Lerner, and Scott Stern. Cambridge, MA: The MIT Press.

Arora, Ashish, V. S. Arunachalam, Jai Asundi, and Ronald Fernandes. 2001. "The Indian Software Services Industry." *Research Policy* 30 (8): 1267–1287.

Atrostic, B. K., and Sang Nguyen. 2005. *Computer Input, Computer Networks, and Productivity*. Washington, DC: Center for Economic Studies, CES Discussion Paper 05–01.

Aubert, Patrick, and Patrick Sillard. 2005. *Offshore Outsourcing and Employment in French Manufacturing Industries*. INSEE (National Institute for Statistics and Economic Studies).

Avi-Yonah, Reuven S. 2006. *Prepared Testimony before US Senate Permanent Subcommittee on Investigations Hearing on Offshore Transactions*. August 1.

———. 1998. *Globalization, Tax Competition and the Fiscal Crisis of the State*. Havard Law School, manuscript.

Baicker, Katherine, and M. Marit Rehavi. 2004. "Policy Watch. Trade Adjustment Assistance." *Journal of Economic Perspectives* 18 (4): 239–255.

Baker, Dean, Gerald Epstein, and Robert Pollin, eds. 1998. *Globalization and Progressive Economic Policy*. Cambridge, UK and New York: Cambridge University Press.

Baldwin, Richard. 2006. *Globalization: The Great Unbundling(s)*. Prime Minister's Office, Economic Council of Finland, September 20, http://www.vnk.fi/hankkeet/talousneuvosto/tyo-kokoukset/globalisaatioselvitys-9–2006/artikkelit/Baldwin_06–09–20.pdf.

Barbosa-Filho, Nelson H., Codrina Rada, Lance Taylor, and Luca Zamparelli. 2005. *US Macro Imbalances: Trends, Cycles and Policy Implications*. New York: Schwartz Center for Economic Policy Analysis, New School for Social Research. Policy Note. December.

Bardhan, Ashok Deo, and Cynthia Kroll. 2003. *The New Wave of Outsourcing*. Berkeley, CA: FCREUE (Fisher Center for Real Estate and Urban Economics), Fisher Center Research Reports No. 1103.

Bartels, Frank L. 2005. "Outsourcing Markets in Services: International Business Trends, Patterns and Emerging Issues," paper presented at Outsourcing Trend and Development Conference, Shenzhen, China.

Bartik, Timothy J. 2004. *Incentive Solutions*. Kalamazoo, MI: W.E. Upjohn Institute for Employment Research, W.E. Upjohn Institute Staff Working Paper No. 04–99.

Barysch, Katinka. 2006. *East versus West? The EU Economy after Enlargement*. London: Centre for European Reform.

Bates, Thomas W., Michael L. Lemmon, and James S. Linck. 2006. "Shareholder Wealth Effects and Bid Negotiation in Freeze-Out Deals: Are Minority Shareholders Left Out in the Cold?" *Journal of Financial Economics* 81 (3): 681–708.

Benner, Mats, and Torben Bundgaard Vad. 2000. "Sweden and Denmark: Defending the Welfare State." In *Welfare and Work in the Open Economy. Volume II: Diverse Responses to Common Challenges*, ed. Fritz W. Scharpf and Vivien A. Schmidt. New York and Oxford: Oxford University Press.

Bernstein, Jared. 2006. *All Together Now; Common Sense for a Fair Economy*. San Francisco, CA: Barrett-Koehler Publishers, Inc.

Bernstein, Jared, and Dean Baker. 2003. *The Benefits of Full Employment; When Markets Work for People.* Washington, DC: Economic Policy Institute.

Best, Michael. 2001. *The New Competitive Advantage: The Renewal of American Industry.* New York and Oxford: Oxford University Press.

Bhagwati, Jagdish, Arvind Panagariya, and T. N. Srinivasan. 2004. "The Muddles over Outsourcing." *The Journal of Economic Perspectives* 18 (4): 93–114.

Bivens, Josh L. 2005. *Truth and Consequences of Offshoring; Recent Studies Overstate the Benefits and Ignore the Costs to American Workers.* Washington, DC: Economic Policy Institute, Briefing Paper No. 155.

Bivens, Josh L., and Christian E. Weller. 2006. "The 'Job-Loss' Recovery: Not New, Just Worse." *Journal of Economic Issues* 40 (3): 603–628.

Blanchflower, David G., and Andrew J. Oswald. 2005. *The Wage Curve Reloaded.* National Bureau of Economic Research, NBER Working Paper No. 11338.

Blinder, Alan S. 2006. "Offshoring: The Next Industrial Revolution?" *Foreign Affairs* 85 (2): 113–128.

———. 2005. *Fear of Offshoring.* Princeton, NJ: Princeton University, CEPS Working Paper No. 119.

Brainard, Lael, and Robert E. Litan. 2005. *Services Offshoring, American Jobs, and the Global Economy.* Washington, DC: Brookings Institution, Perspectives on Work.

Bronfenbrenner, Kate. 2000. *Uneasy Terrain: The Impact of Capital Mobility on Workers, Wages and Union Organizing.* Cornell University, Report to the U.S. Trade Deficit Review Commission, mimeo.

Brown, Sherrod. 2004. *Myths of Free Trade; Why American Trade Policy Has Failed.* New York: The New Press.

Bundesagentur für Arbeit. 2007. *Der Arbeits-und Ausbildungsmarkt in Deutschland.* Nürnberg. January, page 26.

Burke, James. 1997. *The Effects of Foreign Direct Investment on Investment, Employment and Wages in the United States.* Department of Economics, University of Massachusetts, Amherst, mimeo.

Burke, James, and Gerald Epstein. 2006. *Employment Losses in US Manufacturing, 1987–2003.* Political Economy Research Institute, Working Paper, http://www.peri.umass.edu/.

———. 2002. "Threat Effects and the Internationalization of Production." In *Work and Well-Being In the Age of Finance,* ed. Jayati Ghosh and C. P. Chandrasekhar. New Delhi: Tulika Books.

Cai, Wei. 2006. "Rethinking R&D Centers Fever Amid MNEs." China Economic Net. January 2, http://en.ce.cn/Insight/200601/02/t20060102_5705717.shtml.

Campa, Jose, and Linda Goldberg. 1997. *The Evolving External Orientation of Manufacturing Industries: Evidence from Four Countries.* National Bureau of Economic Research, NBER Working Paper 5919.

Chalk, Nigel. 2001. *Tax Incentives In the Philippines: A Regional Perspective.* Washington, DC: IMF, IMF Working Paper No. 01/181.

Clausing, Kimberly. 2005. *The Role of US Tax Policy in Offshoring.* Portland, OR: Reed College.

Commission for Africa. 2005. *Our Common Interest: An Argument.* London: Penguin Books Ltd.

Crotty, James. 2005. "The Neo-Liberal Paradox: The Impact of Destructive Product Market Competition and Modern Financial Markets on Non-financial

Corporation Performance in the Neo-Liberal Era." In *Financialization and the World Economy*, ed. Gerald Epstein. Cheltenham, UK and Northampton, MA: Edward Elgar Publishing, Inc.

Crotty, James, and Gerald Epstein. 1996. "In Defense of Capital Controls." *The Socialist Register.* 118–149.

Crotty, James, Gerald Epstein, and Patricia Kelly. 1998. "Multinational Corporations in the Neo-Liberal Regime." In *Globalization and Progressive Economic Policy*, ed. Dean Baker, Gerald Epstein, and Robert Pollin. Cambridge, New York and Melbourne: Cambridge University Press.

Damijan, Joze P., and Matija Rojec. 2004. *Foreign Direct Investment and the Catching-Up Process in New EU Member States: Is There a Flying Geese Pattern?* WIIW Research Reports, No. 310.

D'Costa, Anthony P. 2003. "Uneven and Combined Development: Understanding India's Software Exports." *World Development* 31 (1): 211–227.

Deloitte Research. 2003. *The Cusp of a Revolution: How Offshoring Will Transform the Financial Services Industry.* New York: Deloitte.

de Mello Jr., Luiz R. 1997. "Foreign Direct Investment in Developing Countries: A Selective Survey." *Journal of Development Studies* 34 (1): 1–34.

de Mooij, Ruud A., and Sjef Ederveen. 2003. "Taxation and Foreign Direct Investment: A Synthesis of Empirical Research." *International Tax and Public Finance* 10 (6): 673–693.

Der Spiegel. 2007. *Sprudelnde Gewinne, mickrige Löhne.* January 11, http://www.spiegel.de/wirtschaft/0,1518,459132,00.html.

Dicken, Peter. 1998. *Global Shift: Transforming the World Economy.* Third edition. New York and London: Guilford Press.

Djankov, Simeon, and Peter Murrell. 2002. "Enterprise Restructuring in Transition: A Quantitative Survey." *Journal of Economic Literature* 40 (3): 739–792.

Dossani, Rafiq, and Martin Kenney. 2003. *Went for Cost, Stayed for Quality: Moving the Back Office to India*, mimeo.

Economics and Statistics Administration. 2002. *Digital Economy 2002.* Washington, DC: U.S. Department of Commerce, https://www.esa.doc.gov/reports/DE2002r1.pdf.

Epstein, Gerald. 2005. *Central Banks as Agents of Economic Development.* Political Economy Research Institute, Working Paper Series No. 104.

Epstein, Gerald, Irene Grabel, and K. S. Jomo. 2005. "Capital Management Techniques in Developing Countries." In *Capital Flight and Capital Controls in Developing Countries*, ed. Gerald Epstein. Cheltenham, UK and Northampton, MA: Edward Elgar Publishing, Inc.

Esping-Andersen, Gosta. 1990. *Three Worlds of Welfare State Capitalism.* Cambridge, UK: Polity Press.

European Commission. 2006a. *European Globalization Adjustment Fund* (Updated December 14, 2006; cited January 20, 2007), http://www.eubusiness.com/Employment/european-globalisation-adjustment-fund-egf/.

———. 2006b. *Eurobarometer 65: Public Opinion in the European Union.* First Results, http://www.eosgallupeurope.com/doc_.php?link=pdf/2006/Eurobarometer_65.pdf.

———. 2006c. *Eurobarometer 66: Public Opinion in the European Union.* First Results, http://www.eosgallupeurope.com/pdf/2006/Standard_Eurobarometer_66_en.pdf.

———. 2006d. *Financial Report 2005*. Luxembourg: Amt für amtliche Veröffentlichungen der Europäischen Gemeinschaften, page 26.

———. 2005. *Eurobarometer 63: Public Opinion in the European Union*. Final Results, http://www.eosgallupeurope.com/pdf/2005/Standard_Eurobarometer_63_Full_report.pdf.

Evans, Peter. 1995. *Embedded Autonomy: States and Industrial Transformation*. Princeton, NJ: Princeton University Press.

Farrell, Diana. 2006. "Don't Be Afraid of Offshoring." *Business Week Online*, March 22, http://www.businessweek.com/globalbiz/content/mar2006/gb20060322_649013.htm.

Faux, Jeff. 2006. *The Global Class War: How America's Bipartisan Elite Lost Our Future—and What It Will Take to Win It Back*. New York: John Wiley & Sons, Inc.

Feenstra, Robert, and Gordon Hanson. 1999. "The Impact of Outsourcing and High-Technology Capital on Wages: Estimates for the United States, 1979–1990." *Quarterly Journal of Economics* 114 (3): 907–940.

Ferrera, Maurizio, and Elisabetta Gualmini. 2004. *Rescued by Europe? Social and Labor Market Reforms in Italy from Maastricht to Berlusconi*. Amsterdam, The Netherlands: Amsterdam University Press.

Financial Times Deutschland. 2005. "EU-Kompromiß erhöht deutschen Nettobeitrag." December 23, http://www.ftd.de/politik/deutschland/36096.html.

Fisher-Vanden, Karen, and Gary H. Jefferson. 2005. *Technology Diversity and Development: Evidence from China's Industrial Enterprises*. manuscript.

Foster, Lucia, John Haltiwanger, and C. J. Krizan. 2002. *The Link between Aggregate and Micro Productivity Growth; Evidence from Retail Trade*. National Bureau of Economic Research, NBER Working Paper No. 9120.

Frankfurter Allgemeine Zeitung. 2007a. "Reallöhne sinken trotz guter Konjunktur." January 30, page 9.

———. 2007b. "Petra Roth bleibt Frankfurter Bürgermeisterin." January 29, page 1.

Freeman, Richard B. 2007. *America Works: Critical Thoughts on the Exceptional US Labor Market*. New York: Russell Sage Foundation.

———. 2006a. *Investing in the Best and Brightest: Increased Fellowship Support for American Scientists and Engineers*. Washington, DC: The Brookings Institution, the Hamilton Project Discussion Paper 2006–09.

———. 2006b. "Does Globalization of the Scientific/Engineering Workforce Threaten US Economic Leadership?" In *Innovation Policy and the Economy (Volume 6)*, ed. Adam Jaffe, Josh Lerner, and Scott Stern, 123–157. Cambridge, MA: The MIT Press.

———. 2005a. "The Great Doubling: America in the New Global Economy." Georgia State University, paper presented at the W. J. Usery Lecture Series on the American Workplace.

———. 2005b. "What Really Ails Europe (and America): The Doubling of the Global Workforce." *The Globalist*, June 3.

———. 2005c. "China, India and the Doubling of the Global Labor Force: Who Pays the Price of Globalization?" *The Globalist*, June 3.

———. 1999. *The New Inequality: Creating Solutions for Poor America*. Boston, MA: Beacon Press.

Freeman, Richard B., and Joel Rogers. 2006. *What Workers Want*. Updated Edition. Ithaca, NY: Cornell University Press.

Friedman, Joel, and Katharine Richards. 2006. *Capital Gains and Dividend Tax Cuts: Data Make Clear that High-Income Households Benefit Most.* Washington, DC: Center on Budget and Policy Priorities, http://cbpp.org/1-30-06tax2.htm.

Friedman, Thomas. 2005. *The World Is Flat.* New York: Farrar, Straus and Giroux.

Fröbel, Folker, Jürgen Heinrichs, and Otto Kreye. 1977. *Die Neue Internationale Arbeitsteilung.* Hamburg: Rowohlt Verlag.

Fung, Archon, Dara O'Rourke, and Charles Sabel, eds. 2001. *Can We Put an End to Sweatshops?: A New Democracy Form on Raising Global Labor Standards.* Boston, MA: Beacon Press.

Galax, Virginia. 2007. "In the Shadow of Prosperity: Hard Truths about Helping the Losers from Globalization." *The Economist,* January 20, 32–34.

GAO (U.S. Government Accountability Office). 2004. *Current Government Data Provide Limited Insight into Offshoring of Services.* Washington, DC: U.S. Government Accountability Office, GAO 04-932, http://www.gao.gov/new.items/d04932.pdf.

Gao, Jian, and Gary H. Jefferson. Forthcoming. "Science and Technology Takeoff in China? Sources of Rising R&D Intensity." *Asia Pacific Business Review.*

Gardes, Francois, and Christophe Starzec. 2004. *Income Effects on Services Expenditures.* Amsterdam, The Netherlands: AIAS (Amsterdam Institute for Advanced Labour Studies), Dempatem Working Paper No. 7.

Garner, C. Alan. 2004. *Offshoring in the Services Sector: Economic Impact and Policy Issues.* Kansas City, MO: Federal Reserve Bank of Kansas City, Economic Review, Third Quarter 2004.

Garretsen, Harry, and Jolanda Peeters. 2006. *Capital Mobility, Agglomeration and Corporate Tax Rates: Is the Race to the Bottom for Real?* De Nederlandsche Bank, De Nederlandsche Bank NV Working Paper No. 113.

Gereffi, Gary. 2001. *Beyond the Producer-Driven/Buyer-Driven Dichotomy: The Evolution of Global Value Chains In the Internet Era.* Sussex, England: Institute of Developmental Studies, IDS Bulletin 32, No. 3.

———. 1999. "International Trade and Industrial Upgrading in the Apparel Commodity Chain." *Journal of International Economics* 48 (1): 37–70.

GfK Gruppe. 2006. *Arbeitslosigkeit bleibt größte Sorge der Europäer.* July 17. http://www.gfk.com/group/press_information/press_releases/new/00851/index.de.html.

———. 2003. *Arbeitslosigkeit ist Thema Nummer 1 in Europa.* August 6. http://www.gfk.com/group/press_information/press_releases/new/00494/index.de.html

Gilboy, George J. 2004. "The Myth behind China's Miracle." *Foreign Affairs* (July/August).

Gong, Yundan, and Gary H. Jefferson. 2007. *The Impact of FDI on the Incidence and Intensity of R&D Spending in China.* manuscript.

Gordon, Philip, and Sophie Meunier. 2001. *The French Challenge: Adapting to Globalization.* Washington, DC: Brookings Institution Press.

Görg, Holger, and David Greenaway. 2004. "Much Ado about Nothing? Do Domestic Firms Really Benefit from Foreign Direct Investment?" *World Bank Research Observer* 19 (2): 171–197.

Görg, Holger, and Eric Strobl. 2005. "Foreign Direct Investment and Local Economic Development: Beyond Productivity Spillovers." In *Does Foreign Direct Investment Promote Development,* ed. Theodore H. Moran, Edward

M. Graham, and Magnus Blomström. Washington, DC: Institute for International Economics.

Grabel, Irene. 2005. "Averting Crisis? Assessing Measures to Manage Financial Integration in Emerging Economies." In *Financialization and the World Economy*, ed. Gerald Epstein. Cheltenham, UK and Northampton, MA: Edward Elgar Publishing, Inc.

Gray, John. 2004. "Senegal Calls: Outsourcing a la Française." *Reuters*, July 18.

Groshen, Erica L., Bart Hobijn, and Margaret M. McConnell. 2005. "US Jobs Gains and Lost Through Trade: A Net Measure." *Current Issues in Economics and Finance* 11 (8).

Guttentag, Joseph, and Reuven S. Avi-Yonah. 2006. "Closing the International Tax Gap." In Max B. Sawicky, ed., *Bridging the Tax Gap: Addressing the Crisis in Federal Tax Administration*. Washington: Economic Policy Institute.

Hage, Simon. 2007. *Rückkehr der Reumütigen*, Der Spiegel Online. February 2, http://www.spiegel.de/wirtschaft/0,1518,460703,00.html.

Hanson, Gordon. 2005. "Comment." In *Does Foreign Investment Promote Development?* ed. Theodore H. Moran, Edward M. Graham, and Magnus Blomström, 175–178. Washington, DC: Institute for International Economics.

Harrison, Ann E., and Margaret S. McMillan. 2006. *Outsourcing Jobs? Multinationals and US Employment*. National Bureau of Economic Research, NBER Working Paper 12372.

Hausmann, Ricardo, and Dani Rodrik. 2006. *Doomed to Choose: Industrial Policy as Predicament*, mimeo.

Hay, Colin. 1999. *The Political Economy of New Labor: Laboring Under False Pretences?* Manchester, UK: Manchester University Press.

Hay, Colin, and Nicola J. Smith. 2005. "Horses for Courses? The Political Discourse of Globalization and European Integration in the UK and Ireland." *West European Politics* 28 (1): 124–158.

Hemerijck, Anton, Jelle Visser, and Brigitte Unger. 2000. "How Small Countries Negotiate Change. Twenty-Five Years of Policy Adjustment in Austria, the Netherlands, and Belgium." In *Welfare and Work In the Open Economy. Volume II: Diverse Responses to Common Challenges*, ed. Fritz W. Scharpf and Vivien A. Schmidt. New York and Oxford: Oxford University Press.

Herzog, Roman, and Lüder Gerken. 2007. "Europa entmachtet uns und unsere Vertreter." *Die Welt*, January 13, Page 1.

Hines Jr., James R. 2005. *Corporate Taxation and International Competition*. Ross School of Business Working Paper No. 1026.

Hira, Ron, and Anil Hira. 2005. *Outsourcing America: What's behind Our National Crisis and How We Can Reclaim American Jobs*. New York: American Management Association.

Holmes, Thomas J. 1995. "Analyzing a Proposal to Ban State Tax Breaks to Businesses." *Federal Reserve Bank of Minneapolis Quarterly Review* 19 (2): 29–39.

Hölzl, Werner, Andreas Reinstaller, and Paul Windrum. 2005. *Organizational Innovation, Information Technology, and Outsourcing to Business Services*. University of Maastricht: Maastricht Economic Research Institute on Innovation and Technology (MERIT).

Hu, Albert G., and Gary H. Jefferson. 2006. *A Great Wall of Patents: What Is behind China's Recent Patent Explosion?* manuscript.

Hu, Albert G., Gary H. Jefferson, and Qian Jinchang. 2005. "R&D and Technology Transfer: Firm-Level Evidence from Chinese Industry." *Review of Economics and Statistics* 87 (4): 780–786.

Hummels, David, Jun Ishii, and Kei-Mu Yi. 2001. "The Nature and Growth of Vertical Specialization in World Trade." *Journal of International Economics* 54 (1): 75–96.

Hunya, Gabor. 2002. "Restructuring through FDI in Romanian Manufacturing." *Economic Systems* 26 (4): 387–394.

Hunya, Gabor, and Magdolna Sass. 2005. *Coming and Going: Gains and Losses from Relocations Affecting Hungary.* The Vienna Institute for International Economic Studies, 323.

ILO (International Labour Organisation). 2006. *Offshoring and the Internationalization of Employment: A Challenge for Fair Globalization.* Lanham, MD: Bernan, Proceedings of the France/ILO Symposium April 2005.

———. 2004 and 2005. *ILO Socio-Economic Security Program, Economic Security for a Better World.* Geneva: International Labour Organization.

———. 2003. *Employment and Social Policy in Respect of Export Processing Zones (EPZs).* Geneva: International Labour Organisation, GB.286/ESP/3.

Indian Institute of Foreign Trade. 2006. "IIFT-NASSCOM Discuss the Future and Challenges Faced by the Indian It Industry." August 21, http://www.iift.edu/iift/IT_Press.asp.

Jaffe, Adam, and Josh Lerner. 2004. *Innovation and Its Discontents: How Our Broken Patent System Is Endangering Innovation and Progress, and What to Do about It.* Princeton, NJ: Princeton University Press.

Jaffee, Dwight M. 2004. "Globalization, Offshoring, and Economic Convergence: A Synthesis," paper presented at Understanding Global Outsourcing, Stern School of Business.

Javorcik, Beata. 2004. "Does Foreign Direct Investment Increase the Productivity of Domestic Firms? In Search of Spillovers Through Backward Linkages." *American Economic Review* 94 (3): 605–627.

Javorcik, Beata, and Bartlomiej Kaminski. 2006a. "Multinational Corporations and Export Competitiveness of New Europe." In *Competitiveness of New Europe*, ed. J. Winiecki. Rzeszow: University of Information Technology Press.

———. 2006b. "How to Attract FDI and Maximize Its Benefits." In *Competitiveness of New Europe*, ed. J. Winiecki. Rzeszow: University of Information Technology Press.

———. 2004. "The 'EU Factor' and Slovakia's Globalization: The Role of Foreign Direct Investment." *Czech Review of Economics and Finance* 54 (9–10): 456–472.

Jefferson, Gary H., and Zhong Kaifeng. 2004. "An Investigation of Firm-Level R&D Capabilities in East Asia." In *Global Production Networking and Technological Change in East Asia*, ed. Shahid Yusuf, M. Anjum Altaf, and Kaoru Nabeshima. A World Bank Publication edition. New York and Oxford: Oxford University Press.

Jensen, J. Bradford, and Lori G. Kletzer. 2006. *Tradable Services: Understanding the Scope and Impact of Services Outsourcing.* Institute for International Economics, May, http://www.iie.com/publications/print.cfm?doc = pub&ResearchID = 638.

———. 2005. "Tradable Services: Understanding the Scope and Impact of Services Offshoring." In *Brookings Trade Forum 2005: Offshoring White-Collar Work—the*

Issues and the Implications, ed. Lael Brainard and Susan M. Collins. Washington, DC: The Brookings Institute.

Jones, Ronald W. 2000. *Globalization and the Theory of Input Trade.* Cambridge, MA: The MIT Press.

Joseph, K. J. 2002. *Growth of ICC and ICT for Development: Realities of the Myths of the Indian Experience.* Helsinki, Finland: UNU/WIDER (United Nations University, World Institute for Development Economics Research), Discussion Paper No. 2002/78.

Kaminski, Bartlomiej, and Francis Ng. 2005. "Production Disintegration and Integration of Central Europe into Global Markets." *International Review of Economics and Finance* 14 (3): 377–390.

———. 2004. *Romania's Integration into European Markets: Implications for Sustainability of the Current Export Boom.* World Bank Policy Research Working Paper 3451.

———. 2001. *Trade and Production Fragmentation: Central European Economies in European Union Networks of Production and Marketing.* Washington, DC: World Bank, World Bank Policy Research Working Paper No. 2611.

Kaminski, Bartlomiej, and Michelle Riboud. 2000. *Foreign Investment and Restructuring: the Evidence from Hungary.* Washington, DC: The World Bank, World Bank Technical Paper No. 453.

Kaplinsky, Raphael. 2000. "Globalization and Inequalization: What Can Be Learned from Value Chain Analysis." *Journal of Development Studies* 37 (2): 117–146.

Kapur, Devesh, and John McHale. 2005. "Sojourns and Software: Internationally Mobile Human Capital and the Software Industry in India, Ireland and Israel." In *From Underdogs to Tigers: The Rise and Growth of the Software Industry in Brazil, China, India, Ireland and Israel,* ed. Ashish Arora and Alfonso Gambardella. New York and Oxford: Oxford University Press.

Katzenstein, Peter. 1985. *Small States in World Markets: Industrial Policy in Europe.* Ithaca, NY: Cornell University Press.

Katz, Jorge, M. 1996. *Estabilización Macroeconómica, Reforma Estructural y Comportamiento Industrial.* Santiago de Chile and Buenos Aires: CEPAL and Alianza Editorial S.A.

Kearney, A.T. 2004. *Making Offshore Decisions: A.T. Kearney's 2004 Offshore Location Attractiveness Index.* A.T. Kearney.

Kerr, William R. 2006. *Ethnic Scientific Communities and International Technology Diffusion.* (June 29), Working Paper.

Kierzkowski, Henryk. 2001. "Joining the Global Economy: Experience and Prospects of the Transition Economies." In *Fragmentation: New Production Patterns In the World Economy,* ed. Sven W. Arndt and Henryk Kierzkowski. New York and Oxford: Oxford University Press.

Kirkegaard, Jacob Funk. 2005. *Outsourcing and Offshoring: Pushing the European Model over the Hill rather than over the Cliff.* Washington, DC: Institute for International Economics, IIE Working Paper No. 05–1.

Kirkegaard, Jacob Funk, and Martin J. Baily. 2004. *Transforming the European Economy.* Washington, DC: Institute for International Economics.

Kletzer, Lori G. 2002. *Imports, Exports and Jobs: What Does Trade Mean for Employment Job Loss?* Kalamazoo, MI: W.E. Upjohn Institute for Employment Research.

Kletzer, Lori G., and Howard Rosen. 2005. "Easing the Adjustment Burden on Us Workers." In *The United States and the World Economy; Foreign Economic Policy for the Next Decade*, ed. C. Fred Bergsten. Institute for International Economics.

Konings, Jozef. 2001. "The Effects of Foreign Direct Investment on Domestic Firms: Evidence from Firm-Level Panel Data in Emerging Economies." *Economics of Transition* 9 (3): 619–633.

Krugman, Paul R. 1979. "A Model of Innovation, Technology Transfer, and the World Distribution of Income." *Journal of Political Economy* 87 (2): 253–266.

Krupa, Matthias. 2007. "Demokratie in Zahlen." *Die Zeit* 4: 3.

Kumar, Nagesh. 2001. "Indian Software Industry Development: International and National Perspective." *Economic and Political Weekly* 36 (45): 4278–4290.

Kumar, Nagesh, and K. J. Joseph. 2005. "Exports of Software and Business Process Outsourcing from Developing Countries: Lessons from the Indian Experience." *Asia Pacific Trade and Investment Review* 1 (1): 91–110.

Lall, Sanjaya. 2003. *Reinventing Industrial Strategy: The Role of Government Policy in Building Industrial Competitiveness*, for the Intergovernmental Group on Monetary Affairs and Development (G-24).

———. 2001. *Competitiveness, Technology, and Skills*. Cheltenham, UK and Northampton, MA: Edward Elgar Publishing, Inc.

———. 1992. "Technological Capabilities and Industrialization." *World Development* 20 (6): 165–186.

Lankes, Hans-Peter, and Nicholas Stern. 1998. *Capital Flows to Eastern Europe and the Former Soviet Union*. London: The European Bank for Reconstruction and Development, EBRD Working Paper, No. 27.

Lankes, Hans-Peter, and Anthony J. Venables. 1996. "Foreign Direct Investment in Economic Transition: The Changing Pattern of Investments." *Economics of Transition* 4 (2): 331–347.

Leamer, Edward E., and Michael Storper. 2001. "The Economic Geography of the Internet Age." *Journal of International Business Studies* 32 (4): 641–665.

Leick, Romain. 2005. "Philosophen: Panik als Lebensform." *Der Spiegel* 47: 162.

Levin, Senator, Carl. 2006. Statement on "Hearing on Deconstructing the Tax Code: Uncollected Taxes and Issues of Transparency." U.S. Senate. September 26.

Levy, Frank, and Richard J. Murnane. 2004. *The New Division of Labor: Now Computers Are Creating the Next Job Market*. Princeton, NJ: Princeton University Press.

Levy, Jonah. 1999. "Vice into Virtue: Progressive Politics and Welfare Reform in Continental Europe." *Politics and Society* 27 (2): 239–273.

Lipsey, Robert E., and Fredrik Sjoeholm. 2005. "The Impact of Inward FDI on Host Countries: Why Such Different Answers?" In *Does Foreign Investment Promote Development?* ed. Theodore H. Moran, Edward M. Graham, and Magnus Blomström, 23–43. Washington, DC: Institute for International Economics.

Lohr, Steve. 2006. "Outsourcing Is Climbing Skills Ladder." *The New York Times*, February 16, C1.

Madrick, Jeffrey, and William Milberg. 2006. *A New Social Safety Net for America*. New York: Schwartz Center for Economic Policy Analysis, Policy Paper.

Mahoney, Melissa, William Milberg, Markus Schneider, and Rudi von Arnim. 2006. *Spurring Growth Dynamics from Services Offshoring*. New York: Schwartz Center for Economic Policy Analysis, New School for Social Research, Policy Note.

Mankiw, N. Gregory, and Philip Swagel. 2006. *The Politics and Economics of Offshore Outsourcing*. National Bureau of Economic Research, NBER Working Paper 12398.

Mann, Catherine L. 2006. *Information Technology, Productivity Growth, and International Trade in Services*, paper presented at Research Institute for Industrial Economics Stockholm Conference, November.

———. 2003. *Globalization of IT Services and White-Collar Jobs: The Next Wave of Productivity Growth*. Washington, DC: Institute of International Economics, Policy Brief No. PB03–11.

Mann, Catherine L. with Jacob Funk Kirkegaard. 2006. *Accelerating the Globalization of America: The Role for Information Technology*. Washington, DC: Institute for International Economics.

Manow, Philip, and Eric Seils. 2000. "Adjusting Badly: The German Welfare State, Structural Change and the Open Economy." In *Welfare and Work In the Open Economy. Volume II: Diverse Responses to Common Challenges*, ed. Fritz W. Scharpf and Vivien A. Schmidt. New York and Oxford: Oxford University Press.

Marin, Dalia. 2004. *A Nation of Poets and Thinkers—Less So with Eastern Enlargement? Austria and Germany*. London: Centre for Economic Policy Research, CEPR Discussion Paper No. 4358.

Markusen, James R., and Anthony J. Venables. 1999. "Foreign Direct Investment as a Catalyst for Industrial Development." *European Economic Review* 43 (2): 335–356.

Mattoo, Aaditya, and Sacha Wunsch. 2004. "Pre-Empting Protectionism in Services: The GATS and Outsourcing." *Journal of International Economic Law* 7 (4): 765–800.

Mayer, Jörg. 2003. *The Fallacy of Composition: A Review of the Literature*. New York and Geneva: United Nations Conference on Trade and Development, UNCTAD Discussion Papers. No 166.

McCarthy, John C. 2004. *Near Term Growth of Offshoring Accelerating: Resizing US Services Jobs Going Offshore*. Cambridge, MA: Forrester Research, Inc. May 14.

McKinsey & Company, Inc. 2005. *The McKinsey Quarterly*. Washington, DC: McKinsey & Company, Inc.

McKinsey Global Institute. 2005. *The Emerging Global Labor Market*. Washington, DC: McKinsey & Company, Inc.

———. 2003. *Offshoring: Is It a Win-Win Game?* Washington, DC: McKinsey & Company, Inc.

Meyer, Klaus E. 2000. "International Production Networks and Enterprise Transformation in Central Europe." *Comparative Economic Studies* 42 (1): 135–150.

Meyer, Thomas. 2006. *Offshoring to New Shores: Nearshoring to Central and Eastern Europe*. Frankfurt, Germany: Deutsche Bank Research, Economics No 58.

Milberg, William. forthcoming. "The New Social Science Imperialism and the Problem of Knowledge in Contemporary Economics." In *Economics and Anthropology*, ed. Stephen Gudeman. New York and Oxford: Oxford University Press.

Milberg, William, and Markus Schneider. 2007. *Employment Effects of Us Trade Balance Deterioration*. NSSR mimeo.

Milberg, William, and Rudi von Arnim. 2007. *US Offshoring: Implications for Economic Growth and Income Distribution*. New York: Schwartz Center for Economic Policy Analysis, New School for Social Research, mimeo.

Moran, Theodore H. 2001. *Parental Supervision: The New Paradigm for Foreign Direct Investment and Development*. Washington, DC: Institute for International Economics.

Moran, Theodore H., Edward M. Graham, and Magnus Blomström. 2005. *Does Foreign Investment Promote Development?* Washington, DC: Institute for International Economics.

Morisi, Teresa L. 1996. "Commercial Banking Transformed by Computer Technology." *Monthly Labor Review* 119 (8): 30–36.

Mun, Sung-Bae, and M. Ishaq Nadiri. 2002. *Information Technology Externalities: Empirical Evidence from 42 US Industries*. National Bureau of Economic Research, NBER Working Paper No. 9272.

Murphy, Kevin M., Andre Shleifer, and Robert W. Vishy. 1989. "Industrialization and the Big Push." *Journal of Political Economy* 97 (5): 1003–1026.

NAPA (National Academy of Public Administration). 2006. *Offshoring: An Elusive Phenomenon*. Washington, DC: National Academy of Public Administration, a report of the Panel of the National Academy of Public Administration for the US Congress and the Bureau of Economic Analysis.

NASSCOM (National Association of Software and Service Companies). 2006. *Strategic Review 2006*. New Delhi, India: National Association of Software and Service Companies.

———. 2004. *Indian ITES-BPO Industry Handbook*. New Delhi, India: National Association of Software and Service Companies.

NASSCOM and Hewitt Associates. 2005. *Total Rewards Study*. New Delhi, India: National Association of Software and Service Companies.

NASSCOM and McKinsey & Company, Inc. 2005. *NASSCOM-McKinsey Report 2005—Extending India's Leadership In the Global IT and BPO Industries*. New Delhi, India: National Association of Software and Service Companies.

Natali, David, and Martin Rhodes. 2004. "Trade-offs and Veto Players: Reforms Pensions in France and Italy." *French Politics* 2 (1): 1–23.

Naughton, Barry. 2007. *The Chinese Economy: Transitions and Growth*. Cambridge, MA: The MIT Press.

NBS (National Bureau of Statistics of China). 2005. *China Statistical Yearbook*. Beijing: China Statistics Press.

NBS-MOST (National Bureau of Statistics and the Ministry of Science and Technology). 2006. *China Statistical Yearbook on Science and Technology*. Beijing: China Statistics Press.

Nelson, Richard R., and Sidney J. Winter. 1982. *An Evolutionary Theory of Economic Change*. Cambridge, MA: Harvard University Press.

Nolan, Marcus, and Howard Pack. 2003. *Industrial Policy in an Era of Globalization: Lessons from Asia*. Washington, DC: Institute for International Economics.

Ocampo, José Antonio. 2004. "Beyond the Washington Consensus: What Do We Mean?" *Journal of Post Keynesian Economics* 27 (2) (Winter): 293–314.

OECD (Organization for Economic Co-operation and Development). 2006. *The Share of Employment Potentially Affected by Offshoring: An Empirical Investigation*. Paris: Organization for Economic Co-operation and Development, DSTI/ICCP/IE(2005)8/Final.

———. 2005a. National accounts. Paris, http://www.oecd.org/std/national-accounts.

———. 2005b. *Potential Offshoring of ICT-Intensive Using Occupations*. Paris: Organization for Economic Co-operation and Development, DSTI/ICCP/IE (2004)19/FINAL.

———. 2004. *OECD Economic Outlook*. Paris: Organization for Economic Co-operation and Development.

———. 2003. *The Source of Economic Growth in OECD Countries*. Paris: Organization for Economic Co-operation and Development.

The Outsourcing Institute. 2005. *The New Workplace: Outsourcing in Japan*, http://www.outsourcing.com/.

Pandey, Geeta. 2004. "Call of India Lures European Workers." *BBC News*, November 24, http://news.bbc.co.uk/1/hi/world/south_asia/4038069.stm.

Parker, Andrew C. 2004. *TwoSpeed Europe: Why 1 Million Jobs Will Move Offshore*. Cambridge, MA: Forrester Research, Inc. August 18.

Paus, Eva. 2005. *Foreign Investment, Development, and Globalization. Can Costa Rica Become Ireland?* New York and Houndmills: Palgrave Macmillan.

Paus, Eva, and Kevin Gallagher. 2006. *Missing Links between Foreign Investment and Development: Lessons from Costa Rica and Mexico*. Boston, MA: Global Development and Environment Institute, Tufts University, Working Paper No. 06–01.

Polanyi, Karl. 1944. *The Great Transformation: The Political and Economic Origins of Our Time*. Boston, MA: Beacon Press.

politics.co.uk. "Institute of Directors: Offshoring Is Here to Stay." January 23, 2006, http://www.politics.co.uk/issueoftheday/institute-directors-offshoring-here-stay-$370499$367012.htm.

Pollin, Robert. 2003. *Contours of Descent: US Economic Fractures and the Landscape of Global Austerity*. New York: Verso.

Pollin, Robert, Gerald Epstein, James Heintz, and Léonce Ndikumana. 2006. *An Employment-Targeted Economic Program for South Africa*. New York: United Nations Development Program.

Pollin, Robert, Mark Brenner, Stephanie Luce, and Jeannette Wicks-Lim. Forthcoming. *A Measure of Fairness: The Economics of Living Wages and Minimum Wages in the United States*. Ithaca, NY: Cornell University Press.

Porter, Michael. 1990. *The Competitive Advantage of Nations*. New York: Free Press.

PressEecho.de. 2006. Angst vor Kündigung unverändert hoch—Trendwende am Arbeitsmarkt kommt nicht bei Beschäftigten an. August 29, http://www.pressee-cho.de/finanzen/NA3730879567.htm.

Primo Braga, Carlos A. 1996. "The Impact of the Internationalization of Services on Developing Countries." *Finance & Development* 33: 34–37.

Radwan, Ismail, and Fernando Gihani. 2005. *Sri Lanka Offshoring Professional Services: A Development Opportunity*. Washington, DC: The World Bank, SASFP.

Rhodes, Martin. 2000. "Restructuring the British Welfare State: Between Domestic Constraints and Global Imperatives." In *Welfare and Work in the Open Economy. Volume II: Diverse Responses to Common Challenges*, ed. Fritz W. Scharpf and Vivien A. Schmidt. New York and Oxford: Oxford University Press.

Ricardo, David. 1951. "Essay on the influence of a low price of corn on the profits of stock (1815)." In *The Works and Correspondence of David Ricardo: Volume IV*, ed. Piero Sraffa. Cambridge, UK: Cambridge University Press.

Richardson, Ranald. 1999. "Call Centers and the Prospects of Export-Oriented Work In the Developing World: Evidence from Western Europe." In *Europe and Developing Countries in the Globalized Information Economy*, ed. Swasti Mitter and Maria Ines Bastos. New York: Routledge.

Richet, Xavier. 2004. "Réseaux Internationaux de Production et Nouvelles Économies de Marché: Les Stratégies des Constructeurs Automobiles dans les Pays D'Europe Centrale et Orientale." Université de la Sorbonne Nouvelle.

Rodriguez-Clare, Andres. 1996. "Multinationals, Linkages, and Economic Development." *American Economic Review* 86 (4): 852–873.

Rodrik, Dani. 2006a. *Industrial Development: Stylized Facts and Policies*, mimeo.

———. 2006b. *The Social Cost of Foreign Exchange Reserves*. National Bureau of Economic Research, NBER Working Paper No. 11952, January.

———. 1997. *Has Globalization Gone Too Far?* Washington, DC: Institute for International Economics.

———. 1995. "Getting Interventions Right: How South Korea and Taiwan Grew Rich." *Economic Policy* 10 (20): 53–107.

Ros, Jaime. 2001. *Industrial Policy, Comparative Advantages, and Growth*. Santiago de Chile: CEPAL, CEPAL Review No. 73.

———. 2000. *Development Theory and the Economics of Growth*. Ann Arbor, MI: University of Michigan Press.

Sachs, Jeffrey. 2005. *Investing in Development: A Practical Plan to Achieve the Millenium Development Goals*. London and Sterlin: Earthscan Publications Limited.

Saggi, Kamal. 2002. "International Technology Transfer and Economic Development." In *Development, Trade, and the WTO: A Handbook*, ed. Bernard Hoekman, Aaditya Mattoo, and Philip English. Washington, DC: The World Bank.

Saigol, Lina, and James Politi. 2006. "M&A in 2006 Beats Tech Boom." *Financial Times*, December 20.

Samuelson, Paul A. 2005. "Response from Paul A. Samuelson." *Journal of Economic Perspectives* 19 (3): 242–244.

———. 2004. "Where Ricardo and Mill Rebut and Confirm Arguments of Mainstream Economists Supporting Globalization." *Journal of Economic Perspectives* 18 (3): 135–146.

Sands, Anita. 2005. "The Irish Software Industry." In *From Underdogs to Tigers: The Rise and Growth of the Software Industry in Brazil, China, India, Ireland and Israel*, ed. Ashish Arora and Alfonso Gambardella. New York and Oxford: Oxford University Press.

Sapir, André. 2005. *Globalization and the Reform of European Social Models*. Brussels, Belgium: Breugel, background document for the presentation at ECOFIN Informal Meeting in Manchester, www.bruegel.org/Files/media/PDF/Publications/Papers/EN_SapirPaper080905.pdf.

Scharpf, Fritz W. 2000. "Economic Changes, Vulnerabilities, and Institutional Capabilities." In *Welfare and Work in the Open Economy. Volume I: From Vulnerability to Competitiveness*, ed. Fritz W. Scharpf and Vivien A. Schmidt. New York and Oxford: Oxford University Press.

Scharpf, Fritz W., and Vivien A. Schmidt, eds. 2000. *Welfare and Work in the Open Economy. Volume I: From Vulnerability to Competitiveness*. New York and Oxford: Oxford University Press.

Schmidt, Vivien A. 2002. *The Futures of European Capitalism.* New York and Oxford: Oxford University Press.

———. 2000. "Values and Discourse in the Politics of Welfare State Adjustment." In *Welfare and Work In the Open Economy. Volume I: From Vulnerability to Competitiveness,* ed. Fritz W. Scharpf and Vivien A. Schmidt. New York and Oxford: Oxford University Press.

———. 1996. *From State to Market? The Transformation of French Business and Government.* New York and London: Cambridge University Press.

Schultze, Charles L. 2004. *Offshoring, Import Competition, and the Jobless Recovery.* Washington, DC: The Brookings Institution, Policy Brief No. 136.

Shapiro, Helen. 2003. "Bringing the Firm Back In." In *Development Economics and Structuralist Macroeconomics,* ed. Amitava Krishna Dutt and Jaime Ros. Cheltenham, UK and Northampton, MA: Edward Elgar Publishing, Inc.

Shapiro, Helen, and Lance Taylor. 1990. "The State and Industrial Strategy." *World Development* 18 (6): 861–878.

Smith, Timothy B. 2004. *France in Crisis: Welfare, Inequality and Globalization Since 1980.* Cambridge, UK: Cambridge University Press.

Spencer, David. 2005. "The Cost of Capital Flight". *Accountancy Business and the Public Interest* 4 (2): 151–160.

Srinivasan, T. N. 2005. *Information Technology Enabled Services and India's Growth Prospects.* September 16, mimeo.

Standing, Guy. Forthcoming. "Labor Recommodification in the Global Transformation." In *The Market Economy as a Political Project: Reading Karl Polanyi For the 21st Century,* ed. Ayse Bugra and Kaan Agartan. New York and Houndmills: Palgrave Macmillan.

———. 2002. *Beyond the New Paternalism: Basic Security as Equality.* London: Verso.

Statistisches Bundesamt (Hrsg.). 2006. *Datenreport 2006: Zahlen und Fakten über die Bundesrepublik Deutschland.* Bonn: Bundeszentrale Für Politische Bildung, Schriftenreihe Band 544: 483.

Stefanova, Boyka M. 2006. "The Political Economy of Outsourcing In the European Union and the East-European Enlargement." *Business and Politics* 8 (2).

Stiroh, Kevin. 2002. "Information Technology and the US Productivity Revival: What Do the Industry Data Say?" *American Economic Review* 92 (5): 1559–1576.

Sturgeon, Timothy. 2006. *Why We Can't Measure the Economic Effects of Services Offshoring: The Data Gaps and How to Fill Them.* Industrial Performance Center, MIT, Services Offshoring Working Group. September 10.

Sturgeon, Timothy, and Richard K. Lester. 2003. *The New Global Supply-Base: New Challenges for Local Suppliers in East Asia.* Industrial Performance Center, MIT, paper prepared for the World Bank's Project on East Asia's Economic Future.

Suri, Navdeep. 2005. "Outsourcing and Development," paper presented at Experts Meeting on Strengthening the Participation of Developing Countries in Dynamic and New Sectors of World Trade, Geneva.

Sutcliffe, Bob. 2004. "World Inequality and Globalization." *Oxford Review of Economic Policy* 20 (1): 15–37.

Szanyi, Miklós. 2004. "Competitiveness and Industrial Renewal: The Role of Foreign Direct Investments in the Development of the Hungarian Electrical Industry," paper presented at Seminar on Foreign Direct Investment and Multinational Corporations in Enlarged Europe, Universidad Complutense de Madrid.

Tanzi, Vito. 1995. *Taxation in an Integrating World.* Washington, DC: The Brookings Institution.

Taylor-Gooby, Peter (ed.). 2005. *New Risks, New Welfare: The Transformation of the European Welfare State.* New York and Oxford: Oxford University Press.

Thompson Financial. 2006. *Mergers and Acquisitions Review.* Third Quarter.

Uchitelle, Louis. 2006. *The Disposable American. Layoffs and Their Consequences.* New York: Alfred A. Knopf.

UK National Statistics. 2005. http://www.statistics.gov.uk.

UNCTAD (United Nations Conference on Trade and Development). 2006. *World Investment Report 2006.* New York and Geneva: United Nations.

———. 2005a. *World Investment Report 2005.* New York and Geneva: United Nations.

———. 2005b. *Report on the Expert Meeting on Strengthening the Participation of Developing Countries in Dynamic New Sectors of World Trade: Trends, Issues and Policies,* paper presented at TD/B/COM.1/EM.26/3, Palais des Nations, Geneva.

———. 2005c. *Business Process Offshore Outsourcing: Untapped Opportunities for SMEs.* New York and Geneva: United Nations, the United Nations Conference on Trade and Development, Document UNCTAD/SDTE/TIB/2005/6.

———. 2004. *World Investment Report 2004.* New York and Geneva: United Nations.

———. 2003a. *E-Commerce and Development Report 2003.* New York and Geneva: United Nations.

———. 2003b. *Investment and Technology Policies for Competitiveness: Review of Successful Country Experiences.* New York and Geneva: United Nations.

———. 2002. *World Investment Report 2002.* New York and Geneva: United Nations.

———. 2001. *World Investment Report 2001: Promoting Linkages.* New York and Geneva: United Nations.

———. 2000. *The Competitiveness Challenge: Transnational Corporations and Industrial Restructuring in Developing Countries.* New York and Geneva: United Nations.

van Welsum, Desiree, and Xavier Reif. 2006. *We Can Work It Out—the Globalisation of ICT-enabled Services.* National Bureau of Economic Research, NBER Working Paper 12799.

Visser, Jelle, and Anton Hemerijck. 1997. *A Dutch Miracle: Job Growth, Welfare Reform and Corporatism in the Netherlands.* Amsterdam, The Netherlands: Amsterdam University Press.

Wade, Robert. 1990. *Governing the Market: Economic Theory and the Role of Government in East Asian Industrialization.* Princeton, NJ: Princeton University Press.

Welfens, P. J. J., and D. Borbely. 2006. *Structural Change, Innovation and Growth in the Context of EU Eastern Enlargement,* paper presented at European Institute for International Economic Relations, University of Wuppertal.

Williams, Frances. 2005. "WTO Seeks to Allay Fears on Moving IT Services Offshore." *Financial Times,* July 1, p. 11.

Wilson, Daniel J. 2004. *IT and Beyond: The Contribution of Heterogenerous Capital to Productivity.* San Francisco, CA: Federal Reserve Bank of San Francisco, Working Paper 2004–13.

Wilson, John D. 1999. "Theories of Tax Competition." *National Tax Journal* 52 (2): 269–304.

World Bank. 2002. *World Development Report 2002: Building Institutions for Markets.* New York and Oxford: Oxford University Press.

———. 1995. *Global Economic Prospects and Developing Countries*. Washington, DC: World Bank.

Wort & Bild Verlag Presse-Service. 2005. "Angst vor Arbeitslosigkeit nahezu verdreifacht." *Apotheken Umschau*, September, http://www.wortundbild.de/PGD/PGDP/pgdp_05.htm?snr = 21483.

Wösler, Martin. 2002. "30 Jahre deutsch-chinesische diplomatische Beziehungen 1972–2002—Brief aus Peking." *China Journal*, http://dcg.de/woesler/brief.html, accessed Jan 5, 2007.

WTO (World Trade Organization). 2005. *World Trade Report 2005*. Geneva: World Trade Organization.

Yusuf, Shahid. 2003. *Innovative East Asia: The Future of Growth*. A World Bank Publication edition. New York and Oxford: Oxford University Press.

Zöhlnhofer, Reimut. 2004. "Destination Anywhere? The German Red-Green Government's Inconclusive Search for a Third Way in Economic Policy." *German Politics* 13 (1): 106–131.

Zukowska-Gagelmann, Katarzyna. 2000. "Productivity Spillovers from Foreign Direct Investment in Poland." *Economic Systems* 24 (3): 223–256.

INDEX

Indian Copyright Act, protections in, 177

Indian Institute of Foreign Trade, 170

Indian Institutes of Technology (IITs), migration of graduates of to U.S., 165

Indian ITES-BPO sector growth: boost for air travel through, 169; employment and income effects of, 167–68; empowering impact of on women, 168; faster than in IT sector, 167; future skilled labor shortage in, 173–74; healthy foreign exchange earnings on, 170–71; impact of on income growth and consumption, 167; modern competitive telecommunications facilities needed for, 169; learning and spillovers from, 168–69; progressive transfer of skills to domestic operations through, 168–69; quality awareness in, 175; rapid rise in wages in, 178

Indonesia, Nusantara-21 Project in, 160

Industrial citizenship: era of, 42; obsolescence of, 52

Industrial restructuring, impact of North-South deep integration on, 181

Informal sector, increased income and standards as goal for, 36

Information: improved access to, 143; worldwide dissemination of, 37

Information Communications technology (ICT), 6–7; central role of, 63, 64–66; creation of infrastructure in India, 14; development of, 24; diffusion of in economy, 159; impact of ICT hardware on the economy, 6; introduction of tradability into range of services through, 163; as

promoter of decentralized growth, 14; quantification of role of, 63

Information Security Management Systems, independent third-party certification scheme for, 177

Information technology (IT): Act of 2000, as forward looking legislation dealing with information security and cyber crimes, 177; diffusion of networked, and productivity growth, 64; four channels to enhance economic growth with, 65–66; -enabled services, trade in, 217; hardware, increased business purchase of, 64, 82; increased application of to service activities, 64; intensity and aggregate productivity growth, relation between, 66; investment, electronics as leader in, 66–68; products and services, 64; services, global increase in, 64; and worldwide software expenditures, estimates of, 150. See also IT TNCs; IT Workforce Development Initiative

Information technology (IT) products and services: offshoring of, as catalyst for economic development, 14; three characteristics of, 6–7; value added in, 16

Information technology-enabled back office processes sector (ITE-BOP), 149, 150, 163; development benefits from (India), 166–77; less demanding skill levels of, 159; mechanization of, 154; potential for skill upgrading in, 157; as "Trojan Horse," 171

Infosys, training programs of, 174

Printed in the United States
129616LV00001B/20/P